Medicine's Strangest Cases

Michael O'Donnell

PORTICO

First published in the United Kingdom in 2002

This edition published in 2009 by Portico
10 Southcombe Street
London
W14 0RA

An imprint of Anova Books Company Ltd.

ISBN 9781906032906

A CIP catalogue record for this book is available from the British Library.

10 9 8 7 6 5 4 3 2 1

Printed and bound by CPI Mackays, Chatham, Kent, ME5 8TD

This book can be ordered direct from the publisher.
Contact the marketing department, but try your bookshop first.

www.anovabooks.com

CONTENTS

Medicine's Strangest Cases

INTRODUCTION

A paediatrician once described in the *Lancet* how, when travelling by train, he had tried to diagnose what was the matter with a tiny girl sitting on the lap of the woman opposite him. Only after twenty minutes' careful observation did he realise that the child had a condition that rarely came his way: she was perfectly normal.

That's one problem with defining strange cases in medicine. To those who live relatively normal lives, everything that doctors do is strange. Doctors also work in a pretty strange environment in which people they may have met only minutes before will, if asked, remove their clothes and then allow the doctor's hands to explore their bodies in ways that haunt the dreams of fantasists.

If that weren't enough, I'll confess to a personal difficulty in diagnosing 'strangeness', or what the cover of this book calls 'extraordinary incidents'. Not only was any sense that I may have had of the ordinary knocked out of me by my twelve years as a doctor, but my working life since has done little to diminish my tolerance of quirkiness and odd behaviour.

Nine years working with Frank Muir and Denis Norden on Radio Four's *My Word* and sixteen sharing the company of Robert Robertson and his other guests on *Stop the Week* – none of them chosen for their sedateness or conformity of view – ensured that, for a good chunk of my life, 'strangeness' was the normal currency of conversation. I even wrote a radio series, *Relative Values,* based on my belief that you don't have to dig too deep beneath the surface of what may seem the most ordinary of families to find extraordinary goings-on.

When I started this book, I found I was having to make arbitrary decisions. Was a Yorkshire GP, for instance, describing a 'strange case' when he told me what happened in the 1950s after he'd had a difficult time delivering a baby in a Yorkshire farmhouse?

When the baby was safe in the mother's arms and she was lying comfortable and content in a freshly made bed, the doctor broached a subject that had long intrigued him: 'This is the sixth child you and Harry have had. Why don't you marry him?'

'I could never do that, doctor.'

'Don't you think it might be better for the children?'

'Maybe. But I could never marry him, doctor.'

'Why not?'

'Because I've never really liked him.'

A strange case or a mundane strand from the warp and woof of general practice?

And how about the consultant physician who, in the seventies, had to visit a member of a large family in a tower block in Liverpool? As he was leaving, the family matriarch thanked him profusely for his kindness and, as a token of her gratitude, handed him a box of eggs. 'Nice and fresh,' she said. 'And we'd like you to have them.'

A glance out the window confirmed he was in a concrete ghetto with not a blade of grass in sight. 'Don't tell me you keep chickens here,' he said.

'Oh no, doctor, but my daughter works in the hospital canteen.'

That sounds less strange than warp and woof to me, but these distinctions are never clear. In the end, I decided to award the accolade of strangeness to cases that tickled the tiny clutch of cells in my brain that some call their 'fancy', even though I realised that strangeness, like eccentricity, is a condition we recognise in others but rarely in ourselves.

Looking at the final text, I realise that my fancy has been tickled not just by bizarre, amusing or mischievous incidents, but by a handful of anger-provoking happenings where doctors given to moralising or playing political games, or motivated by self-aggrandisement, sought to distort history, to mis-award honour, or to do down those of whom they didn't approve.

In assembling this collection, my main source has been the commonplace book that I have kept for the half-century that has passed since I qualified as a doctor. That book went through two expansionist phases, the first when I was editor of *World Medicine,* the second when I wrote a weekly column for the *British Medical Journal* and a couple of other medical publications. I've just totted up that, during those two spells, I received letters from over three thousand doctors who wanted to pass on accounts of their struggles to survive in the unpredictable, sometimes bizarre, but often endearing world of clinical medicine. I remain grateful to all of them and, when writing this book, have tried to echo their voices. I'm particularly grateful to two GPs, John Oldroyd and Bev Daily, who kept me in touch with the realities of general practice during the 1970s and 1980s.

I'm also grateful to many friends who have fed my appetite for anecdotal evidence, especially Paul Vaughan, Bernard Dixon, Geoff Watts, Colin Tudge, Richard Leech, Robin Steel, Phil Hammond, Richard Gordon, and the late John Rowan Wilson. I have a particular indebtedness to Albert Hoffman, who became a pen friend after I visited Basle in 1989 to make a television programme about his life and work, and who sent me excerpts from his research diaries, some of which I quote on pages 120–2.

Finally, I would like to offer this book as a token of gratitude to another troupe of old friends with whom I occasionally lunch or dine at a London club of ambiguous reputation and whose tolerance of my loquacity means they have to put up with a lot of this sort of thing.

Loxhill, March 2002.

THE CASE OF THE VANISHING FATHER FIGURE

COS, GREECE, 460–377 BC

For the elders of nineteenth-and twentieth-century medicine, the ancient Greek physician Hippocrates seemed the ideal role-model: part priest, part physician, always portrayed as elderly, paternalistic, jealous of his privileges, and addicted to pious utterance. It came as a relief to less reverent doctors to discover that the putative Father of Medicine was a man not of history but of fable.

Everything we know about Hippocrates is legend. He is said to have been born in the fifth century BC on the Greek island of Cos, where he practised as a physician and led a long and virtuous life. Yet no one is sure of his dates to within twenty or thirty years and, though he is alleged to be the author of the Hippocratic oath, some scholars claim that none of the texts of the Hippocratic corpus, many of which are contradictory, were written by the man after whom they are named.

The oath itself is a rich source of medical mythology. Despite what many people believe, it is not a fixed and definitive statement of medical ethics but has been modified relentlessly down the centuries. It has never been widely sworn by medical students or graduands; indeed, most British doctors have never even seen it. Nor has the swearing of it been imposed as a condition for obtaining a medical degree or entering practice.

The earliest certain evidence of the oath being sworn in a university comes from 1558, and not until 1804 is there evidence of it being sworn by newly fledged doctors. As Vivian Nutton told the Royal College of Physicians in 1995, 'The demand for medical oaths and declarations is largely a feature of the second half of the twentieth century, favoured by physicians but often viewed with suspicion by patients.'

As for the contents of the oath, in the form in which it was printed in the late nineteenth century, it reads like a catalogue of restrictive practices dressed up as a solemn promise to Apollo. In 1973, the science writer Dr Robert Reid wrote: 'It takes little consideration of the Hippocratic oath to conclude that it is a bigoted and dangerous document. It embraces hardline early trade union practices, including the closed family shop, intended to establish a mystery about the men who practised the art which would separate them from other beings. As well as encouraging nepotistic incompetent hierarchies, it hands out totally ambiguous ethical advice.'

The role that Hippocrates plays in modern medicine seems to be that of a paternalistic god, and belief in his existence is a comforting source of ritual for doctors who like that sort of thing. Paul Vaughan, one-time press officer of the British Medical Association (BMA), has described how, one afternoon in the mid-1950s, there was one of those ceremonies on which the BMA is rather keen. The Greek Ambassador and any number of medical notables gathered in the Garden Court at BMA House to watch a distinguished representative of the Greek medical profession plant a small sprig brought from the island of Cos and said to have come from the very plane tree under which Hippocrates sat uttering aphorisms. Polite applause, says Vaughan, pattered around the garden as the ceremonial sod was lifted and the frail specimen gently placed in the alien soil, symbolising the handing-on of a centuries-old tradition, a noble ideal for the BMA to guard. A few weeks later, the cutting was dead.

One dangerous effect of the Hippocratic inheritance is the way it is used by those who think that, because they have acquired a medical degree, a divine light sparkles somewhere about their person. In 1978, Paul Vickers, a consultant surgeon who was a prominent BMA man and also a member of the

General Medical Council, told a medical audience: 'What the public and we are inclined to forget is that doctors are different. We establish standards of professional conduct. This is where we differ from the ragtag-and-bobtail crew who like to think of themselves as professionals in the health field.' Three years later, Vickers was found guilty of murdering his wife with an anti-cancer drug.

In 1985, the ebullient medical journalist Dr Donald Gould proposed a safer role model: 'Doctors are not gods, and function best as loyal, devoted, skilful servants, advising, persuading, supporting, but never usurping. The best doctor is a kind of Jeeves.'

TRUST ME, I'M A DOCTOR

TARSUS, CILICIA, 334 BC

Alexander the Great led his troops on their conquering march through Asia Minor like a pop idol at the head of an army of fans. Before they left home, he won the loyalty of his young Macedonian followers by ordering his treasurers to provide for their families while they were away, then won their adoration with his charismatic leadership. Some historians claim it was only at the insistence of the fans that he proclaimed himself to be a god.

When the army reached Tarsus, the capital of Cilicia, Alexander paused his march and the spies who were tracking his progress reported that he seemed reluctant to move on. Darius, the Persian king, attributed this dallying to cowardice, and prepared to move against him. Alexander had, in fact, been struck down by a debilitating illness, which some attributed to accumulated fatigue, others to his habit of bathing in the ice-cold waters of the River Cydnus.

The young king's doctors were afraid to treat him. They could see that he was desperately ill and knew that, if he died, his adoring followers would accuse them of being in league with his enemies and of murdering their king and living god. Only one physician, Philip the Acarnanian, was willing to take the risk. According to Plutarch, 'Seeing how critical his case was, but relying on his own well-known friendship for him, he resolved to try the last efforts of his art, and rather hazard his own credit and life than suffer him to perish for want of physic.'

While Philip was preparing his medicinal brew, Alexander received a letter from one of the physician's enemies, warning him that the Persian king had bribed the Acarnanian to poison him, offering Philip great sums of money and the promise of his daughter in marriage. Alexander read the letter and slipped it under his pillow without showing it to anyone.

When Philip entered the king's tent with the medicine, Alexander took the cup and handed his doctor the letter. Then, while Philip read it, Alexander drank the potion 'with great cheerfulness and assurance'. As he finished the draught and Philip finished the letter, the two friends looked at one another. Alexander's look was cheerful, radiating gratitude and confidence in his physician; Philip's was one of alarm. He appealed to the gods to witness his innocence, 'sometimes lifting up his hands to heaven, and then throwing himself down by the bedside, and beseeching Alexander to lay aside all fear, and follow his directions without apprehension'. Alexander sought to calm his doctor. 'Fear not,' he said, 'I have complete confidence in your honour.'

There followed two critical days for patient and physician. 'The medicine at first worked so strongly as to drive, so to say, the vital forces into the interior,' Plutarch reports. 'He lost his speech, and falling into a swoon, had scarce any sense or pulse left.' On the third day, however, Alexander's strength returned and he was able to reappear before his soldiers who had been 'in continual fear and dejection until they saw him abroad again'. Without delay, Alexander rallied his army and led it into battle against Darius, who panicked and rode away, leaving behind his mother, his wife and daughters, his chariot, his bow, his shield, his mantle, his army, and 110,000 Persian casualties.

One of the received truths of medicine is that trust between patient and doctor is an essential ingredient of treatment. So was it the doctor's brew or the patient's trust that brought about Alexander's recovery? Anyone who asked the question at the time would have faced a charge, not of treason, but of sacrilege. Alexander's followers *knew* that their leader had survived because he was a god.

THE MAN WHO KNEW EVERYTHING

ROME, 170 AD

The physician Galen, a dominant figure in medical history, was born and trained in Greece but moved to Rome because he felt that a man as gifted as he should be at the centre of the world. He established a fashionable practice in the city and eventually became doctor to a succession of emperors. Galen is often described as a founding father of Western medicine, if only because he wrote so much. Some 350 of his texts survived and their mixture of erudite philosophising, astute observation, dogmatic assertion and irritating polemic remained unchallenged for over a thousand years: indeed, they were Western medicine's standard textbooks right up until the Renaissance.

Galen was an arrogant man – those who didn't agree with him were treated as idiots – and a frightful snob: his texts carry regular reminders that his patients came from the very top drawer. He bequeathed much that was good to medicine but also much that was dangerous. Many who later revered him as a founding father fashioned themselves in his image and developed an inflated sense of their own dignity, maybe even their divinity. They behaved like priests graciously pleased to offer the ignorant the benefits of their superior intellect and mystical power. Some would say that that part of the Galen legacy has yet to be wholly expunged.

His case histories offer a glimpse of the character of the man who wrote them:

Something really amazing happened when the Emperor himself was my patient. Just when the lamps were lit, a messenger came and brought me to the Emperor as he had bidden. Three doctors had watched over him since dawn, and two of them felt his pulse, and all three thought that a fever attack was coming. I stood alongside, but said nothing. The Emperor looked first at me and asked why I did not feel his pulse as the other two had. I answered: 'These two colleagues of mine have already done so and, as they have followed you on the journey, they presumably know what your normal pulse is, so they can judge its present state better.'

When I said this, he bade me, too, to feel his pulse. My impression was that – considering his age and body constitution – the pulse was far from indicating a fever attack, but that his stomach was stuffed with the food he had eaten, and that the food had become a slimy excrement. The Emperor praised my diagnosis and said, three times in a row: 'That is it. It is just as you say. I have eaten too much cold food.'

He then asked what measures should be taken. I replied what I knew of a similar case, saying: 'If you were any plain citizen of this country, I would as usual prescribe wine with a little pepper. But to a royal patient I would recommend milder treatment. It is enough for a woollen cover to be put on your stomach, impregnated with a warm spiced salve.'

Though his tone is often self-congratulatory, Galen came close to achieving the objective he set himself: a philosophy of medicine that melded logic to experience. The main flaw in the philosophy that he evolved was that, like the man himself, it offered an explanation for everything, and Galen's need for explanation drove him to false conclusions.

One way to understand the workings of the body, he suggested, was to dissect it. A physician without anatomy was an architect without a plan. Yet because human dissection was forbidden in Rome, he had to restrict himself to sheep, pigs,

7

goats and Barbary apes. These animal dissections led him to false assumptions about human anatomy. He claimed, for instance, that humans had a five-lobed liver, as dogs do, and that the heart had only two chambers instead of four. He was equally mistaken about the workings of the body. He concluded that blood originates in the liver, passes through the heart, where it is mixed with air, then slops around the body. This misinterpretation led him to introduce blood-letting, an occasionally beneficial but often dangerous treatment that persisted well into the nineteenth century.

Galen was also a great student of the pulse. He wrote voluminously about its value in diagnosis – as in the case of the emperor's over-stuffed stomach – and attended Roman courts to offer an opinion on the veracity of witnesses using their pulse rate as a lie-detector.

Medical scientists credit him with being the first physician to introduce experimentation into medicine. Family doctors like to quote one of his cases that must have seemed strange and mysterious at the time but can now be seen as the first recorded venture into territory that they tread every day.

Galen was called to attend the wife of Servius Paulus, one of his aristocratic patients. Other doctors had been treating her for an organic disease but she had not improved. While taking her pulse, Galen mentioned the name of an actor with whom her name was linked in the gossip of the town. Her pulse immediately quickened. Then Galen leaned down and whispered something in her ear that made her laugh.

What he said remains unrecorded but the laugh began her cure and, 'tis said, is the earliest instance of psychotherapy being used to treat psychosomatic illness.

ON WHOM THE DREADFUL
LOT DID FALL

VERONA, ITALY, 1530

Medical students were once taught – maybe they still are – that syphilis was a gift from the New World to the Old, conveyed to Europe by Columbus's returning sailors. Yet the search for the source of the pox is bedevilled by Man's instinct to blame others for anything of which he feels ashamed. Native Americans have claimed that Columbus's sailors were infected by the natives in Haiti, Spaniards that the disease existed in Europe before the discovery of America and was brought to their south coast by sailors from west Africa.

Though the truth is unlikely ever to be known, it seems certain that when Charles VIII of France laid siege to Naples in 1495 he did so with a pox-ridden army, and his mercenaries further disseminated the disease when they returned to France. As a result, the French called it the Neapolitan disease but the Italians called it the French disease. In the end, a Veronese physician, Hieronymous Fracastorius, aka Girolamo Fracastoro, put an end to these territorial disclaimers by giving the disease a name.

Fracastorius was a true son of the Renaissance, an astronomer, philosopher, geographer, botanist and mathematician who also produced erudite texts on the temperature of wines and on the rise of the Nile. As a physician, he was particularly interested in diseases that spread from one person to another, such as leprosy and plague. When he happened upon one that could be passed

9

during sexual intercourse, he grew so excited that he wrote a poem about it in Latin hexameters.

In the poem, a young shepherd angers the sun god with an act of impiety and is punished by being struck down by a loathsome and contagious disease. In search of a name for the shepherd, Fracastorius turned to Ovid and settled upon Syphilus, the second son of Niobe. When he published his poem *Syphulus* in 1544, it became a bestseller and the name of the mythical character became the name of the distinctly unmythical disease.

As an Italian, Fracastorius referred, of course, to the French disease, and the poem's flavour is conveyed in these excerpts, translated – or, as he put it, 'attempted' – from the Latin by Nahum Tate in 1686.

A shepherd once (distrust not ancient fame)
Possest these Downs, and Syphilus his Name
Some destin'd Head t'attone the Crimes of all,
On Syphilus the dreadful Lot did fall

Through what adventures this unknown Disease
So lately did astonisht Europe seize,
Through Asian coasts and Libyan Cities ran,
And from what Seeds the Malady began,
Our Song shall tell: to Naples first it came
From France, and justly took from France his Name

He first wore bubos dreadful to the sight
First felt strange pains and sleepless passed the night
From him the malady received its name,
The neighbouring shepherds caught the spreading flame.

And also, presumably, the neighbouring shepherdesses.

The notion that syphilis was a deserved punishment for sin survived into the seventeenth century supported enthusiastically by the likes of John Bunyan. Eighteenth-century gentlemen, however, began to speak openly of having a dose of the pox, but the sense of shame and of divine retribution with which Fracastorius invested the disease was rediscovered by the Victorians. In 1860, Samuel Solly, President of the Royal College of Surgeons, pronounced syphilis a blessing because it restrained unbridled passion. If the disease were exterminated, which he hoped it would not be, 'fornicators would ride rampant through the land'. (Did he, I wonder, realise the image he created in his listeners' imaginations?)

The French bourgeoisie were equally intolerant of fornication. In 1833, when the French surgeon Baron Dupuytren asked a patient, 'Have you been with prostitutes?' the patient replied, 'Of course not. How could you even think of that?' To which Dupuytren replied, 'Then they have been with you.'

The eagerness to equate sex with sin persisted well into the second half of the twentieth century. Many made efforts to treat sufferers of syphilis and gonorrhoea in a civilised way, but only in the 1970s did medicine finally erase the shabby but honourable image of the pox doctor and replace it with the sharper, smarter one of a specialist in genitourinary medicine.

In the forties and fifties public information about 'venereal disease' had been confined to notices that local councils were permitted to exhibit only in public conveniences, and these were mere lists of local VD clinics offering confidential treatment. In most hospitals, the clinics, usually signposted as 'special departments', were housed in shabbier premises than those inhabited by more respectable specialities, their entrances often hidden down alleys. True, they offered a confidential service, but a person needed courage not just to go for treatment but to enquire where the clinic was.

Yet the sporting spirit of the eighteenth century was not completely crushed. One evening in 1949, a music-hall baritone, fresh from his performance at a West End theatre, arrived at the special department at the old Charing Cross Hospital, still in the clothes that he wore in his act: white tie, tails, top hat and white gloves. He doffed his topper to the receptionist and announced in beautifully modulated tones, 'I've come in answer to your advertisement in the gentlemen's lavatory in Leicester Square.'

THE BIRTH OF PROFESSIONAL FEEMANSHIP

LYONS, FRANCE, 1533

What little we know of the lives of doctors who practised in ill-documented times is often an indistinguishable mix of fact and legend. There seems, however, to be general accord that one such doctor introduced the concept of the professional fee.

The occasion was provided in October 1533 by Jean du Bellay, Bishop of Paris, when he was on his way to Rome to receive his cardinal's hat. By the time he reached Lyons, he was so afflicted by pain in his back and hips that he had to be carried from his coach to a local inn. There, the innkeeper sent an urgent message to the local teaching hospital, the Hotel-Dieu, but grew distinctly worried when he saw who responded. For along came a lecturer in anatomy who was thought by his colleagues to be dangerously mad because of his habit of picking fights with the Church and its philosophers. He would argue, cheerfully rather than angrily, with priests about the worth of their spiritual cures, with doctors and apothecaries about the value of their medicines, and with patients about the seriousness of their illnesses.

The innkeeper relaxed a little when the bishop seemed to take to this cheery man, middle-aged but young for his years, wearing a fur-edged robe and a skull cap decorated with a golden scarab. The doctor quickly diagnosed the bishop's pain as sciatica, probably brought on by sitting too long in a cramped position in the coach, rubbed in some balm that he said would give temporary relief, advised his patient to get out of his coach occasionally and walk a mile or two, then demanded a fee of ten gold Louis.

The bishop was outraged. 'That's a fortune,' he complained. (And, indeed, it was a quarter of the doctor's annual stipend from the Hotel-Dieu.) 'Your fee is unjustified because of the brevity of your visit and the amount of attention you've given me.'

'For the time and the balm the fee is one Louis,' said the doctor. 'The other nine are for my ability to tell you the nature of your illness.'

And thus was born a maxim that has since served the profession well. In 1952, for instance, when a patient accused a London anaesthetist of charging an exorbitant fee of fifty guineas 'just for putting me to sleep', the anaesthetist replied, 'The fee for putting you to sleep was only five guineas; the other forty-five were for waking you up.'

The doctor who begat the maxim was Francois Rabelais. And he profited from his encounter with the bishop to much greater measure than the ten Louis. Jean du Bellay was so taken with the cheerily eccentric doctor that he invited him to accompany him as his personal physician. Rabelais readily agreed. He had recently published the first collection of his stories about the giants Gargantua and Pantagruel, and was enjoying the sense of freedom that can come with an independent income. He resigned from his job at the Hotel-Dieu and left for Rome with the bishop. They became good friends. Later, when Rabelais gave up medicine and spent much of his time travelling around Europe, he often stayed with Cardinal du Bellay and, when his third book was condemned as heresy by the Sorbonne, his friend's protection saved him.

It is sometimes said that Rabelais was the first doctor-writer to make use of his encounters with his patients. True, his stories make fun of vices and foolishness that doctors often see, but his mockery is aimed not so much at people as at institutions, particularly the Catholic Church. And for that he could draw on other personal experience because, before he became a doctor, he was a priest. The humour he unleashes in his books is genial and bawdy, yet often beneath the ribaldry lies acerbic mockery of self-regarding teachers, politicians and philosophers – so acerbic that he had to spend some time in hiding from those who sought to prosecute him for heresy, the catch-all charge used at the time to silence unwelcome voices.

His books were enormously popular, their sales promoted by people like Pope Clement VII, who pronounced them as forbidden reading and thus provoked a special edition, printed and bound to look like a holy book, to be read by those who feared excommunication. The author's imaginative description of bodily functions, his exploration of the quirks of human anatomy, particularly of the genitalia, and his erudite, if irreverent, references to philosophy led many commentators to say, 'Only a doctor could have written such a book.' The French medical establishment, however, was not best pleased. It responded in the traditional way of medical establishments by deciding to expel Rabelais from the profession, only to be thwarted by the fact that he no longer claimed to be a doctor.

ALCHEMY AS PERFORMANCE ART

LONDON, 1579

Some doctors still refer to patients as cases: 'a case of jaundice' or 'a case of diabetes', as if patients were not people but receptacles of disease. The custom is deeply engrained. Reginald Hilton, a physician at London's St Thomas's Hospital in the 1940s, would greet the arrival of 'a case of syphilis' with a relish that suggested it had been delivered by his wine merchant.

If we applied the same tradition to nominating medicine's 'strangest case', the first candidate would be Simon Forman, variously described in history books as an Elizabethan doctor, womaniser, astrologer, theatre-goer, necromancer and purveyor of love potions – all of which occupations he pursued with energetic dedication. Historians treasure his diaries because they include descriptions of the plays he saw at the Globe Theatre, including *Macbeth, The Winter's Tale, Cymbeline* and *Richard II,* but the diaries have also much to offer any seeker of oddity in medicine.

Forman was born near Salisbury but, after an unhappy spell as a teacher, moved to London and, at the age of 27, set himself up as a practitioner of physic, surgery and magic. Unlike most London doctors, he stayed in the capital during the plagues of 1592 and 1594, when he is said to have saved many lives and acquired a reputation as a courageous man and a good physician. His success drew the attention of the Royal College of Physicians, which, angered by his 'alternative' methods of healing, summoned him for an examination. His scanty knowledge of anatomy and the medical dogma of the day provoked 'great mirth and sport among the auditors' and the College banned him from practising in London.

Nine months later, when he defied the ban and prescribed a potion to a man who died after consuming it, he was sent to prison. For seven years after his release, he conducted a guerrilla war against the College, which responded by employing spies to watch his house and by sending phoney patients to consult him. Forman won the war in 1603 when Cambridge University granted him a licence to practise 'the cure of ills of all kindes and substances of the human boddy'.

Forman's practice made use of three rooms in his house in Lambeth. In the first, his main consulting room, he offered the standard medical treatments of the day supplemented by 'metoposcopy', a form of soothsaying which used the techniques of palmistry to analyse markings on the face, particularly the lines on the forehead and the position of warts. This was also the room in which he concocted love philtres and aphrodisiacs for those who felt the need of them. In the second room Forman cast astrological charts and told fortunes, and in the third, he arranged assignations between those seeking partners. If things went well in the third room, the couple would move to the second for an astrological assessment of their compatibility, and then to the first to receive the potions that would enhance their relationship.

Forman had a large and fashionable practice. He treated the impresario Philip Henslowe for an itching face, Robert Burton – for melancholy, of course – and Archbishop Whitgift for jaundice. He also treated Shakespeare's lover Emilia Lanier (probably the Dark Lady of the sonnets) before persuading her to become his own mistress, and Shakespeare's landlady, Mrs Mountjoy. Her tenant was behind with his rent and she wanted a prediction of his prospects. Forman offered her a posset 'to ease her humor'.

One regular patient was Frances Howard, daughter of Lord Howard of Bindon, who first consulted him as a young girl with 'night flutterynges of the heart'. He asked her to visit him one night when her heart was actually fluttering and he then 'devoided me of my nyght-gowne and, having give me a potion to drive out devills, soothed me uponn my breasts until I was plees'd'.

A few years later, she asked him to cast her horoscope so 'that I might see to what estate I should be raysed'. With the help of astrolabes, charts and almanacs, Forman, 'his beard brystlyng and his eye bryte' told her she should change her estate three times. She readily complied. First she married the son of a wealthy alderman who 'dy'd leaving me unchilded', then an earl who also conveniently died, and finally bagged a duke.

Forman's reputation for necromancy attracted rich merchants wishing to heap ill luck upon competitors, churchmen seeking preferment, gamblers needing a change of fortune, and lovers seeking to attract their beloved or to murder their rivals. Yet most of his 2,000 consultations a year, half of them with women of child-bearing age, were with poor people, many of whom he saw for free.

His reputation for what modern tabloids call 'sex in the surgery' may have been created by women who offered sexual favours in lieu of a fee. He made no secret of his womanising, and recorded each encounter in his diaries, using the codeword 'halek' for coition. His diary for 9 July 1607, when he was aged 55, records: 'Halek 8 a.m. Hester Sharp, and halek at 3 p.m. Anne Wiseman, and halek at 9 p.m. Tronco [his pet name for his wife]'. He was also happy to oblige ladies who suspected their husbands were infertile and to exploit the empathy he established with young women who consulted him. 'He bedded me,' said one, 'and there was no more to it than that. Now I am round with child, and it is his doing.' He was proud of his sexual profligacy and dreamed of seducing Queen Elizabeth.

Despite Forman's reputation as a magician, most of his patients came to him with common ailments – sore throats, toothache, cut fingers, warts, 'coffs & chokyngs', broken bones – all recorded punctiliously in his notebooks and treated with the usual remedies of the day. He pulled teeth, bound wounds and practised the great medical cure-all of the time – bleeding patients with leeches or by lancing a vein to drain off 'infected'

17

blood. His treatment books record that he used euphorbium for palsy, turpeth for croup, white arsenic for lipuria, and snake venom for 'dropsicall afflictions'.

Indeed, his books suggest Forman shouldn't be written off as an exploitative quack. He kept detailed diaries and medical casebooks, made voluminous notes from medical and scientific texts, and defined protocols for conducting scientific research. He published a pamphlet on ways of determining longitude and showed fine discrimination by taking an interest in everything except politics. His writings build a picture of Renaissance medical science that may seem strange to us only because we look at it in retrospect. After all, when Forman got his Cambridge licence, Galileo, whom no one would dismiss as a quack, was teaching astrology to medical students in Padua who believed that they needed to know what the stars foretold for their patients if they were to diagnose and treat them successfully and prepare their medicines at favourable times.

Like the respected doctors of Padua, Forman believed that astrology helped him evaluate his patients. Women were particularly difficult to treat, he claimed, because their health was regulated by their wombs and their sexual activity, subjects on which they were notoriously duplicitous. Astrology revealed to him whether a woman was sexually active and enabled him to assess her disease. And by showing he knew she was being honest or dishonest about her sexual life, he could win her confidence. That has the makings of a convincing story, which is more than can be said for many of the tales told to their patients by Forman's enemies at the Royal College of Physicians.

RUINOUS INHERITANCE

SOUTH AFRICA, 1685; LONDON, 1738

Alan Bennett's play *The Madness of George III*, and the film that followed, drew on a remarkable piece of detective work by two British psychiatrists, Ida Macalpine and her son Richard Hunter. After studying contemporary accounts of the king's behaviour and what records remained of his illness, they concluded that he had suffered from porphyria, an inherited disorder in which a defect in the manufacture of haemoglobin, the oxygen-carrying red pigment in the blood, creates excessive amounts of porphyrin.

The disease often reveals itself when the excess porphyrin is excreted in the urine, turning it the colour of port wine. The excess also gets deposited in other parts of the body – in the skin, which it makes oversensitive to light, in the abdomen, where it causes attacks of pain, and in the brain, where it can cause convulsions and the bouts of madness suffered by the king. These symptoms often appear in intermittent spells, some-times with years passing between each attack – King George enjoyed a gap of 23 years between his first and second bouts of illness, though in the end he spent his last nine years of life 'sick in both body and mind'.

Some historians believe that Ida Macalpine and her son failed to make a convincing case that King George suffered from porphyria. No one has doubts about the disease investigated in another remarkable piece of detective work, by the British epidemiologist Geoffrey Dean. Maybe his work would be better

19

known if it had involved a royal or two, but his central character was a Dutch commoner called Gerrit Jansz whom Dean encountered – retrospectively – in South Africa where, after training as a doctor in Liverpool, he worked as senior physician at Provincial Hospital in Port Elizabeth.

Nothing is known of Jansz's history before 1685, when he left for the Cape. Yet, thanks to Dr Dean, we can now trace the effect on that country of one of the genes that Jansz brought with him, the one that carries susceptibility to a form of porphyria less dramatic and less dangerous than that thought to have been suffered by Mad King George. Its main characteristic is not madness but blotched hands.

In the 1960s, nearly 300 years after Jansz's arrival, some 8,000 white South Africans and 2,000 'coloureds' suffered from 'van Rooyen hands', an inflammation and pigmentation of the skin. The condition occurred more commonly in Dutch than in British descendants, and Geoffrey Dean's detective work was helped by the passionate interest that the Boers took in their forbears, recording in the front pages of their bibles who had given birth to whom down through the generations. These records enabled Dean to trace the direct ancestors of nearly all the Afrikaners and most of the non-Afrikaners who were suffering from 'van Rooyen hands', and each family line led back eventually to Gerrit Jansz. The Dutch immigrant's single malfunctioning gene – only one gene is thought to be involved – had bestowed an immortal inheritance upon his adopted country.

Attempts to trace the inheritance trail of King George's illness have been less successful. Mary Queen of Scots and her son King James I are said to have suffered from it and, if James did have the disease, the malfunctioning gene would have passed to both the Hanoverian and Prussian royal lines. So when England later imported a Hanoverian king, it also re-imported the gene that, in 1738, endowed a newborn babe with the genetic defect that would later earn him the soubriquet Mad King George.

As Alan Bennett's play movingly reveals, George was not mad all the time, and managed to reign for sixty years. Thanks to one of the oddities that infiltrate history when it's viewed through medical eyes, the only monarch to reign longer, Queen Victoria, was a carrier of another nasty malfunctioning gene, the one that bestows haemophilia.

THE MAN WHOM HISTORY PASSED BY

WORTH MATRAVERS, ISLE OF PURBECK, 1774

A painting on display in the foyer of the World Health Organisation office in Copenhagen during the 1980s portrayed a proud moment in medical history: English country doctor Edward Jenner inoculating eight-year-old James Phipps with matter he had taken from a pustule on the skin of dairymaid Sarah Nelmes, who was suffering from cowpox. The painting was captioned 'The First Vaccination'.

That caption, though doctors don't like to admit it, is a lie.

Jenner, so the story goes, knew that 'countryfolk' in his native Gloucestershire believed that dairy-maids who accidentally got infected with cowpox, a disease of cattle, never got smallpox. (Countryfolk was a word that doctors of the time used to denote people who were a notch down from gentility; in conversation, they might call them peasants.) Because cowpox was a relatively benign condition while smallpox, the 'speckled monster', caused 10 per cent of the deaths in Europe, Jenner reasoned that inoculating the contents of a cowpox pustule into a healthy human might confer immunity against the more serious disease. So he went ahead with the experiment that was later hailed as the first vaccination.

Soon after it, James Phipps developed a slight fever from which he quickly recovered. Six weeks later when Jenner inoculated Phipps with a small dose taken from a smallpox pustule, the inoculation did not 'take'. Jenner repeated this test several times but it never 'took' and he concluded that James Phipps had become immune to smallpox.

When Jenner published his account of the experiment, it generated great excitement. Over the next two years, more than 5,000 people were vaccinated in England, and the technique was taken up even more eagerly abroad. In Sweden it became compulsory, as it did in Napoleon's army. When Jenner later begged a favour of Napoleon, the Emperor responded, 'Anything Jenner wants shall be granted. He has been my most faithful servant in the European campaigns.'

Vaccination programmes proved enormously successful and eventually, thanks to the thoroughness with which they were pursued, the World Health Organisation was able to announce in 1980 its greatest ever victory in its war against disease, the complete eradication of smallpox from this planet. Small wonder that 14 May 1796 has become a golden day in medical history, the date on which Edward Jenner performed 'The First Vaccination'.

Yet if you visit the graveyard beside the church of St Nicholas at Worth Matravers in Dorset, you will find a tombstone bearing this inscription:

Sacred
to the memory
of
Benjamin Jesty (of Downshay)
who departed this life
April 16, 1816
aged 79 years.
He was born in Yetminster in this
County, and was an upright honest
man particularly noted for having
been the first Person (known) that
introduced the Cow Pox
by Inoculation, and who from
his great strength of mind made the
Experiment from the (Cow)
on his Wife and two Sons in the Year 1774

So who was this man who performed 'the first (known) vaccination' 22 years before Jenner's revered experiment? Benjamin Jesty was a Dorset farmer who, like Jenner, was aware of the local belief that an attack of cowpox gave protection against smallpox, indeed had first-hand evidence because some of his servants had been treated for cowpox caught through milking.

In 1774, the county of Dorset suffered a severe outbreak of smallpox and Jesty feared for the safety of his wife and his two small sons, aged two and three. When he heard that a neighbour's cows were infected with cowpox, he took his family to the infected farm and scratched their arms with a stocking needle that he had contaminated by pricking it into an infected cow's udders. The vaccine 'took' strongly, particularly in his wife, who ran such a fever that an alarmed Jesty called in medical help, probably from Surgeon Trowbridge of Cerne. Certainly it was Surgeon Trowbridge who, after Mrs Jesty had recovered, used the same test that Jenner was to use over twenty years later on James Phipps to confirm that she and her sons had become immune to smallpox.

So why was the Copenhagen picture called The First Vaccination? And why does Jesty's name appear so rarely in accounts of medicine's 'war' against smallpox? In 1979, Bryan Brooke, then professor of surgery at St George's Hospital in London, where Jenner had been a student, wrote: 'It seems to me that Jenner must have heard what Jesty did; but there was never a mention, never an acknowledgement by him, nor is there by those who write today about the history of vaccination. Can it be a conspiracy of silence by the medical profession – starting possibly with Jenner – because the first known vaccinator was not a medical man?'

Professor Brooke claimed that whenever he tried to win Jesty the recognition that was his due, he ran into a stone wall. In the mid-1970s, for instance, *The Times* published a centre-page article celebrating the news that smallpox was near to eradication. It told the traditional tale of Jenner, James Phipps and Sarah Nelmes but made no mention of 'the first vaccinator (known)'. Brooke wrote to *The Times*. As professor of surgery at St George's, he wanted, he said, 'to make amends to Jesty from one George's man on behalf of another. But the conspiracy of silence prevailed yet again; my letter wasn't published. It is the convention that unpublished letters receive a reply from the editor, usually courteous, but on this occasion somewhat tart. Their correspondent of course knew all about Jesty but considered that he had no significant part in the story. From which I was able to deduce that their correspondent had not done his homework and knew little or nothing about him.'

In 1802, Parliament voted to give Jenner £10,000 and the following year the Royal Jennerian Society was founded to promote vaccination. Meanwhile, the 'upright honest' Benjamin Jesty lived out his life in Downshay, no doubt content that he had saved his wife and sons from the clutches of the speckled monster. Though he may have occasionally reflected that when it comes to the pursuit of fame and fortune, doctors have as little respect as other professionals for the peasant – beg its pardon, countryfolk – dictum, credit where credit is due.

LONDON'S CELESTIAL
HEALTH CENTRE

LONDON, 1779

In the late summer of 1779, two huge men wearing gold-trimmed livery, and quickly nicknamed Gog and Magog, walked the streets of London distributing handbills advertising Dr James Graham's Temple of Health.

The Magnificent Electrical Apparatus and the supremely brilliant and Unique decorations of this Magical Edifice – of this enchanting Elysian Palace! where wit and mirth, love and beauty – all that can delight the sound and all that can ravish the senses, will hold their Court, this and every Evening this Week, in chaste and joyous assemblage. The Celestial Brilliance of the Medico-Electrical Apparatus in all the apartments of the Temple will be exhibited by Dr Graham himself, who will have the honour of explaining the true Nature and Effects of Electricity, Air, Music and Magnetism when applied to the human body.

Precisely at eight o'clock the Gentleman Usher of the Rosy Rod, assisted by the High Priestess, will conduct the rosy, the gigantic, the STUPENDOUS Goddess of Health to the Celestial Throne.

The blooming Priestess of the Temple will endeavour to entertain Ladies and Gentlemen of candour and good nature, by reading a Lecture on the simplest and most efficacious means of preserving health, beauty, and

26

personal loveliness, and a serene mental brilliancy even to the extremest old age.

VESTINATHE GIGANTIC, on the Celestial Throne, as the Goddess of Health, will exhibit in her own person a proof of the all-blessing effects of virtue, temperance, regularity, simplicity, and moderation; and in these luxurious, artificial and effeminate times, to recommend those great virtues.

The Temple stood in the Royal Terrace in the newly built Adelphi. For two shillings and sixpence, patrons could savour the Elysian sensuality of the main hall; if they wished to explore further and enjoy the loin-stirring ritual of the Gentleman Usher of the Rosy Rod and his Goddess of Health, they had to invest ten shillings and sixpence.

Those who paid the full half-guinea could wander through extravagantly decorated rooms, illuminated by scented candles and lined with erotic paintings and sculpture. The air was filled with perfume, pumped in through hidden tubes, and with celestial music produced off-stage by mechanical wind instruments. In alcoves between the stained-glass windows were collections of walking sticks, crutches, spectacles, ear trumpets and other aids discarded by those who, thanks to Dr Graham's electrical and magnetic treatment, no longer needed them.

At certain hours in the Chamber of Apollo, Dr Graham, robed in Greco-Roman style, would proclaim the secrets of a healthy life and rejuvenated sexual performance – fresh air, exercise and a frugal diet. In this he was assisted by young Gods and Goddesses of Youth and Health. The young women, recruited through newspaper advertisements and chosen for their looks, delivered homilies written by the doctor on the nature of love and loveliness, illustrating the themes by striking classical poses, sometimes wearing white silk robes, sometimes wearing nothing.

One of the Temple's first Goddesses was a sixteen-year-old housemaid, Amy Lyon, whose pose as the Goddess Hygiea was captured in a Rowlandson cartoon. In her most popular performance, she frolicked naked in a health-giving mud bath.

Later she became a professional plaything of rich men and eventually, after becoming Lady Hamilton, of Lord Nelson.

A Temple bookstall offered Graham's books. The most popular was *Private Advisers*, which detailed the 'darkest secrets of gentlemen and ladies', cost a guinea, and came in a plain brown wrapper. Another strong seller was *Treatise on Health,* designed to encourage happy marriages. In it, Graham advised couples to bar the moon from their bedchamber and to sing along together while engaging in sexual sport: 'Music softens the mind of a happy couple, makes them all love, all harmony. Joined together in lyric concord while engaged in Moll Pratly's Jig, the happy couple will become inhabitants of a superior region.'

They could further enhance their performance, he explained, with Dr Graham's Divine Balsam, available from the Temple shop – as were phials of Electrical Ether, designed to protect against the city's noxious atmosphere, and Imperial Pills to purify the blood. The shop's best seller was Nervous Ethereal Balsam, the elixir for 'worn-out constitutions' in both sexes, which claimed not just to cure impotence but to be a powerful aphrodisiac, and to guarantee procreation.

Aside from the underclad tableaux, the feature most attractive to Graham's aristocratic clientele was the 'magnetico-electric' Celestial Bed claimed to have magical properties found nowhere else on earth.

> The truly divine energy of this celestial and electrical fire, which fills every part of the bed, as well as the magnetic fluid, are both of them calculated to give the necessary degree of strength and exertion to the nerves. Besides the melodious tones of the harmonica, the soft sounds of a flute, the charms of an agreeable voice and the harmonious notes of the organ, being all joined, how can the power and virtue of such a happy conjunction fail in raising sentiments of admiration and pleasure in the soul of the philosopher and even of the physician?

The bed, twelve feet long and nine feet wide, rested on glass pillars and its oriental canopy was decorated with large crimson tassels. Celestial blue curtains hung from the canopy and the silk sheets and pillows were deep purple. The blankets were impregnated with Arabian essences; other perfumes were blown gently into the bedchamber through hidden glass tubes. Emblazoned above the bed and 'sparkling with electrical fire' was the command *Be Fruitful; Multiply And Replenish The Earth*.

Beneath the bed were the magnetic lodestones that provided the celestial fire, and an electrically activated vacuum tube that created mysterious luminosity and crackled like lightning whenever touched by a speck of passing dust. The couple's performance was accompanied by celestial music and, when they were done, a gigantic engine hidden beneath them tilted the bed to assist conception.

Though Graham claimed he prevented 'wantons and mere pleasure-seekers' from using the bed, he never turned away men of noble family who sought a night of celestial bliss, not necessarily with their wives. Indeed, it was rumoured that a quiet word and the handing of a consideration to the Gentleman Usher of the Rosy Rod would ensure a celestial experience with one of the maidens from Vestina's Fairy Train.

Later, when Graham moved to Pall Mall and renamed his establishment the Temple of Health and Hymen, he had holes dug in the ground and recommended warm earth baths to all who wished 'to see their hundredth birthday'. People would lie in them for hours and a contemporary engraving shows four women entering them wearing nothing but their modish hats.

James Graham had studied medicine in Edinburgh but dropped out of medical school and went to America, where he eventually set himself up in Philadelphia as an eye specialist. Impressed by Benjamin Franklin's electrical experiments, he adopted electricity as a treatment that 'invigorates the whole body and remedies all physical defects'. Equipped with this panacea, he moved to London and quickly built a fashionable practice. He was mellifluous, handsome and an instinctive showman, and he quickly persuaded London society to inhale his ethereal balsams, sit on his 'magnetic throne', and lie in baths filled not with water but with crackling electrical sparks.

When he expanded his practice by creating the Temple of Health, it was not to everybody's taste. Horace Walpole wrote: 'It is the most impudent puppet-show of imposition I ever saw, and the mountebank himself the dullest of his profession. A woman, invisible, warbled to clarinets on the stairs. The decorations are pretty and odd, and the apothecary, who comes up a trap-door (for no purpose, since he might as well come up the stairs), is a novelty. The electrical experiments are nothing at all singular.'

Two years after moving to Pall Mall, Graham fell out of fashion as quickly as he had fallen into it. He closed the Temple and returned to Edinburgh where he got religion, turned peculiar and 'remained naked in the earth for nine successive days' before he died at the age of 49. Despite that last attenuated earth bath, he failed to fulfil even half his promise of a hundredth birthday.

AN AFTER-DINNER CONSULTATION

LONDON, 1780

George Fordyce, educated in Aberdeen and Edinburgh during the 'golden age' of Scottish medicine, was elected a physician at St Thomas's Hospital in London in 1770. He became an authority on fevers, and his work was highly regarded during his lifetime. Yet he was no great hit with the capital's medical establishment because he showed little concern for the social graces. The 1827 biography of Fordyce in the archives of the Royal College of Physicians regards it as a failing that he engaged in little private practice and explains that, 'His manners were less refined, and his dress in general less studied than is expected in this country in the physician. In the earlier years of his life to render the enjoyment of its pleasures compatible with his professional pursuits, he used to sleep but little. He was often known to lecture for three consecutive hours without having undressed himself the preceding night.'

Fordyce's place in medical history rests heavily on his eating and drinking habits and on one strange but celebrated case. For over twenty years, he dined every day at Dolly's chophouse in Paternoster Row. At four o'clock in the afternoon, the doctor would take his seat at his regular table, which already bore a silver tankard of strong ale, a bottle of port and a quarter of a pint of brandy. The moment he entered, the cook put a pound and a half of rump steak on the gridiron and, as soon as he was seated, the waiter served a *bonne bouche*. This was followed sometimes by half a boiled chicken, sometimes by a plate of

31

fish. After this, he took one glass of brandy and then proceeded to the steak, with which he drank the tankard of ale and the bottle of port. After his meal, he would finish the brandy before tottering off to his house in Essex Street. He would then eat no other meals until four o'clock the next day when he would return to Dolly's. His oft repeated maxim was, 'One meal a day is enough for a lion, and it ought to be for a man.'

The case for which he is remembered arose one evening when he was in Dolly's and, somewhere between the port and the brandy, received an urgent call to attend to a lady taken ill with an unspecified complaint. He arrived at the patient's house aware that he was far from sober and tried to put on as good a show as he could. Yet when the time came for him to examine her, he had considerable difficulty locating her pulse and, when he did locate it, was unable to count the beats. Muttering under his breath, 'Drunk, by God', he wrote out a prescription and hurriedly left the room.

The following morning, an urgent letter arrived from his patient. Fordyce opened it with some anxiety, expecting a severe rebuke. Instead he found an apology. His patient confessed that she well knew the unfortunate condition in which he had found her the previous evening and begged him to keep the business confidential 'in consideration of the enclosed'.

The enclosed was a bank note for a hundred pounds, which in those days was, as the saying goes, a considerable fortune.

A MOMENT OF TRUTH

BATH, 1781

Doctors who specialise in diseases of the rich learn early in their careers that a sound private practice needs an adequate supply of regular patients. Medical emergencies and exotica may provide for luxury – the Bentley, the opera, the Caribbean winter holiday – but a sufficiency of regular patients protects practitioners from the relentless tyranny of household bills.

In the golden age of private practice, before the coming of the NHS, a Regular Patient was one who figured on the Regular Visiting List and was visited at the same time each week, each fortnight, or each month. Most were lonely women, often widows, who yearned for someone to talk to. They didn't need, indeed often resented, any form of clinical examination, other than the doctor holding their wrists in pulse-taking mode while they told long, rambling, self-centred stories.

The excuse for the Regular Visit was the Agreed Illness. The ideal Agreed Illness was not too incapacitating to interfere with the pleasures of a well-upholstered life, yet serious enough to need regular attention and to allow for occasional spectacular 'attacks' that demanded dramatic medical intervention and sympathetic clucking from friends.

The Agreed Illness also had to be specific both to patient and doctor. Patients talking to impressionable friends needed to be able to say, 'My liver (kidney/womb/metabolism) is unique, you know. Every doctor, and I've seen the very best, my dear, has been quite baffled by my X-rays.' But unless they could add,

'Indeed they're so complicated that only dear Dr Handholder can understand them,' dual specificity had not been established and patients could, after a minor tiff, take their profitable illnesses elsewhere.

That's why private practitioners grew not so much protective as possessive of their Regular Patients. Possession was nine tenths of the income.

Sir Walter Farquhar (1738–1819) earned his citation in medical history when one of his Regular Patients decided to take the waters at Bath. When she expressed concern at the idea of being separated from the only physician who really understood her, Farquhar assured her he had a 'wholly reliable' colleague in Bath and gave her a letter of introduction setting out the details of her case.

During her journey, the woman realised that, though Sir Walter had been her doctor for many years and had assured her that her condition was one of the most complicated with which he had ever had to deal, he had never told her exactly what it was. The answer clearly lay in the letter. Overcome with curiosity, and despite the protests of her travelling companion, she steamed it open.

It read: 'Dear Davis. Keep the old lady for three weeks then send her back.'

THE SILENT CORE OF CONSULTATION

LONDON, 1798

John Abernethy, an eighteenth-century surgeon, was notorious for his brusqueness when dealing with wealthy patients. One of them, the duke of somewhere or other, was so angered by what he perceived as the surgeon's rudeness that he barked, 'I will make you eat your words, sir,' only for Abernethy to respond, 'It will be of no use for they will be sure to come up again.'

Yet, despite his abrasive attitude to private patients, Abernethy was always kind to those under his care in charity hospitals. Once when he was leaving to do a hospital round and a wealthy patient tried to detain him, he explained that the man would have to call another day. 'Private patients, if they do not like me, can go elsewhere; but the poor devils in the hospital I am bound to take care of.'

His selective brusqueness was rarely calculated, more often an instinctive reaction to pomposity. When he was after a job as surgeon at St Bartholomew's Hospital, he called on each of the governors in turn to make himself known to them. During his visit to one palatial home, the governor, a wealthy grocer, said rather loftily, 'I presume you are after my vote at this important point in your career.'

'No, I am not,' said Abernethy. 'I want a pennyworth of figs. Look sharp and wrap them up – I want to be off.'

Abernethy had two great dislikes. The first, strange for a man celebrated as 'a daring surgeon', was of operating. An assistant described how he once found him, 'in the retiring room, after a severe operation, with big tears in his eyes, lamenting the possible failure of what he had just been compelled to do by dire necessity and surgical rule'.

His second great dislike was of what he called 'idle chatter'. One evening, after visiting a woman he'd been treating for some weeks, he spoke to the daughter who'd been nursing her. 'I have witnessed your devotion and kindness to your mother. I am in need of a wife, and I think you are the very person who would suit me. My time is incessantly occupied, and I have therefore no leisure for courting. Reflect upon this matter until Monday.' She did and they got married. Their subsequent harmonious relationship confirmed he'd made a shrewd diagnosis.

John Abernethy earned a place in countless anthologies on the afternoon he told a melancholic patient that he needed to get out more and learn to laugh. 'Go and see the clown Grimaldi,' he said, only for the patient to reply, 'I am Grimaldi.' He earns a place in this collection of strange cases with his account of the ideal consultation for a hater of 'idle chatter'.

A young woman entered his consulting room and, without a word, held out an injured finger for examination. Abernethy dressed the wound in silence.

The woman returned a few days later.

'Better?' asked Abernethy.

'Better,' said the patient.

Subsequent visits were conducted in much the same way. On her last visit, the woman held out her finger, now healed.

'Well?' asked Abernethy.

'Well,' she replied.

'Upon my word, madam,' said Abernethy, 'you are the most rational woman I have ever met.'

THE SURGICAL TRIPLE WHAMMY

LONDON, 1840

Before the coming of anaesthetics, patients, heavily dosed with rum or opium, had to be held down or strapped to the operating table. Hence the most useful, and most admired, of a surgeon's skills was his operating speed. One man whose reputation as a surgical speedster spread from his native Scotland to Europe and North America was Robert Liston, a daring and successful surgeon who often took on patients whom other surgeons had rejected.

Liston's operating speed was such that one observer wrote, 'the gleam of his knife was followed so instantaneously by the sounds of sawing as to make the two actions appear almost simultaneous'. Others described how, to free both hands during an operation, he would clasp the bloody knife between his teeth. His achievements were many but he earned an ineradicable place in medical folklore with one of the strangest operations of all time.

It happened near the end of his career and was the culmination of many adventures he had had along the way. Born in 1794 at Ecclesmachan in Linlithgow, Liston studied medicine at Edinburgh University and became a surgeon at the Royal Infirmary where he was rumoured, as were other surgeons, to 'resurrect' corpses. He was a vain, argumentative and abrasive man and, although he was unfailingly kind and gentle with the poor and the sick, he soon made enemies of his fellow surgeons.

They complained about his arrogance – a charge that in

Edinburgh must have raised questions about the relative blackness of pots and kettles – but what really upset them was his habit of operating successfully in the tenements of the Grassmarket and Lawnmarket on patients they had discharged as incurable. When eventually they barred him from the wards, he packed his bags and travelled south to become professor of surgery at University College Hospital in London.

There, he built his reputation as the fastest surgeon in town, and his dramatic operating sessions attracted packed galleries of students and their friends. An impressive man, six-foot-two tall, Liston would stride across the bloodstained floor of the operating theatre wearing Wellington boots and his bottle-green operating coat, calling to the students who stood in the galleries, pocket watches in hand, 'Time me, gentlemen, time me.'

His speed sometimes had 'side-effects'. Once, when he amputated a patient's leg in his standard time of two and a half minutes, his flashing knife also removed the poor man's testicles. Yet, despite such occasional setbacks, his reputation for speed built him an enormous private practice. He took a house opposite Bucks club in Clifford Street, Mayfair, and his crowded waiting room had a butler in attendance to serve Madeira and biscuits.

The operation that won him his place in medical student lore was another leg amputation which this time he accomplished in under two and a half minutes. Sadly, the patient died later in the ward from surgical gangrene, as patients often did in the days before antiseptics and asepsis. During the operation, Liston inadvertently amputated the fingers of his young assistant, who also later died of gangrene, and slashed through the coat tails of a distinguished surgical spectator, who, terrified that the knife had pierced his vitals, dropped dead from fright. As modern surgeons point out, with a relish that borders on pride, Liston thus performed the only operation in surgical history to have a 300 per cent mortality rate.

Soon after that historic occasion, the arrival of anaesthesia, first introduced in America, gave surgeons more time to operate, and the high-speed skills of men like Liston became redundant. Ironically, Liston himself performed the first operation under anaesthesia in Europe. On 21 December 1846, disregarding the time advantages conferred by the new technique, he amputated a leg in his usual two and a half minutes before growling, 'This Yankee dodge beats mesmerism hollow.'

HAIL HAPPY HOUR

HARTFORD, CONNECTICUT, USA, 1844

On 10 December 1844, Gardner Quincy Colton, failed medical student but successful entertainer, appeared 'by special request' at the Union Hall in Hartford, Connecticut, to present a scientific evening that he guaranteed would be 'in every respect a genteel affair'. His demonstration of 'Nitrous Oxide, Exhilarating or Laughing Gas!' that would make people 'Laugh, Sing, Dance, Speak or Fight, &c, &c, according to the leading trait of their character', was much like the performance put on by modern stage hypnotists.

'Eight Strong Men' would fill the front seats to protect the audience from the 'frenzy' of the 'Twelve Young Men' who would volunteer to inhale from the rubber bag, and who, as a precaution against vulgarity, would be 'gentlemen of the first respectability'.

The effects of nitrous oxide were no secret. In England, the chemist Sir Humphry Davy used it to treat his headaches and enjoyed the experience: 'Vivid ideas passed rapidly through the mind, and voluntary power was altogether destroyed, so that the mouthpiece generally dropt from my unclosed lips.' He encouraged his friends to savour the effects, and enthusiastic inhalers included the poet Robert Southey, who wrote of the experience, 'The atmosphere of the highest of all possible heavens must be composed of this gas.' Davy also offered the gas to Dr Roget, he of the *Thesaurus,* who likened the effect to that of champagne and said it made him feel like the sound of a harp.

On the December evening in Union Hall, one of the Twelve Young Men who inhaled the gas was a local dentist, Horace Wells, whose only achievement till then had been the invention of a taste-free adhesive for false teeth that had failed to sell despite a money-back guarantee. Spotting another business opportunity, Wells persuaded Colton to come to his surgery the following morning and give him the gas while his partner Dr Riggs extracted one of his troublesome wisdom teeth. The nitrous oxide rendered him oblivious to the operation and Horace Wells announced the dawn of 'a new era in tooth-pulling'.

Wells's former partner Thomas Morton arranged for him to give a demonstration in Boston on a Harvard student with an aching tooth. This time the gas didn't work. The audience is reported to have laughed (could the gas have escaped into the auditorium?) and Horace Wells returned to Hartford.

But Morton was alive to the commercial possibilities. Nitrous oxide wasn't the only inhalant used at parties – 'ether frolics' were even more popular than laughing-gas parties. So Morton tried ether on a dog, which 'wilted completely away'. For a short time, the animal couldn't be aroused by shaking or pinching, but a few minutes later was as lively as normal. Morton hoped to patent the technique and make his fortune so he continued to experiment in secret, on dogs, his apprentices and himself.

Then on the evening of 30 September 1846, he came into the open. Eben H Frost arrived at his surgery with violent toothache, sniffed ether from a pocket-handkerchief, and woke to discover his tooth on the floor. Sixteen days later, Morton gave ether at the Massachusetts General Hospital while a surgeon removed a tumour from a young man's jaw. This time the experiment was a success. Morton had succeeded where Wells had failed because ether is a more powerful anaesthetic than nitrous oxide, which tends to asphyxiate before it anaesthetises.

Anaesthesia was now an acceptable technique, and it spread rapidly to Europe. *The People's London Journal* ran the headline, 'Hail happy hour! We have conquered pain!' Yet Morton, much to the disgust of Boston's doctors and dentists, spent most of his time not on anaesthesia but trying to establish sole patent rights to ether. Proud Boston was even more discomfited when Dr Crawford Williamson Long, a country GP in faraway Jefferson, Georgia, quietly announced that he had been performing minor surgical operations under ether anaesthesia since March 1842, almost five years before Morton started.

It's a strange quirk of medical history that the most significant advance in nineteenth-century medicine came not through scientific endeavour but through man's determination to indulge the party spirit. 'Ether frolics' and laughing-gas parties were the ancestors of twentieth-century cocktail parties, and as the novelist – and anaesthetist – Richard Gordon points out, 'Anaesthesia, like drunkenness, was born of mankind's ageless desire to escape from himself.'

The next place to turn pleasure-seeking to good use was the staid city of Edinburgh. On 4 November 1847, Professor J Y Simpson, of Edinburgh University, gave a dinner party after which he persuaded two of his young assistants to join him in sniffing chloroform. The two young men were seized with 'unwonted hilarity' before collapsing into unconsciousness, and just before Simpson himself slid snoring to the floor, he muttered, 'Far stronger than ether.' When the three recovered, Simpson's niece, Miss Petrie, insisted on having a go and went under exclaiming, 'I am an angel! I am an angel!'

Chloroform quickly took over from ether, which was unpopular because of its smell and the way it irritated the eyes, throat and lungs. Yet when Simpson gave chloroform to women in childbirth, he had to battle with the Church, which believed that women were born to labour in pain. Simpson won the battle – and a baronetcy – when Queen Victoria inhaled chloroform during the birth of Prince Leopold.

By then, anaesthesia had been established as a necessary adjunct to surgery, though there were, as always, doctors who resented the passing of the old ways. Sir John Hall, principal medical officer in the Crimea, claimed, 'The smart of the knife is a powerful stimulant, and it is better to hear a man bawl lustily than to see him sink silently into his grave.'

Horace Wells had ushered in more than a new era in tooth-pulling. Dramatic advances in twentieth-century surgery would be enabled by advances in anaesthesia. Yet the new technique's first effect on surgeons was to devalue their most prized skill, their speed. As George Bernard Shaw put it, chloroform 'enabled every fool to be a surgeon'.

EMBROIDERED TALES FROM THE PARISH PUMP

SOHO, LONDON, 1854

One of the great romantic tales of medicine is the story of Dr John Snow and the Broad Street pump. In 1854, the story goes, a cholera epidemic devastated the Soho parish of St James. On the fringe of Soho lived John Snow, an anaesthetist at St George's Hospital, who had a special interest in cholera because, as an apprentice doctor, he had watched an epidemic wreak havoc in Newcastle-upon-Tyne. One evening, he appeared at a parish meeting and advised the elders to remove the handle from the pump in Broad Street. In the words of his biographer, Sir Benjamin Ward Richardson, 'A stranger asked in modest speech for a brief hearing . . . He advised the removal of the pump handle . . . The vestry was incredulous but had the good sense to carry out the advice. The pump handle was removed and the plague was stayed.'

One minor flaw in the story is that it isn't true. Nor is the alternative version, still purveyed in medical schools, that Snow himself removed the handle from the pump, thus stopping people from drinking the water and halting the epidemic.

If you read what Snow wrote, you discover that, when the pump handle was removed, the epidemic was virtually over. The people of Soho had taken the traditional preventive action against pestilence and fled the city. The evidence that incriminated the pump came later when Snow mapped the houses occupied by cholera victims and found them linked by their source of drinking water. His investigation was, in the parlance of today, a retrospective study.

In Snow's time, Broad Street was the commercial hub of the parish of St James, housing a bakery, a brewery and a small factory. Snow's map of the disease defined it as the centre of the epidemic; only one of the street's buildings had been spared its share of victims and that was the brewery, where the workers didn't drink much water. The epidemic wasn't confined to Broad Street, but all who had suffered cholera in outlying parts of the parish had drunk the clean 'sweet water' for which the Broad Street pump was known.

The immobilisation of the pump played little part in the control of the disease. As Snow wrote, 'There is no doubt that the mortality was much diminished by the flight of the population . . . The attacks had so far diminished before the use of the water was stopped that it is impossible to decide whether the well still contained the cholera poison in an active state or whether, from some cause, the water had become free from it.'

Luckily, Snow's achievement is too significant to be damaged by the romantic accretions it acquired in Victorian times from Sir Benjamin and others. Maybe they sought to compensate for the way that Snow's contemporaries had cold-shouldered his discovery. At the time of the Soho epidemic, doctors believed that cholera descended from a miasma, an invisible disease cloud that hovered above afflicted communities. When Snow proposed that the cause was not a miasma but polluted water, few doctors were prepared to accept his circumstantial evidence. Only thirty years later, after the germ that causes cholera had been identified, did the medical establishment accept that the disease occurred when germs from the bowels of infected people contaminated drinking water.

When Snow died in 1858, four years after the Soho epidemic, few people accepted his hypothesis. A parliamentary committee of enquiry set up to investigate the epidemic took evidence from the medical heavyweights of the day before concluding, 'After careful enquiry we see no reason to adopt this belief.' Instead, it backed the established view, 'the supposition that the choleraic infection multiplies rather in air than in water'.

Luckily for Londoners, when their city suffered another cholera epidemic in 1866, it proved to be its last. The 'Great Stink' of 1858 had finally persuaded a long-dithering Parliament to allow Joseph Bazalgette, Chief Engineer to the Metropolitan Board of Works, to go ahead with his plans for a comprehensive sewerage system. So, although John Snow showed the way, the man who banished cholera from London was Bazalgette. The massive sewers he constructed still insulate its water supply from its sewage and protect London's citizens from waterborne diseases.

Because of its notoriety, Broad Street was later renamed Broadwick Street, and today the site of the pump is marked by a red kerbstone outside a pub. In 1955, after persuasive pressure from a group of epidemiologists, the pub, formerly the Duke of Newcastle, was renamed the John Snow to mark the centenary of Snow's publication of his *Observations on Cholera*. For years, a visitors' book, kept behind the bar, accumulated the signatures of international pilgrims who had come to pay homage at the birthplace of epidemiology.

The persuasive epidemiologists of '55 included Austin Bradford Hill who, with Richard Doll, had used the technique pioneered by Snow to establish the link between cigarette smoking and lung cancer. The pub's change of name was marked by a small ceremony. A tiny clutch of respectful epidemiologists gathered on the pavement while the 58-year-old Bradford Hill made a perilous ascent up a rickety ladder to unveil a new sign bearing Snow's picture.

The centenary was also marked by an exhibition at the London School of Hygiene that featured a fine portrait of Snow lent by his great nieces, who lived in Yorkshire. They were distinctly unpleased, however, when they heard that a pub had been named after their ancestor. They claimed that he, like them, was a strict teetotaller. Austin Bradford Hill tried to assuage them by reminding them that Snow had been reported to take 'a little wine for his stomach's sake' and by pointing out that you had to be a pretty important man to have a pub named after you.

The great nieces remained unpersuaded and, after their

deaths, the epidemiologists discovered that the portrait had been bequeathed not to them but to the Faculty of Anaesthetists. The official reason was that Snow had made the use of chloroform during childbirth acceptable to the nation by administering it to Queen Victoria for the painless delivery of Prince Leopold. Bradford Hill suspected there might be another reason, though, as a punctilious epidemiologist, he would never claim a direct causal connection.

I wonder how that tale will be embellished a hundred years from now.

THE DISEASE THAT DARE NOT SPEAK ITS NAME

BRITAIN AND USA, 1857–1974

A dread debilitating disease, first described by nineteenth-century British and American physicians, still threatened the flower of British youth in the first half of the twentieth century. Dr William Acton had predicted the outbreak when he described the symptoms in 1857: 'The frame is stunted and weak, the muscles underdeveloped, the eye is sunken and heavy, the complexion is sallow, pasty, or covered with spots of acne, the hands are damp and cold, and the skin moist. The boy shuns the society of others, creeps about alone, joins with repugnance in the amusements of his schoolfellows. He cannot look anyone in the face, and becomes careless in dress and uncleanly in person. His intellect has become sluggish and enfeebled, and if his evil habits are persisted in, he may end in becoming a drivelling idiot or a peevish valetudinarian.'

The disease, of course, was masturbation though, in his monumental work *The Function and Disorders of the Reproductive Organs, in Childhood, Youth, Adult Age, and Advanced Life, Considered in their Physiological, Social and Moral Relations,* Dr Acton preferred to call it onanism after poor old Onan, the character in Genesis, whom the Lord slew for spilling his seed upon the ground. Acton was not alone in his prognosis of the fate awaiting those who persisted in the habit. In 1874, Bucknill & Tuke's textbook on psychological medicine stated authoritatively that, 'Onanism is a frequent accompaniment of Insanity and sometimes causes it.'

North American youth was also at risk. There, the most widely publicised warnings came from the ebullient Dr John Harvey Kellogg, who gave the world cornflakes and was the first medical superintendent of a health farm created by Seventh Day Adventists at Battle Creek in Michigan. In *Man, the Masterpiece, or Plain Truths Plainly Told about Boyhood,Youth, and Manhood,* first published in the 1880s and reprinted in a near unending series of editions, Kellogg described 39 'suspicious' symptoms of the disease. He also pointed out that the disease could afflict both sexes. His advice on treatment of young women included 'application of carbolic to the clitoris as an excellent means of allaying abnormal excitement'. For boys, he suggested 'tying the hands', 'covering the organs with a cage', or circumcision performed without an anaesthetic – 'the brief pain attending the operation will have a salutary effect upon the mind, especially if connected with the idea of punishment, as it well may be in some cases'.

At the start of the twentieth century the public-spirited Baden-Powell, founder of the Scout movement, sought to prescribe a preventative rather than a punitive approach. Unlike Dr Kellogg, Baden-Powell, an English gentleman, assumed that ladies never went in for that sort of thing. He wanted to protect his beloved scouts, but when the first edition of his *Scouting for Boys* was on the brink of publication, the printer, Horace Cox, refused to handle it unless some 'far too explicit' advice was removed.

One passage to which he objected ran: 'The result of self-abuse is always – mind you, always – that the boy after a time becomes weak and nervous and shy, he gets headaches and probably palpitations of the heart, and if he carries on too far he very often goes out of his mind and becomes an idiot. A very large number of the lunatics in our asylums have made themselves mad by indulging in this vice although at one time they were sensible, cheery boys like any one of you.'

The printer objected on the grounds of indecency rather than inaccuracy.

Another deleted paragraph began: 'Remember too that several awful diseases come from indulgence – one especially that rots away the insides of men's mouths, their noses, and eyes, etc.' Saddest of all was the deletion of wholesome advice offered to boys who felt the urge coming on: 'Just wash your parts in cold water and cool them down.'

The version Cox eventually printed was so enigmatic that many a scout may have wondered what exactly was the dangerous activity against which he was being warned. 'This "beastliness" is not a man's vice; men have nothing but contempt for a fellow who gives way to it.'

The high prevalence of the disease still concerned some doctors in the second half of the twentieth century. In May 1974, Patrick K Fitzgerald wrote in the *Irish Medical Times:* 'I feel that the major cause of masturbation is bad genital hygiene. In the United States masturbation is rare. This I believe is due to two factors: a) circumcision of all males at birth; b) a high standard of genital and general hygiene.' His assertion that the condition was rare in the US was, to say the least, interesting.

A sign of diminishing concern about the disease came in a newspaper report in 1984 of an elderly woman who had named her budgie Onan because of its habit of scattering its seed upon the carpet.

ENDURING REMEDIES

THE BRITISH EMPIRE, 1866

A reader browsing through *Burke's Landed Gentry* in 1866, or reading the *Surrey Advertiser* – or, 'tis said, a hundred other newspapers and magazines – would have encountered an advertisement:

DR J. COLLIS BROWNE'S CHLORODYNE
the great specific for CHOLERA, DIARRHOEA, DYSENTERY.
GENERAL BOARD OF HEALTH, LONDON, REPORT that it
ACTS AS A CHARM, one dose
generally sufficient.
Dr Gibbon, Army Medical Staff, Calcutta, states,
'TWO DOSES COMPLETELY CURED ME OF DIARRHOEA'

Dr Browne did not restrict himself to catering to English people's obsession with their bowels.

Dr J. Collis Browne's Chlorodyne is the true palliative in
NEURALGIA, GOUT,
CANCER, TOOTHACHE, RHEUMATISM
... a liquid medicine which assuages PAIN OF EVERY KIND,
affords a calm refreshing sleep WITHOUT HEADACHE and
INVIGORATES the nervous system when exhausted
... rapidly cuts short all attacks of EPILEPSY, SPASMS, COLIC,
PALPITATION, HYSTERIA

There followed an 'Important Caution' that drops a hint about problems that Dr Browne was having with his competitors.

The immense sale of the REMEDY has given rise to many UNSCRUPULOUS imitations.
DR J. C. BROWNE (Late Army Medical Staff) DISCOVERED A REMEDY to denote which he coined the word CHLORODYNE. Dr Browne is the SOLE INVENTOR, and, as the composition of Chlorodyne cannot possibly be discovered by Analysis (organic substances defying elimination), and since the formula has never been published, it is evident that any statement to the effect that a compound is identical with Dr. Browne's Chlorodyne *must be false*.
This caution is necessary as many persons deceive purchasers by false representations.
Vice-Chancellor Sir W. PAGE WOOD stated publicly in Court that
DR. J. COLLIS BROWNE WAS UNDOUBTEDLY the INVENTOR OF CHLORODYNE, that the whole story of the defendant Freeman was deliberately untrue and he regretted to say it had been sworn to. – See *The Times,* 13 July 1864

Most of what we know of Dr Browne, apart from the fact that he lived in Ramsgate and died in 1884, comes from the ads. Yet his remedy lives on, its popularity down the years assured by its none-too-secret ingredient, morphine. It's not surprising that he had to fight off competition. As GPs were told on a recent postgraduate course, 'If you were a general practitioner in London in 1850, just about the only things you had in your pharmacopoeia that actually worked were opium for treating diarrhoea, rhubarb for treating constipation, and J Collis Brown's Chlorodyne, which contained morphine, ether, cannabis and treacle and certainly should have had a generally cheering effect.'

The mixture continued to contain morphine until the 1960s when the Home Office discovered that many pensioners were addicted to the contents of a small brown bottle that was readily available over chemists' counters, was relatively cheap, and made them very happy. The morphine was removed but the mixture continued to sell.

The strangest thing about Dr Browne's creation is not the length of its survival – the morphine and the cannabis ensured that – but the endorsements printed in the leaflet that was still packed with it in the 1970s long after it had been reformulated.

Edward Whymper, Esq, the celebrated mountaineer, writes on February 16, 1897, 'I always carry Dr J Collis Browne's Chlorodyne with me on my travels, and have used it effectively on others on Mont Blanc.'

'During my fifteen years' active service in South Africa, I found your medicine of the greatest value to myself and comrades.'
– Troop Sgt A E Rogers et al, Kitchener's Fighting Scouts.

'Gaunter and gaunter grew the soldiers of the Queen. Hunger and sickness played havoc with those fine regiments. But somehow the RAMC managed to patch the men up with chlorodyne and quinine.'
– Cassell's History of the Boer War, page 542.

That 1970s leaflet was a symptom of an even stranger phenomenon: the negligible effect the pharmaceutical revolution of the second half of the twentieth century had on the 'household remedies' sold in chemists' shops. These nostrums seemed to rely for their appeal more on nostalgia – 'the treatment mother gave me' – than on modern pharmacology.

In 1983, the year that pharmacists were at last granted permission to sell drugs previously available only on prescription, middle-aged shoppers could create a litany of nostalgia just by reading the labels on the shelves at their local chemist's: Elliman's Universal Embrocation, Scott's Emulsion, Iron Jelloids, Andrew's Liver Salts, Veno's Lightning Cough Cure, Potter's Catarrh Pastilles, Milk of Magnesia, Lofthouse's Original Fisherman's Friend . . .

Even the descriptive words and phrases on the labels came

from the pre-pharmaceutical years: rubbing oils, camphor, balsam, teething jelly, 'children's cooling powders', capsicum and eucalyptus, iron tonic and syrup of figs . . .

Read out loud, they sound like lines from a Betjeman poem, evoking sun-kissed days when Len Hutton was at the Oval, Henry Hall was on the wireless, the *Wizard* and the *Hotspur* were on the counter in the corner shop, and Robert Donat, Jean Harlow and Will Hay were on the silver screen.

THE BIRTH OF AN EPITHET

PRUSSIA, 1870

In the second half of the nineteenth century, Germany became a dominant force in European medicine and the pathologist Rudolph Virchow became a dominant force in German medicine. His enduring legacy is that he taught doctors to use the methods of natural science rather than those of natural philosophy, to observe and experiment rather than rely on the works and teachings of the past.

Those who adopt a familial approach to history describe Virchow as the father of modern pathology because he pioneered the concept that disease arises not in organs but in the cells of which they are composed. But pathology was not his only child. He is also described as the father of social medicine because he insisted that students be taught that disease is inseparable from the social conditions in which it occurs. He claimed he had only one career: being a doctor included being a social reformer.

In 1848, when Virchow was 27, the Prussian government sent him to investigate a typhus epidemic in Upper Silesia, where he concluded that the disease had spread rapidly because of the appalling living conditions of the destitute Polish minority. Instead of delivering the report that the government wanted – an anodyne mixture of humanitarian aspiration and unenforceable medical guidelines – Virchow recommended political freedom and sweeping educational and economic reforms for the people of Upper Silesia.

The report brought him into the first of many conflicts with the government, and his continuing anger at social injustice led him eventually, at the age of sixty, to enter the Reichstag, where he was an outspoken critic of Prussian conservatism and one of Bismarck's bitterest opponents. Some claim, though there is no record, that he so exasperated Bismarck that the Chancellor challenged him to a duel. When Bismarck's seconds called on Virchow, he explained that, as the challenged party, he had the choice of weapons. 'I choose these,' he said, and held aloft two large sausages. 'One is infected with deadly germs; the other is perfectly sound. Let His Excellency decide which he wishes to eat, and I will eat the other.' The seconds returned with the message that the Chancellor had decided to laugh off the affair.

The story could be true because Virchow, unlike Bismarck, regarded irreverence as a virtue. Late in his life, when appendicectomy became a fashionable operation and one of his students asked him if humans really could survive without an appendix, he answered, 'Humans, yes, but not surgeons.'

One of Virchow's strangest cases involved him both as pathologist and politician. It arose when the French ethnologist Armand de Quatrefages, incensed by the damage done by German shells to Paris's natural history museum during the Franco-Prussian War of 1870, declared that the Prussians were by race neither Nordic nor Teutonic but descendants of the barbaric Huns who ravished eastern Europe during the Middle Ages.

Virchow responded by using the scientific methods that he promoted. He introduced a bill in the Prussian Parliament enabling researchers to measure the physical characteristics of all six million Prussian schoolchildren – head measurements, bone lengths, hair colour and so on. When the data were analysed, he was able to brandish scientific proof that the Prussians were, in origin, Franks – cousins of the French.

But he was too late. The derogatory epithet Hun had stuck . . . and still does.

A BRACE OF MEDICAL'WILSONISMS'

DUBLIN AND CORK, 1870 AND THE 1930s

Before Antony Jay became celebrated as co-author of *Yes, Minister,* he was an ubiquitous presence in the smoke-filled backrooms of television, where he regularly produced ideas that prompted others to say, 'Why on earth didn't I think of that?' One of his memorable contributions was the concept of the Wilsonism – his name for those practical wrinkles known to insiders in every profession and cherished because they regularly prove their worth in the front line of experience.

Jay encountered the phenomenon when, on coming down from Oxford, he tried his hand at teaching and spent a depressing first morning in a classroom of boys who remained determinedly noisy despite his shouted commands to 'Shut up' or 'Be quiet'.

During the break, a wise old schoolmaster, who had heard the disruptive clamour coming from Jay's class, took him aside and told him it was no use shouting general exhortations; a teacher had to be specific and direct his command at a name. Jay should add a surname to his order and shout, 'Shut up, Wilson'. It wouldn't matter if there was no Wilson in the class, everyone would quieten and look around to see who was being admonished. Jay tried the phrase and found that 'Shut up, Wilson' could silence the noisiest of classrooms.

Medical Wilsonisms are rarely written down, for they rarely flatter the doctor, but are passed by word of mouth within the craft or handed down as heirlooms from doctor fathers to

57

their doctor sons. Two classic examples have, however, been recorded in medical journals. Both, by chance, come from Ireland.

The first formed part of the inheritance of the actor and writer Richard Leech, who, before he embarked on his theatrical career, qualified as a doctor to please his parents and maintain a family tradition. Richard's nugget of practicality came from his grandfather Richard Leeper, a distinguished Dublin physician and one-time physician superintendent of Swift's Hospital in Dublin.

Leeper's gift to his grandson went something like this:

'Never give medicine to a dying man. Always give him brandy, for everyone knows that brandy never harmed anyone. Give the patient medicine and someone will say, "God forgive me if I wrong him, but Leeper's draught was the last thing the poor man took".'

Grandfather Leeper must have received that advice round about 1870, and no one knows how many generations had passed it on. It could well have started with Hippocrates, for that quality of learning has an imperishable validity.

The second Wilsonism was nurtured within one of Cork's best-known medical families, the Carneys. In the 1930s and '40s, a member of the family was a GP in the Montenotte district of Cork, where he was always referred to as Doctor Carney, as if Doctor were his first name. His Wilsonism was to say to the relatives of a sick man, 'We'll be a little bit worried about him for the next twenty-four hours.'

Any GP who hears that sentence immediately recognises its power. It leaves the relatives with a reassuring image of the kindly doctor going about his business with part of his mind constantly concerned about the health of their loved one. And whatever the outcome, the doctor will appear to have anticipated it.

If the patient takes a turn for the worse, the relatives will say to themselves, 'The doctor gave us a hint of what might happen but was kind enough to break it gently.' And if the patient recovers, as patients have a tendency to do despite the most rigorous of treatment, the doctor's 24 hours of concern is, in some mysterious way, seen to have played a part in the miraculous recovery.

It is indeed such a valuable Wilsonism that one wonders how many generations of Carneys treasured it before an astute observer picked it up in the 1930s.

LOVE LOCKED IN

PENTONVILLE, 1884; ISLE OF WIGHT, 1947

In the early hours of one morning in 1947, a young man and woman arrived at the Royal Isle of Wight County Hospital. The ambulance men who transported them faced unusual mechanical problems and a considerable threat to their professionally serious demeanour. The couple were on their honeymoon and, while they were making love, the woman's vagina had gone into a continuous vigorous spasm that had trapped her husband's penis. After a painful wait of several hours, he'd been unable to withdraw it.

The case was reported by Dr Brendan Musgrave in a letter to the *British Medical Journal (BMJ)* and his account of the incident was confirmed by Dr S W Wolfe. Both had been housemen in the County Hospital at the time and remembered the ambulance drawing up and the two young people being carried into the casualty department on a single stretcher. The woman was given an anaesthetic, which relieved the vaginal spasm and enabled the man to remove his organ. Both patients were discharged later the same morning.

Until Dr Musgrave's letter appeared, the condition 'penis captivus' was suspected to be one of medicine's urban myths. The story of a couple locked in inseparable sexual intercourse until their anguished cries lead to mortifying discovery has been doing the rounds for a long time. In 1935, a search for published cases found that the first reports had appeared in medieval texts, which described its occurrence in sinners who had indulged in

60

clandestine intercourse in churches and were discovered the following day. Prayers or a bucket of cold water were said to have brought liberation. But all the reports were hearsay and almost certainly embellished.

The most recent case the search unearthed was alleged to have occurred in Warsaw in 1923, though the account that Plitzin wrote in *Thèse de Paris* eight years later has the air of romantic tragi-comedy that was fashionable at the time and cannot be wholly attributed to translation.

> It was in the spring, a couple of young students stayed behind in the garden after closing time. In the midst of their amorous sport, a violent spasm occurred, imprisoning the penis. The keeper, alarmed by the desperate cries of the young man, ran up. The doctor of the municipal ambulance, after giving an anaesthetic to the woman, separated the couple. The matter might have been forgotten, but the journalists, in their greed for sensational facts, did not fail to publish the adventure. The next day, two revolver shots put an end to the mental sufferings of the two lovers.

A more prosaic – and less heart-wrenching – case was mentioned in a footnote in Bloch's *The Sexual Life Of Our Time* published in 1902.

> A few years ago a remarkable case of this kind occurred in Bremen. One of the dock labourers was having sexual intercourse in an out-of-the-way corner of the docks, when the woman became affected with this involuntary spasm, and the man was unable to free himself from his imprisonment. A great crowd assembled, from the midst of which the couple were removed in a closed carriage, and taken to the hospital, and not until the chloroform had been administered to the girl did the spasm pass off and free the man.

Until Dr Musgrave wrote to the *BMJ,* the most authoritative report of penis captivus, often quoted in articles and textbooks, appeared in a letter published on 4 December 1884 by the magazine *Philadelphia Medical News*.

Dear Sir: The reading of an admirably written and instructive editorial in the *Philadelphia Medical News* for November 24 on forms of vaginismus, has reminded me of a case in point which bears out, in an extraordinary way, the statements therein contained. When in practice at Pentonville, England, I was sent for, about 11.00 p.m., by a gentleman whom, on my arriving at his house I found in a state of great perturbation, and the story he told me was briefly as follows. At bedtime, when going to the back kitchen to see if the house was shut up a noise in the coachman's room attracted his attention, and, going in, he discovered to his horror that the man was in bed with one of the maids. She screamed, he struggled, and they rolled out of bed together and made frantic efforts to get apart, but without success. He was a big, burly man, over six feet, and she was a small woman, weighing not more than ninety pounds. She was moaning and screaming, and seemed in great agony, so that, after several fruitless attempts to get them apart, he sent for me.

When I arrived I found the man standing up and supporting the woman in his arms, and it was quite evident that his penis was tightly locked in her vagina, and any attempt to dislodge it was accompanied by much pain on the part of both. It was a case *De cohesione in coitu*. I applied water, and then ice, but ineffectively, and at last sent for chloroform, few whiffs of which sent the woman to sleep, relaxed the spasm, and relieved the captive penis, which was swollen, and in a state of semi-erection, which did not go down for several hours, and for days the organ was extremely sore.

The woman recovered rapidly, and seemed none the worse. . . . As an instance of Iago's 'beast with two backs', the picture was perfect. Yours truly,

EgertonY Davis, Ex US Army
Caughnawaga, Quebec

The letter was a hoax and written by one of the great figures of turn-of-the-century medicine, Sir William Osler, a Canadian who was then at the University of Pennsylvania and was later to become Professor of Medicine at Johns Hopkins University before crossing the Atlantic to become Professor of Medicine at Oxford.

Osler believed strongly that research and rational deduction were essential in medicine, and his approach to teaching was practical rather than philosophical. He was on the editorial board of *Philadelphia Medical News* and a fellow board member, the obstetrician Theophilus Parvin, was author of the 'admirably written and instructive editorial'. Osler thought Parvin's airing of his pet subject was strong on dogma and short on fact, and had decided to tease its pompous author.

A contemporary account reveals that, when Osler visited the magazine's office, the editor asked, 'Do you know Egerton Y Davis who lives somewhere near Montreal? Parvin is delighted as he has sent the report of a case just as he thought possible.'

'For heaven's sake,' said Osler, 'don't print anything from that man Davis. He is not a reputable character.'

'Too late now,' said the editor. 'The journal is printed.'

When Osler's hoax became known, penis captivus was written off as a bar-room tale. Yet if it is, as Dr Musgrave's letter suggests, a genuine hazard, doctors on the Isle of Wight may care to offer visitors the practical Oslerian advice suggested by the novelist Richard Gordon. 'Should it strike on the back seat of your Fiesta, it is best to blow up each others' nostrils. It seems to work with horses.'

A BURNING ISSUE

LLANTRISANT, WALES, 1884

If strangeness is endowed by eccentricity, there have been few stranger medical cases than that of Dr William Price, who lived and practised in Llantrisant, Glamorgan, and who, in 1884, stood in the dock at Cardiff Assizes.

The good doctor, then aged 84, had always taken a novel approach to medicine – novel for those times – attempting to treat the causes of disease rather than its symptoms. He spurned all forms of transport and walked miles across the hills visiting patients, often at two or three in the morning, claiming that at that hour a patient's resistance was at its lowest and disease more easily diagnosed. He declined to treat patients who smoked and was fanatical about hygiene: he washed every coin that passed through his hands and refused to wear socks because he thought them unhygienic. He was a dedicated chaser of women and had many children. Yet he never married because marriage, he believed, led to the enslavement of women. He was a vociferous opponent of vaccination and Methodism, a vegetarian, and a dedicated sun-worshipper who liked to walk naked across the Welsh hills accompanied by groups of naked young women eager to share the health-giving exercise.

After qualifying at St Bartholomew's Hospital, London, he had gone straight to Wales but had been dismissed from his first job, as a mining company doctor in the Lower Rhondda, for promoting Chartism among the miners. He had fled into exile in France, where he lived for seven years before returning to

Wales and settling in Llantrisant. As a medical student, he had insisted on taking his final exams in Druidic robes, had later appointed himself Archdruid of Wales, and appeared in court on the first day of his trial wearing a white robe embroidered with cabalistic signs.

Yet it was none of these sins against decent society that put him in the dock in Cardiff. At his trial before Mr Justice Stephenson, he faced two charges: attempting to obstruct the course of an inquest by burning a body; and attempting to dispose of a body by burning when the law required that it should be buried in hallowed ground.

The body was that of Price's own infant son, who had died at the age of five months and who Price had named Jesu Grist – Jesus Christ in Welsh – believing he was the new messiah come to earth to lead the Welsh back to Druidism. Price had cremated him on a local hilltop in accordance with what he believed were ancient Druid rites, accompanying the ritual with 'arcane lamentations'.

When the trial opened, Price announced he would be defending himself and proceeded to do so with gusto. Within a minute, he had demolished the first charge by producing a coroner's certificate proving that there *had* been an inquest and that death had been attributed to 'natural causes'. On the second charge, he challenged the prosecution to name the legislation that made burning a corpse illegal. The prosecution responded by calling the local minister from Llantrisant, who testified that the Church required that the body of any baptised infant be committed to hallowed ground.

'The Church is not the law,' cried Price, rising in the dock, smoothing his Druidical robes and 'wagging' his beard in biblical style as he embarked on a long, impressive, yet wholly incomprehensible speech in what he claimed was the tongue of ancient Welsh bards. The judge threatened to charge him with contempt, then had him 'taken down' to cool off. When he returned, he explained to Mr Justice Stephenson that he had no wish to give offence but that his ruling should take precedence over the judge's. God had appointed him to be all-powerful among the Druids and he thus had greater authority than any newcomer like the Christian Church.

'Nevertheless,' said the judge, 'you will either accept my authority in this court or go to jail.' Price settled for a temporary suspension of his authority to allow the trial to continue.

First, for the prosecution came witnesses to testify to the doctor's 'madness', including sensational tales about the slavering dogs that guarded his house, about his manservant and his housekeeper, mother of several of his children, who used blunderbusses to drive away intruders, and accusations of grave-robbery and the dissection of corpses. Price defused the sensational intent of this testimony by turning up that day not in Druidical robes but in a neatly tailored suit and allowing the evidence to provoke no more than an amused smile as if, wrote one reporter, 'he was hearing of the deeds of someone other than himself'.

The smile grew warmer as a stream of defence witnesses gave evidence of his skill as a doctor. The jury heard how, after he had got his degree at the Royal College of Surgeons in 1821, he returned to Wales to practise among those who needed him most and whom he understood best. The people of Llantrisant may occasionally have been alarmed by his oddities but were fulsome in their praise of his understanding, not just of their ills, but of the way in which they were compelled to live their lives. Two phrases that cropped up often in his patients' testimony were 'he would always come willing' and 'he knew who could pay and who not'. Several women said he was 'gentle as a bird' at their confinements and a miner who'd been trapped by a fall of coal waxed lyrical about the anaesthetising effect of the brandy Dr Price had given him before amputating his leg while he lay at the pit face.

In his summing up, the judge pointed out that Dr Price faced the charge of burning the body of his infant son because he believed that cremation was more wholesome than interment, and that the ancient religion to which he claimed to belong demanded the reduction of a corpse to ashes. 'In these enlightened times,' said the judge, every man was entitled to his beliefs, and it was not an offence to follow the practices of religions more ancient than Christianity; it could, however, become an offence if it transgressed the laws of the land. No law except the law of custom and convention precluded the burning of the corpses of those who had died from natural causes, unless the burning constituted a public nuisance – and that was for the jury to decide.

After a long retirement, the jury failed to agree a verdict. The judge ordered a new trial but, after a recess, the prosecution announced it would proceed no further. The judge recalled the jury and ordered it to discharge the doctor. Price at once brought charges against the police for malicious prosecution, defamation of character and wrongful imprisonment. Six months later, a jury found in his favour but awarded damages of only a farthing.

The Cremation Society had sent an observer to the original trial but, though the case had established the legality of cremation, the campaigners faced a long struggle. The Home Office, as is its way, delayed reform with endless niggling over detail. A crematorium at Woking, 'specially constructed with regenerative and reverberating furnaces according to the Italian models', remained un-reverberate, and eighteen years passed before crematoria were legalised.

Price had died ten years earlier. His will directed that his corpse be burned publicly on Caerlan Hill, seated in an ancient Druidical chair set on top of two tons of Welsh coal. The Home Office, still quibbling with the Cremation Society, decreed that the corpse could be burned but only if it were decently shrouded and placed in a coffin. Nevertheless, 20,000 spectators turned up and paid three pence each to watch the 'hellish spectacle'.

THE RISE AND RISE OF DR KILLJOY

1886–PRESENT DAY

Extraordinary moments in medicine are sometimes born of the paradox that, though doctors strive to help people better to enjoy their lives, the instinctive reaction of some when they see people having fun is to look for the dangers.

In 1895, when bicycling became a fashionable pastime and women were presented with an acceptable form of healthy exercise that allowed them to get out and about, a Dr Herman wrote to the *British Medical Journal* seeking to deny them this simple pleasure.

> If the pedals are too far from the seat, the rider cannot make her feet follow the pedals without inclining the pelvis. Such side to side movement of the pelvis produces unnecessary strain on the muscles of the back and loins, and also friction against the sensitive external genitals. If the saddle is badly shaped, the friction thus produced may lead to bruising, even to excoriations, and short of this, in women of certain temperament, to other effects on the sexual system, which we need not particularise.

Three years later, the *British Medical Journal* used a leading article to emphasise that the risks of this seemingly harmless pastime were not confined to 'women of certain temperament'.

There must be few of us who have not seen the ill effects

68

of over-exertion on a bicycle. The commonest is palpitation and temporary dilatation but even this is sometimes very difficult to cure . . . that temporary dilatation occurs is enough to show the great strain put upon the heart, and it is an added danger that the sense of fatigue in the limbs is so slight. The rider is thus robbed of the warning to which he is accustomed to attend, and repeats or continues the strain upon the heart. As in other similar cases, the effect is to render that dilatation permanent which was at first but temporary, and to cause an increase in the muscle of the heart by repeated exertion. The heart produced is of large dimensions and of thick walls – a condition which may, perhaps, give little uneasiness to its owner, but which a medical man will view with considerable distrust and apprehension.

Cycling was not the only pastime that doctors viewed with distrust and apprehension. Nor was their disquiet confined to one side of the Atlantic. In 1886, Dr Samuel Adams, writing in the *Journal of the American Medical Association,* listed the hazards of another seemingly innocent pleasure:

The dangers of kissing include the transmission of scurvy, diphtheria, herpes, parasitic diseases, ringworm, and ulcerative stomatitis . . . One person kissed on the ear suffered a rupture of the eardrum undoubtedly due to suction . . . frequent kissing of children can induce precocious puberty, undue excitement of sexual organs, and irregular menstruation.

We can't write off that warning as mere nineteenth-century prudishness. Over a hundred years later, in 1993, five Finnish doctors wrote to the *Lancet* warning tourists against kissing Russian girls. Their reason was that one of the 400,000 Finns who visited Russia that year had returned from St Petersburg with diphtheria. True, he 'admitted' that he had kissed a Russian girl, but he had also drunk from unwashed glasses at a birthday party. And even though the Russian girl had remained healthy, the doctors believed the world should be warned of the potential, if improbable, health hazard associated with 'contact with a local inhabitant'.

The 1993 report was not an isolated incident. The tradition of medical censoriousness enjoyed a spectacular revival in the second half of the twentieth century, triggered by the 1950s craze for hula-hooping. Doctors discovered that when they issued gloomy warnings about what hooping could do to the spine, not only did they get their letters in their professional journals but they also got their names in the newspapers read by their patients.

Egged on by journalists, who recognise a good story when they hear one, a new generation of Dr Killjoys, now aided by Mrs Grundys, eagerly sought hazards in fashionable pastimes. In the last three decades of the twentieth century hazards published in learned journals included: Jogger's Nipple, Break-dancer's Neck, Crab-eater's Lung, Swim-goggle Headache, Amusement Slide Anaphylaxis, Cyclist's Pudendum, Dog Walker's Elbow, Space Invaders Wrist, Unicyclist's Sciatica, Jeans Folliculitis, Jogger's Kidney, Welly-thrower's Finger, Flautist's Neuropathy, and Urban Cowboy's Rhabdomyolosis – a painful nastiness in the muscles caused by riding mechanical bucking broncos in amusement arcades.

The 1980s produced more medical articles listing the hazards of jogging than those commending its health-promoting value. A special award should surely go to three punctilious Swiss, Drs Itin, Heanel and Stalder from Kantonsspital Liestal, for reporting the strangest jogging hazard: bird attacks by the European buzzard *(Buteo buteo)*. The attacks occurred during the buzzard breeding season and the birds attacked the joggers from behind, diving at their fleshy moving parts 'for as long as the joggers were in motion'. Sadly the good doctors didn't speculate on what was passing through the buzzards' minds at the time.

As the century drew to its close, the *Independent on Sunday* drew on medical expertise to list the ailments that could afflict clubbers. These included:

PVC Bottom: friction burns that manmade fibres inflict on sweating bodies.

Techno Toe: toe lacerations caused by too long toenails during dancing.

Ravers' Rash: what non-ravers call 'heat rash'.

A professor from St Mary's Hospital was wheeled in to offer the expert observation that a combination of amphetamines and 'excessive dancing on concrete floors' could 'put stress on backs and joints'. Well, fancy that.

Dr Killjoy will, I fear, always be alive and well and practising in a newspaper somewhere near you.

THE WAR OF THE BIG TOE

FRANCE, GERMANY, USA, 1896–1911

Doctors have long sought immortality by attaching their names to diseases, instruments, or even operations. The delight an eponym can bring is celebrated in a James Thurber cartoon by a man who cries, 'I've got Bright's disease and he's got mine.'

Now that most diseases have been appropriated, outsiders might think that the chances of an eponym are remote. Far from it. GPs still see vast numbers of patients with indeterminate symptoms. All a doctor needs to do is to collect a few of these – say, headache, pain in the right knee and intermittent constipation – lump them together as a syndrome, then attach his or her name to it.

Seekers after immortality need, of course, to show discretion in their choice of symptoms. No one wants to suffer the fate of Thomas Crapper who displayed his name too proudly and too prominently on his revolutionary water closet.

Doctors who don't mind diluting immortality can share an eponym with a chum. Indeed, the more names attached to a syndrome, the more impressive it becomes. And a chum with a complicated name can add intellectual weight. Names that are difficult to pronounce add even more weight. Creutzfeld-Jakob disease, for instance, acquires gravitas on its first mention. Once again, doctors need to show discretion and resist the temptation to overcook as in the operation named, 'The Finsterer-Lake-Lahey modification of the Miculicz-Kronlein-Hofmeister-Reichal-Polya improvement of the Billroth II gastrectomy'.

The strangest example of doctors striving too vigorously to immortalise themselves occurred at the end of the nineteenth century. One hundred years later, Scottish neurologist Roger Grant described how French and German physicians launched a 'neurological assault on the big toe'. They were staking rival claims to one of neurology's enduring signs, the extensor plantar response – the one a doctor elicits by scratching the sole of your foot with his fingernail, his door key, or the blunt end of the hammer with which he taps your knees. (One Harley Street practitioner of the 1930s used to claim that the only reliable instrument for this test was the ignition key of a Bentley.)

The big toe's normal response is to turn up but in certain neurological conditions, it turns down. When Joseph Francois Felix Babinski described this reflex movement in 1896 – it has since been known, of course, as the Babinski Response – his neurological colleagues dismissed it as unimportant. Yet, within a few years, enthusiasm for scratching, pinching and stroking the foot spread across Europe like an epidemic. And each seeker after immortality claimed either that his reflex was new, or that the method he used was so original that it merited separate eponymous recognition.

The heavyweight contenders were two German neurologists, Professors Oppenheim and Schaefer, who refused to accept that their eponymous reflexes were mere modifications of Babinski's. Oppenheim, who had pooh-poohed Babinski's original finding, suddenly 'discovered' the significance of the way ankle and toes responded to a heavy stroking of the inside of the calf; Schaefer provoked the same response by pinching the Achilles tendon.

In the early 1900s, the Americans made their traditional late arrival into a European conflict and began to 'discover' different ways of inducing movement of the big toe. The first American bid for eponymity came in 1904 with Gordon's Leg Sign – much the same as Schaefer's Reflex except that the squeezing was of calf muscle rather than of Achilles tendon. There followed Chaddock's Toe Sign or Chaddock's Manoeuvre – a way of eliciting the Babinski response in people with sensitive soles to their feet. Other American claims were also ways of eliciting a Babinski response by different methods: Bing's Sign – pricking the top of the foot, Strumpell's Phenomenon – pressure over the shin bone, Cornell's Response – scratching a different part of the sole, and Hirschberg's sign – twisting the foot while scraping the sole.

As a result of this fiercely fought competition at the turn of the century, there are now over thirty names associated with skin or tendon reflexes of the foot though, to the relief of most doctors, the only one in common use is Babinski.

LARGE FEES AND HOW TO GET THEM

USA, 1911

Doctors have never found it easy to balance the demands of Hippocrates and Mammon. Those who practise in Europe try to disguise the conflict with the professional nonchalance recommended by Anthony Trollope in *Doctor Thorne:*

> A physician should take his fee without letting his left hand know what his right hand is doing; it should be taken without a thought, without a look, without a move of the facial muscles; the true physician should hardly be aware that the last friendly grasp of the hand had been made more precious by the touch of gold.

Things are not the same on the other side of the Atlantic. In medicine, as in other forms of human endeavour, practices indulged covertly in Europe are proclaimed overtly in the United States.

In the late nineteenth and early twentieth centuries, a posse of American doctors published textbooks offering guidance to their colleagues on how to exploit their patients. The least inhibited author, Dr Albert V Harmon, whose seminal text *Large Fees and How to Get Them* appeared in 1911, had little time for Trollopian reticence: 'One of the most potent causes of professional poverty is the mania of the doctor for a pretense of well-doing. He exhibits this in many ways. One of the most pernicious is an affectation of contempt for money.'

Harmon was echoing a sentiment expressed in 1891 by Dr J J Taylor in *How to Obtain the Best Financial Results in the Practice of Medicine:* 'Never allow sentiment to interfere with business. The "thank-you" is best emphasised by the silvery accent of clinking coins.'

Most of the authors laid great stress on presentation. Dr T F Reilly, author of *Building a Profitable Practice,* told his readers:

> Try to look like a doctor. The doctor in the minds of most city dwellers to-day is tall and thin and wears a Van Dyke beard, or at least approaches this style . . . Always seem serious and busy when patients come into your office; have medical books and journals strewn about, showing that you are studying. Never let patients see you reading novels, or other light literature; you must ever and always appear a serious worker in a serious business.

Dr Harmon warned his readers against allowing waiting patients to talk to one another about their ailments or prescriptions. Discussion might encourage them to find fault with the doctor's work. A wise physician employed a well-trained and faithful receptionist: 'When she finds the conversation drifting into disagreeable channels she can adroitly step in and change the subject.'

Harmon also offered detailed advice on how to drum up business. The doctor should scan local newspapers for reports of sick people and send them unsigned letters enclosing samples of the latest treatments for their ailments. The letters would awaken the recipients' interest in possible medical treatment and the doctor could then write a note mentioning his 'professional curiosity' in their complaint.

Hooking the patient was but the first step. Harmon devoted a whole section to 'Ways of getting additional fees from patients who have already paid well for the original treatment'.

> One man (or woman) needs the eyes looked after and fitted with proper glasses, another should have the teeth fixed up, another requires a special surgical appliance, while still

another should have a special prescription compounded. The doctor always has a list of experts to whom he directs patients on a fee-sharing plan, and these fees are never over-modest.

He recommended even less scrupulous techniques when aiming at lucrative targets: 'You know, the rich are always in a precarious condition. It's a mighty conscientious doctor who will tell a rich man that his trouble is only imaginary.' And a rich man's imagination could be a treasure chest:

It is a well-understood fact among physicians that the average man of fifty or over takes more interest and pride in his sexual virility than in any phase of his physical system. Where men of ordinary means will haggle over a $250 fee for being successfully treated for some annoying, really dangerous ailment, they will pay $1,000 or more cheerfully on anything that seems like a reasonable assurance of having their sexual power restored to its pristine vigour.

Dr Harmon favoured an indirect approach. The doctor should recommend 'a thorough physical examination'.

While performing this, pay no attention to the sexual organs at first, but, when nearing the end of the examination say casually: 'How long have you been in that condition, Mr X?' This is a random shot, but it will strike home 99 times out of a hundred. You have got your human fly stuck on a gummed trap from which he couldn't extricate himself if he would, and he doesn't want to.

A fly in a gum trap is an image rarely used today; modern doctors talk more ponderously about 'the doctor-patient relationship'. But then, Harmon was writing ninety years ago and his techniques could never be used now. Could they?

'THE WORKING CLASS CAN KISS MY ARSE'

BRITAIN, 1911–48

Despite the reassuring message of the proverb, distance, more often than not, lends disenchantment. The first half of the twentieth century was the era of Doctors' Orders – commands that doctors were born to issue and which patients were born to obey. So there were no complaints from patients who qualified for treatment under Lloyd George's National Insurance Act of 1911 – members of the working class earning wages up to £150 a year – when they read the instructions printed on the backs of their medical cards issued by local medical insurance committees:

> *The Committee require an insured person in receipt of Medical Benefit to comply with the following rules as to conduct:*

He shall, when applying to a practitioner for treatment, produce his medical card if required by the practitioner to do so.
He shall obey the instructions of the practitioner attending him.
He shall not conduct himself in a manner which is likely to retard his recovery.
He shall not make unreasonable demands upon the professional services of the practitioner attending him.

He shall, whenever his condition permits, attend at the surgery or place of residence of the practitioner attending him on such days and at such hours as may be appointed by the practitioner.

He shall not summon the practitioner to visit him between the hours of 6 p.m. and 8 a.m., except in cases of serious emergency.

He shall, when his condition requires a home visit, give notice to the practitioner, if the circumstances of the case permit, before 10 a.m. on the day on which the visit is required.

The Rules of the Committee also provide that any complaint by an insured person which is adjudged by them to be frivolous or vexatious, shall be regarded as a breach of their rules.

Any insured person who is guilty of a breach of any of the Committee's rules is liable to a fine not exceeding ten shillings, or in the case of repeated breaches one pound, or to be suspended from Medical Benefit for a period not exceeding one year.

These instructions continued to be printed on medical cards until the coming of the NHS in 1948.

Not only doctors issued orders. Nurses, hospital governors, administrators and, of course, hospital matrons were no slouches when it came to issuing stern instruction to the sick. Here is the notice sent to patients about to be admitted to Ancoats Hospital in Manchester in the 1930s.

If admitted you will be required to observe the following rules:

CLEANLINESS Patients on admission are required to have a bath. They must be clean in person and clothing, and bring with them a change of linen, pair of slippers, soap, towel, toothbrush, comb and brush.

FOOD Eggs, butter, jam, and fruit can be brought for the patients at the discretion of the Ward Sister, except in the case of the Children's Ward, when all food must be handed to either the Sister or the Nurse in charge of the Ward.

CONDUCT Persons are liable to immediate dismissal for serious misconduct, and for wasting or destroying the property of the hospital.

VISITING Patients are requested to inform relatives and friends that visiting is allowed on SATURDAY ONLY, and except in serious cases, this rule is strictly adhered to. Two special permits are issued to each patient for Wednesday.

WORK IN WARDS Patients who are able to do so may be required to assist in the work of the Hospital, but are not allowed to make up the fires.

AND NOW A WORD FROM
OUR DOCTOR

BRITAIN AND USA, 1914–49

Most of us live in two countries, similar yet different. One is the country we actually inhabit, the other is the country promoted by our national tourist office. In much the same way, medicine exists in two worlds: the world in which patients and their doctors struggle to survive and the world promoted by politicians, medicated soap operas and the advertising industry.

I sensed the distinction between the worlds in which I live when I visited a small museum in North London. Displayed within it were magazine advertisements from the first half of the twentieth century, making it a haven where persons of a certain age could wallow in nostalgia. The fading pages conjured up a world that was nearly, but not quite, the world I once inhabited, populated by people almost, but not quite, as I remembered them.

A recurring figure was the all-wise family doctor. My memories of childhood suggest he really did exist, in a benign rather than an all-wise form, but maybe those memories were nurtured by the strip cartoon used to advertise Horlicks, sadly missing from the North London collection.

In the first frame of the strip, tragedy would strike at the heart of middle-class life. Young Daphne's backhand would deteriorate, Daddy would lose his temper with his secretary, Mummy would grow tired and irritable, or Grandpa would stumble over the agenda at the golf club committee. Then some kindly friend would suggest that the person in distress should see a doctor. In the next frame, a serious-faced GP would immediately diagnose 'night starvation' and prescribe a cup of calming Horlicks to be taken at bedtime. The final frame, usually labelled 'A month later', would show Daphne winning the tournament, Daddy being nominated as 'boss of the year' by the typing pool, Mummy being lauded by members of the Women's Institute for organising the fete, or Grandpa driving himself in as the newly elected president of the golf club. And above each proud visage would float the bubble: 'Thinks . . . Thanks to Horlicks.'

The campaign was so successful that Ovaltine had to fight back by founding a children's club of Ovaltineys of which my sister and I were enthusiastic members. Our club song, 'We are the Ovaltineys, little girls and boys,' blared out regularly from Radio Luxembourg and so worried Horlicks that they organised a competition for a song of their own. That contest is still bitterly remembered in my household because a grave miscarriage of justice denied the prize to the schoolgirl who was later to become my wife. Her entry (set to a traditional air) began:

> Men of Horlicks lead the nation.
> Save us all from night starvation.

My visit to the museum reminded me that the all-wise doctor of the advertising world wasn't as clever as we thought he was. One of the best-known claims of 1930s and '40s American advertising was: 'More doctors smoke Camels than any other cigarette.'

But then international athletes also claimed to smoke Camels, 'because they know they're good for their wind'.

And in another 'celebrity endorsement', 'Film star Dolores del Rio, who has her throat insured for $50,000, tells why it's good business for her to smoke Luckies.'

But the saddest – and now sickest – advertisement of them all dates from the First World War: a drawing of a young officer on sick leave, a bandage round his head and a cigarette between his fingers, walking arm in arm with a young woman. Beneath the drawing is the dialogue:

> Gertie: You brave boys would smoke your cigarettes even if you were dying.
> Bertie: You bet we would, you dear old thing – and save our bally lives.

Other exhibits at the museum were reminders that just as fear is the commonest symptom to drive patients to a doctor, so it is the commonest symptom to drive punters to a huckster. Advertisements from the 1930s and '40s reveal just how great was the fear of any form of illness before the coming of antibiotics. And that fear was shamelessly exploited. One ad consists of a line drawing of an over-worried man who tells us, 'I've got to have an operation.' And below the picture comes an explanatory broken sentence: 'More serious than most men realise . . . the troubles caused by harsh toilet tissue.'

The social revolution in which soft lavatory paper took over from the coarser stuff – now found only in backward places like NHS hospitals – was, it seems, triggered by an advertising campaign based on unspecified fears about health. In one ad., an authoritative yet kindly doctor, not unlike the fellow who used to diagnose night starvation, tells us:

> In nearly every business organisation a surprisingly large percentage of the employees is suffering from rectal trouble . . .
> Be safe at home and work.
> Insist on Scott tissue or Waldorf.

In the 21st century, fear is still used to sell alleged antidotes to the dreaded teenage scourges – acne, halitosis and dandruff – but today's commercials seem less cruel than the old magazine ads. They certainly offer nothing to match one on display at the museum which, at first glance, looked like an advertisement for a horror movie.

At its centre was a man who was clearly a social outcast –

haggard, shamefaced and unable to look the artist in the eye. Only when we read the paragraph below – in which his outrageous conduct is emphasised with capitals – do we learn what he has done.

He took his girl to the swimming bath and gave her ATHLETE'S FOOT.

He was . . .

A CARRIER.

BEYOND THE CALL OF DUTY

WASHINGTON, DC, 1919

Doctors have helped to shape history even when they weren't present. Harold Macmillan would not have resigned as prime minister in 1963 if his doctor, Sir John Richardson, had been in London instead of on holiday. Macmillan needed a prostate operation and a doctor looking after him told him that he could be off work for three or four months. Richardson, rightly as it turned out, thought that Macmillan would be fit in six weeks. But Richardson wasn't there to say so and has always maintained that, if he had been, he could have prevented the resignation. If he had, Harold Wilson might not have won the 1964 election. Or, on the other hand, he might. History progresses more by accident than by design, and the results of accidents are often unpredictable.

A few doctors, however, have made deliberate decisions to shape history. When on 2 October 1919, Woodrow Wilson, the 28th President of the United States, suffered a coronary thrombosis and a stroke, Wilson's doctor, Cary Grayson, conspired with the president's wife to hide the true nature of his patient's disability.

On 31 October when the president had to receive the King and Queen of Belgium, Wilson was propped up in bed with the sheets drawn up to the newly grown beard that hid his facial paralysis. Only the bearded face and his right arm were uncovered. The curtains were drawn and the lights dimmed and, as the visitors entered, they were ushered to the right side of the bed so that they could not see the president's paralysed left side. Throughout the visit, Mrs Wilson or Dr Grayson stayed in the room ready to interrupt if the president showed any sign of rambling. As the royal couple left, they told waiting reporters that the president was fine.

Edith Wilson was determined that her husband be remembered as America's greatest president and feared that his illness would sully his reputation. For months she refused White House aides access to her husband, and often conducted presidential business herself, writing instructions in the margins of documents ostensibly after consulting the president.

Dr Grayson played his part by telling a cabinet meeting soon after Wilson's stroke that the president was suffering from 'a nervous breakdown, indigestion and a depleted nervous system'. He dissuaded cabinet members from 'bothering' the president because 'any excitement might kill him'. Later, when Secretary of State Robert Lansing mentioned that the Constitution provided for the vice president to take over if the president were incapacitated, Grayson replied angrily that he would never certify that the president was disabled.

The president's health became the subject of a Washington whispering campaign, and two senators were delegated to visit the president to determine his mental status. Dr Grayson and Mrs Wilson spent a morning preparing their patient and, when the senators arrived, they were led once again into a darkened room with Grayson and Edith Wilson stationed one each side of the bed. The interview was confined to previously submitted questions to which the president had spent the morning learning the answers by heart. Once again, the trick worked: the senators reported to waiting journalists that the president was 'in fine form mentally and physically'.

Wilson grew unhappy with the charade he saw being played around him and twice told his doctor he wanted to resign. But each time, Cary Grayson talked him out of it. Soon, the president had only brief moments of lucidity, followed by long spells of incoherent rambling, and it became clear that he would never recover full use of his affected limbs. Yet Mrs Wilson decided he would continue as president and that the burdens of office would not be allowed to hinder his recovery. Gradually, she took over the reins of government and ran things as best she could, not because she wanted the power but to protect her husband. The official record of Wilson's final days in the White House show that bills were left unsigned and policy left undecided. Said one historian, 'Our government went out of business.'

The charade created by Dr Grayson and Mrs Wilson reached its highest – that is, its lowest – point when the president developed prostatic obstruction and Grayson called in a urologist, Dr Hugh Young from Johns Hopkins Hospital in Baltimore. In Young's opinion, the president needed an operation but was too weak to survive one. Yet Grayson, by now more spin doctor than physician, persuaded him to read a statement to the press: 'The president walks sturdily now, without assistance and without fatigue . . . As to his mental vigor, it is simply prodigious . . . Indeed, I think in many ways the president is in better shape than before the illness came . . . His frame of mind is bright and tranquil and he worries not at all . . . You can say that the president is able-minded and able-bodied, and that he is giving splendid attention to the affairs of state.'

Even as Dr Young spoke, the president was in a wheelchair in a darkened room, rambling and muttering to himself.

The medical charade at the White House was part of Edith Wilson's mission to create a false biography of the man she loved, hiding his shortcomings and exaggerating his achievements. After his death, she appointed an acolyte as his official biographer and, in her own *My Memoir,* offered a glowing account of an heroic presidency. Her efforts were spectacularly successful and crowned in 1944 by the Hollywood film *Woodrow Wilson: The Rise of an American President* which near to canonised its subject. Edith had ensured that the screen-writers were advised by the anointed biographer, whose book had provoked Winston Churchill into denouncing the absurdity of depicting Wilson 'as a stainless Sir Galahad'.

By surviving 37 years longer than her husband, Edith outlived most of his contemporaries who might have questioned her version of history, and her hagiographic creation of

Woodrow Wilson as an intellectual giant victimised by the frailty of others survived even after her death.

Then, on Memorial Day weekend in 1990, it turned to ashes when the sons of Dr Cary Grayson released their father's papers that revealed that the stroke that Wilson suffered on 2 October 1919 was so extensive that it offered no 'more than a minimal state of recovery'. Soon historians were speculating what might have happened in the years between the two World Wars if Edith Wilson had allowed the vice president, Thomas R Marshall, to take over in 1919. Marshall, some argued, might have won the argument with the isolationists and led the United States into the League of Nations.

If Dr Cary Grayson had been franker with the public about his patient's condition, would the United States have played a more responsible, active role in a world that allowed the rise of Adolf Hitler? Speculation is entertaining but unfruitful. All that is certain is that Grayson showed that doctors can influence the course of history – but so, according to Benjamin Franklin, can the makers of nails for the shoes of warhorses.

A PROFITABLE DISEASE
OF THE RICH

LONDON, 1922

For the first two thirds of the twentieth century, the most rewarding postgraduate qualification in British medicine demanded no special learning, attributes or skills. It was not a degree but an address, and any doctor could acquire it by renting a room in what Louis Appleby has described as 'a street that has grown rich on snobbery and second opinions'.

The address, of course, was Harley Street and, in the 1920s, A J Cronin worked there before he established his career as a novelist. Later, in his autobiographical *Adventures in Two Worlds,* he described how, as a young Harley Street doctor, he invented a disease to meet the needs of fashionable London society.

Most of his patients were women, many of them, he says, rich, idle, spoiled and neurotic. He responded, in the best traditions of the romantic novel, by being darkly brooding, stern and bullying. This role went down well with his clientele and ensured that his practice prospered. His greatest triumph, however, was to give a name to his patients' prevailing state of bored, self-centred idleness. By giving their condition a name, he enhanced its status to that of a disease, so he told his patients that they were suffering from 'asthenia'.

'This word became a sort of talisman,' he wrote, 'and procured my entry to more important portals. At afternoon tea in Cadogan Place, or Belgrave Square, Lady Blank would announce to the Honourable Miss Dash – eldest daughter of the Earl of Dot: "Do you know, my dear, this young Scottish doctor – rather uncivilised, but amazingly clever – has discovered that I'm suffering from asthenia. Yes, asthenia. And for months old Dr Brown Blodgett kept telling me it was nothing but nerves.'"

Having created the disease, Cronin proceeded to invent a remedy. At the time, a growing medical fashion was to give medicines like iron, manganese or strychnine and other 'tonics' not by the mouth but by injection through a hypodermic syringe. The technique served Cronin well. 'Again and yet again my sharp and shining needle sank into fashionable buttocks, bared upon the finest linen sheets. I became expert, indeed, superlative, in the art of penetrating the worst end of the best society with a dexterity which rendered the operation almost painless.'

That would have impressed the sort of patient who suffered from asthenia. Well into the 1940s, patients would recommend a doctor because 'he gives a painless injection'. The ritual would have been of more interest to Cronin's patients than the actual substance injected; indeed, he doesn't mention what he used though some of his contemporaries injected minute quantities of sterile water guaranteed to inflict no pain. (Pain might distract the patient from the impressive liturgy of treatment.)

Cronin admits he was a rogue, though no more so than many of his colleagues. Yet his treatment, this 'complex process of hocus-pocus' as he called it, proved remarkably successful, probably because it was administered with such command and vigour. 'Asthenia gave these bored and idle women an interest in life. My tonics braced their languid nerves. I dieted them, insisted on a regime of moderate exercise and early hours. I even persuaded two errant wives to return to their long-suffering husbands, with the result that within nine months they had matters other than asthenia to occupy them.'

EXORCISING THE CURSE OF THE PHARAOHS

LUXOR, EGYPT, 1923; PORT ELIZABETH, SOUTH AFRICA, 1955

In November 1922, the archaeologist Howard Carter was excavating in the Valley of the Kings at Luxor when he found a sealed door that he thought could be the entrance to a pharaoh's tomb. He stopped work and sent a cable to Lord Carnarvon, who had financed the exploration.

Carnarvon came immediately and, on the evening of 26 November 1922, he and Carter stood outside a door bearing the seal of Tutankhamun. Carter inserted a candle through a hole they had made in the door. 'At first I could see nothing, the hot air escaping from the chamber caused the candle flame to flicker, but presently, as my eyes grew accustomed to the light, details of the room within emerged slowly from the mist. Strange animals, statues and gold, everywhere the glint of gold. For the moment, an eternity it must have seemed for the others standing by, I was struck with amazement and when Lord Carnarvon, unable to stand the suspense any longer, inquired anxiously "Can you see anything?", it was all I could do to get out the words "Yes, wonderful things".'

The room was an antechamber beyond which, lined with gold, lay Tutankhamun's burial chamber. Lord Carnarvon was again present when Carter opened this chamber and, soon after, developed lassitude, headache and breathlessness. He grew progressively more ill and returned to the Continental Hotel in

Cairo. There he developed bilateral pneumonia and his condition deteriorated until he died on 6 April.

His death was attributed officially to blood poisoning caused by an infected insect bite. But when two others who had visited the tomb soon after its opening died unexpectedly, newspapers promulgated a different diagnosis: 'The curse of the pharaohs'. They claimed that a small stone tablet discovered in Tutankhamun's tomb was inscribed: 'Death will slay with his wings whoever disturbs the peace of the Pharaoh.'

The story seems unlikely because Tutankhamun was never called Pharaoh, a title invented long after his death. Yet the legend persisted and has since been resurrected every time that anyone remotely connected with the expedition has suffered misfortune. Oddly the only person to survive the 'curse' was the man who first entered the tomb. Howard Carter died of natural causes at the age of 66.

In November 1955, thirty years after Carnarvon's death, Dr Geoffrey Dean, a consultant physician in Port Elizabeth in South Africa, was asked to see John Wiles, who was desperately ill with bilateral pneumonia. Five weeks before, Wiles, a geologist, had explored a complex of caves in Rhodesia to see if the large quantities of bat guano that lay there could be used as fertiliser. He had spent a day underground in caves where the dry and dusty guano was in places over six foot deep.

Twelve days later, Wiles developed pain in his chest and a headache, and thought he was getting malaria. His symptoms got worse during the four-day train journey back to South Africa and by the time he reached home he was feverish, his back and his head ached intolerably, and he was unable to take a deep breath without pain and coughing. His family doctor examined his blood but found no malaria parasites and the young man's condition continued to deteriorate, despite penicillin injections. By the time he was seen by Geoffrey Dean, he had bilateral pneumonia.

While Dean was puzzling over his patient's condition, he was approached by a former British South African policeman who had heard of Wiles's illness. The policeman described a mysterious happening that had taken place some thirty years before when he was in command of the police at Fort Usher in Rhodesia. At the time, the local *njanga,* witch doctors, claimed that some nearby caves were *m 'tagati,* bewitched. Anyone not a *njanga* who went into the caves would die.

As part of a plan to subvert the power of the witch doctors, an African constable entered the caves. Three weeks later he became breathless and ill and three weeks after that was dead. Another policeman, boasting that he was unafraid of the *njanga,* went into the caves to collect some bones that the witch doctors used in their ceremonies. He too developed breathlessness and died six weeks later. The deaths convinced the locals that the caves were *m'tagati* and the police were forbidden to enter them. The retired policeman told Dean that these were the caves that John Wiles had entered and predicted that Wiles would die.

As it happened, Dr Dean was pursuing a less magical line of enquiry. A South African researcher, Professor J F Murray, had investigated a form of pneumonia called 'cave disease' that occurred among cave explorers in the Transvaal and had shown that it was caused by infection with a fungus, *Histoplasma capsulatum,* that grew in the guano and could be inhaled in the dust. Dr Dean tested John Wiles for histoplasmosis and the result was 'markedly positive'. Now at least he had a diagnosis, but no treatment – antibiotics that could kill the fungus had yet to be developed. Yet John Wiles was lucky. His infection proved to be non-lethal, though he took a long time to recover.

Geoffrey Dean had read about the curse of the pharaohs and decided that Lord Carnarvon's 'pneumonia of insidious onset' was remarkably like that suffered by his patient and the Transvaalers with cave disease. Some years later, during a visit to Egypt, he learned that, during the three months Lord Carnarvon had worked in the underground passage leading to Tutankhamun's tomb, it was so filled with bats at night that they had to be driven out in the morning before work could begin.

Dr Dean suggested that Carnarvon could have inhaled dust from dried bat droppings and that these contained the same fungus that had infected John Wiles, that had caused cave disease in the Transvaal, and had probably been present in the bat-infested caves near Fort Usher. He also suggested that people like Howard Carter and the *njanga* who were in frequent contact with the fungus could build up an immunity, while those who inhaled a large dose for the first time, like Carnarvon and the Fort Usher policemen, developed the full-blown disease.

It is a plausible, if prosaic, explanation of the mysterious curse of the pharaohs and the bewitched *m'tagati* caves. But that's what happens when scientists start investigating magic. Their explanations are as much a let-down as that felt by a child who gets a junior conjurer's set and discovers that all the most exciting tricks have a banal explanation.

THE FIRST RADIO DOCTOR

MILFORD, KANSAS, USA, 1923

Britons of pensionable age retain warm memories of the BBC radio doctor, Dr Charles Hill, who in the dark days of the 1940s addressed the Kitchen Front: 'And now for prunes, those black-coated workers in the lower bowel.' I doubt that Dr Hill would have been pleased to hear that he was following in the footsteps of another radio doctor who, not long before, had made a reputation of a different kind on the other side of the Atlantic.

Dr John Brinkley got his medical qualification from the Eclectic Medical University of Kansas City, a notorious 'diploma mill' that, in exchange for $800, awarded him a degree that allowed him to practise medicine in Arkansas, Kansas, and a few other states. In 1917 he was town doctor in Milford, Kansas (population 200) when, so the story goes, an ageing farmer worried by his waning libido suggested that the doctor could 'pep it up' by giving him a couple of goat's testicles. Brinkley at first laughed off the idea but then read how in France Dr Serge Voronoff was making a name, and a fortune, by implanting monkey glands into elderly men to restore their youthful potency. Brinkley decided to have a go and inserted slices of a goat's testicles into the farmer's scrotum. Two weeks later, his patient reported that his sex drive was restored and within a year he had fathered a son whom he unselfconsciously named Billy.

When the word got round, patients came to Brinkley from all over Kansas, each choosing the goat whose virility he wished to share from a herd in the doctor's backyard. Such was the demand that Milford's town doctor soon established the Dr Brinkley Clinic, which employed two other 'diploma mill' graduates, one of them Brinkley's wife. His activities also attracted the attention of the American Medical Association (AMA) which, after Brinkley failed to produce any scientific data about his goat grafts, denounced his treatment as quackery and denied him membership of the Association.

Brinkley ignored the criticism and promoted his clinic, now known as the Kansas General Research Hospital, with a hard-selling national mailing campaign aimed at men over forty. He also planted newspaper stories that portrayed him as a medical maverick, a friend of the ageing American male, a victim of persecution by jealous conservative doctors, and a devout family man. He told interviewers that Saint Luke, apostle and doctor, must have also been a quack because he hadn't belonged to the American Medical Association.

In 1923 Brinkley made his master move, starting the first radio station in Kansas – KFKB, 'Kansas First, Kansas Best' – on which he played the role of a kindly, 'just a country boy at heart' family doctor, a character that went down better with his rural audience than did the slick fast talk they heard on big-city stations. His audience didn't mind, or even notice, if he pronounced words wrongly or seemed to lose the thread of what he was saying, for that was exactly what they did.

KFKB's transmissions reached far beyond Kansas and soon established a huge audience for programmes that mixed country music with fundamentalist sermons and lectures from the station owner on rejuvenation. Brinkley also used KFKB to attack more orthodox doctors. 'Don't let your doctor two-dollar you to death . . . come to Dr Brinkley.' When listeners started to write for advice, he set up a regular item 'The Medical Question Box', in which he named the enquirers' home towns, described their symptoms, and recommended treatment – usually one of the medicines he sold by mail order. He was soon receiving more than 3,000 letters a day, and magnanimously donated a new post office to Milford.

In 1929, KFKB won a gold cup as the most popular radio

station in America and Brinkley was a rich man. He virtually owned Milford, which had expanded to accommodate the flow of visitors to his clinic. He bought a yacht and a private plane, and had friends in high places, including the Vice President of the United States, Charles Curtis.

He also had powerful enemies. The *Kansas City Star* ran an exposé on his clinic and Dr Morris Fishbein, editor of the *Journal of the American Medical Association,* denounced him for 'blatant quackery'. Brinkley filed a libel suit against Fishbein but didn't pursue it after he had squeezed as much publicity from it as he could.

In July 1930, Fishbein was a guest speaker at the annual convention of the Kansas Medical Society and, though he didn't mention Brinkley by name, everyone knew to whom he referred when he described a typical charlatan as 'a man who is likely to have a pleasing personality; a smooth tongue; able to present his case with eloquence. He will claim educational advantages he does not possess . . . always he will produce a large number of testimonials from the professional testimonial givers, or from persons who like to see their names in print . . . The charlatan of the worst type is the renegade physician. That man destroys public confidence in a profession. He destroys, but does not heal.'

There followed a raucous public rumpus. Brinkley defended himself with a massive propaganda campaign, stepping up his radio attacks on Fishbein and seeking to validate his treatment with testimonials from satisfied customers published in full-page newspaper advertisements. Yet, despite his huge expenditure of energy and money, the Kansas Supreme Court recommended that he lose his broadcasting licence. 'The licensee has performed an organised charlatanism quite beyond the invention of the humble mountebank.'

Unfazed by this setback, Brinkley sold KFKB for $90,000 and moved to the sleepy town of Del Rio in Texas. Just across the border in Mexico, out of the range of American restriction, he built a more powerful transmitter than he'd had before. His new station expanded the KFKB mixture of weather, sermons and Brinkley's promotional lectures, with performances from the stars of country music, singing cowboys, a Mexican orchestra and a bizarre collection of hucksters, cult leaders and fascist politicians who bought air time at premium rates to promulgate views that no one else would broadcast.

Brinkley closed the clinic in Milford, indeed razed it to the ground when the doctors working there decided to 'go independent', and moved his operation to Del Rio. There, the new Brinkley Rejuvenation Hospital brought prosperity even in the depths of the Depression. Shops, hotels and restaurants thrived on the stream of patients, their families and friends who were attracted by the perpetual summer of the West Texas climate. Brinkley soon launched two more radio stations and the Brinkley Branch Clinic in San Juan for the treatment of 'piles, fistulas, colitis, and diseases of the female and male rectum'.

By the end of 1937, Brinkley's businesses were said to be grossing $12 million a year. He owned real estate, including citrus groves and oil wells, a dozen Cadillacs, and three yachts, including the huge *Dr Brinkley III,* staffed by a 21-man crew. He prided himself that he was never seen in public undecorated with at least $100,000-worth of diamonds in the form of rings, tie clips and tie pins.

But by now his list of enemies included not just the Internal Revenue Service, which was after him for back taxes, but the US government, which was angered by the way he had flouted so many of its regulations and particularly irritated by the signal from his Mexican radio station, which was so powerful that it devoured everything in its path and could be heard in New York and Philadelphia, sometimes to the exclusion of all other channels.

In 1941, despite Brinkley's lobbying of his friends in high places, the Mexican government yielded to pressure from the US and closed down his radio station. Three days later, Brinkley suffered a massive heart attack and, a month later, he was dead, destined to be remembered not as the first radio doctor but as radio's greatest charlatan.

CREDIT WHERE CREDIT IS DUE

LONDON, 1929

Outside a bullring in southern Spain stands a bronze statue of a benign-looking man gazing into the future. Carved on the plinth are the words: 'Alexander Fleming who gave penicillin to the world'. Similar tributes exist in most countries yet, though Fleming certainly discovered penicillin, he just as certainly didn't give it to the world.

The reason why the world thinks he did is that his discovery was quickly dramatised and turned into a legend to join the tales of Archimedes leaping from his bath and shouting 'Eureka!', the apple falling on Newton's head, and John Snow removing the handle from the Broad Street pump. As with most myths built around a kernel of truth, the real story is stranger, more complex and more interesting.

According to the legend, Fleming prepared a culture of organisms – staphylococci – for a future experiment then left them to multiply in small dishes of nutrient medium while he went away for a few days. One of the dishes was not properly covered and a mould floated in through the window of Fleming's laboratory at St Mary's Hospital in London and contaminated the culture. When Fleming returned and examined the dish, he found a clear area around the mould where the staphylococci had failed to grow or had been killed. He investigated the mould, found that it secreted penicillin, shouted the Scottish equivalent of 'Eureka!' and gave his discovery to the world.

That is the legend. The only truth in it is the contamination of the plate, though the mould didn't float in through the window. As the curator of Fleming's old laboratory, now turned into a museum, will tell you, the old boy never opened the windows. The mould probably came up the stairs on the clothes of one of the people working on fungi and yeasts in a laboratory on the floor below.

Fleming was fascinated by the effect the mould had on the growth of the staphylococci because he was intensely interested in substances called lysozymes that appeared to dissolve germs and could be found in tears and in nasal mucus. The mould was clearly producing a powerful lysozyme, so Fleming cultivated it and then made a broth from it. He injected the broth into animals to ensure it produced no toxic effects then used it as a dressing on skin infections like boils and styes. Though it seemed to help, the substance, which he called penicillin – a name derived from the penicillium mould that produced it – was unstable and quickly lost its effect. Useful antiseptics for skin infections already existed so he decided that, because of its lack of stability, penicillin probably had little clinical value.

Fleming had discovered penicillin and recorded its antibacterial effect but had not produced it in the form in which it later became a life saver. Indeed, over the next ten years, he made no reference to penicillin's potential as a treatment for infection in any of the articles he wrote or the speeches he made, not even in a presidential address to a learned society where he was given an hour to talk on subjects that most interested him. Professor Ronald Hare, who worked with Fleming at St Mary's, maintained that those closely associated with him during the early penicillin days believed he had no notion of its possibilities.

Ten years later, Fleming's account of his original discovery was found in a library in Oxford by Ernst Chain, a young Jew born in Berlin who had fled to England when Hitler came to power and who was working in the university's department of pathology. Chain's professor, Howard Florey, knew about penicillin but, like Fleming, had failed to see its potential. Chain, however, was a biochemist and was attracted by the characteristic of penicillin that had discouraged Fleming and Florey; to him, its instability was a challenge rather than a reason for rejecting it. By chance, a specimen of Fleming's original mould had been brought to Oxford by Florey's predecessor for an experiment for which it proved unsuitable. Chain discovered it was still there and devised a way of extracting its 'juice' in a stable form. In a brilliant piece of research and development, he and Florey turned penicillin from a laboratory curiosity into the first 'miracle drug' – a title it earned in 1941 when in tests on six patients in Oxford, it overcame infections that were beyond any other treatment. Thirteen years after Fleming's original discovery, Florey and Chain had realised its potential.

Yet, though Fleming took no part in the work at Oxford, he got all the glory because he had that most valuable of medical advisers, a spin doctor. The newspaper magnate Lord Beaverbrook was a close friend of Lord Moran, Winston Churchill's doctor and a governor of St Mary's, whose skill as a political manipulator was acknowledged in his nickname Corkscrew Charlie. (St Mary's medical students used to say that Beaverbrook's gratitude to Moran dated from an episode when Corkscrew rescued him from a severe asthmatic attack by inadvertently giving him ten times the usual dose of adrenaline.)

In 1942, St Mary's, heavily dependent on charitable subscription, was as hungry for publicity as wartime Britain was for heroes. Beaverbrook decided to supply both and Fleming was soon the subject of articles portraying him as the hero of a long struggle to harness his discovery. Fleming enjoyed the celebrity and even told journalists, in a moment of self-deception, that he had produced large quantities of penicillin at St Mary's to be used under his direction in the Oxford trial. These distortions, repeated uncorrected for years, created the impression that all the credit for the arrival of penicillin should go to him. Even thirty years later, a BBC television programme showed Fleming in 1928 arguing the case for 'antibiotics', a term only coined in 1941, and preparing penicillin for the Oxford trial.

Florey believed that Moran was up to his usual political tricks and, feeling that his professional reputation was under attack, wrote to the president of the Royal Society explaining that he had evidence, provided by the director-general of the BBC and people at St Mary's, that Fleming was trying to give the impression that he had not only foreseen but had devised the development of penicillin therapy, and that the only contribution the Oxford workers had made was to add a few flourishes. The president replied that little could be done without committing the most heinous crime known to the British establishment – washing dirty linen in public.

Florey got the same response when he wrote to the secretary of the Medical Research Council complaining about St Mary's 'unscrupulous campaign' to credit Fleming with all the work done at Oxford. Fleming, he said, was being repeatedly interviewed and presented as 'the discoverer of penicillin', which he was, but with the implication that he had done all the work leading to the discovery of its therapeutic properties, which he had not. Chain took a more relaxed view. Hospitals were struggling for money, he said. St Mary's could see a pot of gold. If he'd been a manager at St Mary's, he would have done the same.

As Fleming's fame spread, he had to face an uncomfortable question. If he had known the potential of his discovery from the beginning, why had he abandoned it when he did, and so postponed a magical cure for over a decade? He equivocated by replying that, because he wasn't a chemist like Chain, he couldn't produce penicillin suitable for injection and therefore could not test it as widely as he would have liked. The need to create a legend ensured that the questioning went no further and the prejudices of the time showed through when Fleming provoked no comment with his petulant claim that he could have developed penicillin if, like Florey, 'I'd had a tame Jew in my department'.

The final word on who should get the credit for what many would rate the greatest advance in twentieth-century medicine was spoken by those who awarded the 1945 Nobel Prize jointly to Fleming, Florey and Chain.

A MEDICAL CLIP ROUND THE EAR

DUBLIN, 1935

Just as there are patients who think that the more unpleasant a medicine, the greater the good it must be doing, so there are doctors, nurses and hospital staff who believe that the only route to health is through suffering. This prejudice is usually concealed but sometimes declares itself unwittingly, as in an Essex hospital memorandum in 1979:

> OLDCHURCH HOSPITAL, ROMFORD
> Memorandum to: Sisters and Heads of Dept.
> As from 12-11-79 the issue of pre-packs will now contain hard toilet rolls, due to excessive use of soft.

The belief that joy has to be earned through suffering – that some people need 'a good shake-up' to 'bring them back to their senses' – underlies a form of treatment that some call punitive medicine. An example is described in a letter that a consultant at the Bristol Royal Infirmary wrote to a GP in 1954:

> This 16-year-old girl is suffering from hysterical epilepsy as a result of seeing a fit at a football match. I think I have cured her by a firm talk. I told her mother that, if they recur, she should smack her face and pour cold water over her.

In the 1970s, the surgeon-turned-novelist John Rowan Wilson took an interest in punitive medicine inspired, he claimed, by

S J Perelman's suggestion that the most effective way to control thumb-sucking was to nail the infant's hands to the side of the cot. One of his ripest discoveries was in a much revered medical text, John Hilton's *Rest and Pain,* published in 1863 and often recommended to medical students by teachers desperate to give them a veneer of erudition.

One condition that caused Hilton grave concern was masturbation, which he regarded as a source of much serious illness. He admitted it was 'a habit very difficult to contend with in practice', assumed it afflicted only males, and recommended painting the victim's penis with a strong tincture of iodine to ensure that it blistered and became so sore that the patient could not bear to touch it.

Rowan Wilson hoped that Hilton's book would always be recommended to students because, apart from its other virtues, it was a reminder that even the most talented of men can make fools of themselves when they seek to define medicine in terms of conventional morality.

One of the strangest cases of punitive medicine was described by Dr Ellia Berstock, who practised as a GP in Stockport. When he was a medical student in Dublin in the mid-1930s, Berstock often visited The Meath Hospital to listen to a Dr Murphy, 'a perky man, fly-collared and pin-stripe suited'. One morning Berstock was among the watching students when Murphy demonstrated a case of hysterical paralysis in a man who was unable to move his legs and was therefore confined to a wheelchair or his bed. Without warning, Dr Murphy applied a red-hot metal disc to his patient's backside and the paralysed patient leaped out of bed and travelled speedily round the ward with the jerky movements of a character in an over-cranked silent film. To the students' surprise, when the man with the branded buttock made it back to his bed and his paralysis, he just smiled and offered no complaint.

Neither the patient nor his condition appeared to be any better for the experience, but Dr Murphy seemed quite pleased with the result.

STRIVING INOFFICIOUSLY

SANDRINGHAM, 1936

In January 1936, King George V fell ill while on his Christmas holiday at Sandringham and on Friday 17th, Queen Mary sent for his doctor, Lord Dawson of Penn. Later the King wrote in his diary: 'Dawson arrived this evening. I saw him and felt rotten.'

The double meaning is unfortunate because those were the last words the King wrote, and three days later he was dead. Over those days, a respectful nation grew aware of Lord Dawson's presence through the regular bulletins he issued about the monarch's health, copies of which were displayed on the railings in front of Buckingham Palace. All were couched in the lordly tones you would expect of a practised courtier: 'The King's bronchial catarrh is not severe but there have appeared signs of cardiac weakness.'

On the evening of 20 January, Dawson dined at Sandringham in the company of the Prince of Wales, Cosmo Lang the Archbishop of Canterbury, and Stanley Baldwin, the prime minister. Dawson is said to have composed his most quoted bulletin on the back of a menu card during that dinner, though it is more likely that he wrote down a sentence he had been refurbishing for days: 'The King's life is moving peacefully towards its close.'

The bulletin was despatched to the BBC and broadcast that evening. Yet, in truth, Dawson's patient was no better nor worse than he had been for 48 hours. A suspicious person might

105

conclude that the good doctor, having composed a series of bulletins ushering the king towards a graceful exit, had now decided that the time had come to ease His Majesty off stage.

After dinner, when the prime minister and court officials retired to plan the royal funeral, the archbishop and Dawson joined the Queen and the Prince of Wales in the king's bedchamber. We were to learn fifty years later that Dawson had already persuaded the Queen and her eldest son that he should not 'strive officiously' to keep the king alive and, once he had managed to steer the Archbishop of Canterbury out of the room, he injected a massive dose of morphine and cocaine into the king's jugular vein. The family were then assembled at the bedside so the king could exit peacefully in the presence of his wife and children. Queen Mary wrote in her diary: 'Am broken-hearted . . . at five to twelve my darling husband passed peacefully away . . . The sunset of his death tinged the whole world's sky.'

The timing of the lethal dose had been determined by the deadline of *The Times* newspaper. Dawson had decided that it would be more dignified for the King's death to be announced in this traditional forum rather than over the new and as yet undignified airwaves. Earlier that evening, Lady Dawson had phoned the editor of *The Times* advising him to keep the lead space open and, just before the deadline, he was able to fill it with the official announcement. Later that day, Stanley Baldwin told the nation in a broadcast tribute that the King's last words were, 'How is the empire?' Dawson recorded in his diary that the actual last words were 'God damn you.'

The following November, the second reading of a bill enabling euthanasia was defeated in the House of Lords. During the debate, Lord Dawson was one of the bill's most vigorous opponents, arguing that legislation was unnecessary because 'good doctors' already helped their patients to die. He claimed, as indeed he had suggested to the ex-queen and the new king, that the ideal medical practice was defined in the lines, 'Thou shalt not kill; but need'st not strive officiously to keep alive.'

Medical teachers still use the aphorism to define commendable practice, unaware, it seems, that it comes from

Arthur Hugh Clough's *The Latest Decalogue,* a nineteenth-century satirical rewriting of the ten commandments to suit 'market forces'. Other couplets include:

> Do not adultery commit;
> Advantage rarely comes of it.
>
> Thou shalt not steal; an empty feat,
> When it's so lucrative to cheat.
>
> Thou shalt not covet; but tradition
> Approves all forms of competition.

After a decent interval of less than a year, Dawson was created a viscount, an award that, as Richard Gordon remarked later, established the going rate for regicide.

STRANGE ADVENTURES IN THE NIGHT

BRITAIN, 1938–97

Each day's fading of the light ushers in the hours of medical eccentricity – hours which bring out the best, and worst, in patients and their doctors. One night in the border town of Hawick, for instance, local GP Dr Ford Simpson was disturbed in the early hours by a phone call from the local community care alarm centre that responds to signals from panic buttons supplied to elderly people. He was told that a patient had pressed her button but was so distressed, or in so much pain, that she could only wheeze her message over the intercom. Dr Simpson quickly attended the scene and found the patient comfortably asleep in her bed. Her large dog had climbed alongside her and, in falling asleep, had pressed the panic button with his nose.

An even stranger night adventure was described at a West Riding medical society by a GP who hid behind the pseudonym 'Harry'. Soon after qualifying in the 1950s, he had been working as a casualty officer at St Luke's Hospital in Bradford. One night, in those early hours when all lights are dimmed and the hospital buildings seem themselves to sleep, a nurse came down to casualty from one of the wards. She was in a panic because a disturbed elderly lady had vanished from her bed and could be found nowhere in the hospital. Harry, being a kindly soul, offered to get his car out to go and look for the absconder. He'd travelled barely half a mile when he spotted his quarry wandering along the pavement in her nightdress. Though she was highly confused, he managed to get her into the passenger seat and drive her back to the hospital where he left her locked in the car while he went to find her keepers. As he re-entered casualty, the nurse rushed up to him, thanked him for his kindness, and explained there was no need to panic because they'd found the missing woman on another ward.

Were this an apocryphal story, that is where it would end. In real life, Harry and his fellow casualty officer were now in a fix. The old woman was confused and carried no form of identity, so they had no address to which they could return her. Yet they were frightened to admit her because the hospital had only a couple of beds free for emergencies and the surgeon, who was their boss, had promised a slow and painful death to anyone who 'blocked' those beds with non-urgent cases.

Eventually, at 3 a.m., after protracted negotiations, Harry and his colleague managed to get the night wanderer admitted to a Salvation Army hostel. When the cleansing light of day returned the following morning, the leader of Bradford City Council rang St Luke's demanding the names of the doctors who had abducted his aunt when she wandered out for a breath of fresh air.

In general practice most night adventures are provoked by what modern NHS managers refer to as 'out-of-hours commitment' and GPs refer to as night calls. In 1994, when the medical newspaper *Pulse* ran a competition for the strangest night call, one of the winners was a GP who had been called at 1 a.m. by a woman who was suffering an asthma attack and had no inhaler. The GP visited, supplied an inhaler, and waited till the attack had settled. Then, as his patient saw him to the door and thanked him, she explained: 'My own inhaler is in my daughter's bedroom and I didn't want to wake her.'

As it happens, most night calls are justified, sometimes for reasons other than the seriousness of the illness. In the 1960s, a young GP was summoned one night to a seedy terraced house in the poorest part of a Northern town to see a small boy with a mild infestation of scabies. According to the journal that published the case he had recently attended 'a fashionable course on Doctor/Patient Communication', so he addressed the mother in what he hoped were firm yet kindly tones. 'You're supposed to call your doctor at night,' he said, 'only if it's a matter of life or death.'

'I know that,' said the mother. 'But it is. My husband works nights and he's always complaining that I don't look after the kid properly. If I called you in the daytime, he'd be here. And if he heard you say the kid had scabies, he'd murder me.'

The most imaginative response to a night call must be that of 'Dr Jim' who practised in a village near Doncaster in Yorkshire between the wars. In 1938, he told a BMA meeting how, the week before, his bedside telephone had rung at 3 a.m. just after he had settled back into bed after returning from 'a successful maternity case' in a local farmhouse.

'Sorry to bother you, doctor,' said a voice, 'but I can't sleep. Is there anything you can do for me?'

'Keep the phone to your ear,' said Dr Jim, 'and I'll sing you a lullaby.'

TALES OF THE UNEXPECTED

LONDON AND MANCHESTER, 1938, 1980 AND 1998

General practice can be one of the most exhausting yet rewarding of human activities. It is also one of the least boring, because GPs soon discover that they operate in a paradoxical milieu in which the inevitable rarely happens and the unexpected occurs all too regularly.

The modern academic and political view is that GPs should adopt the same evidence-based approach to their craft as those who perform more codified tasks. Yet, as a 1999 article in the *Lancet* pointed out, some 40 per cent of new disorders seen by GPs do not evolve into conditions that meet accepted criteria for a diagnosis.

Here are three published cases that illustrate ways in which the unexpected can intrude: one intriguing, one sad, and one . . . well, judge for yourself.

In the summer of 1998 Dr Kumar Kotegaonkar, who practises in Manchester, had a phone call from a man asking for a visit to his bedridden elderly mother because she'd been 'squeaking' for two days.

An intrigued Dr Kotegaonkar made the visit and, during a careful examination of his patient, could find nothing abnormal. Then, as he was about to remove his stethoscope from her chest, he heard a definite squeak. A repeat of the squeak drove him to even more diligent examination and eventually to diagnostic

111

triumph. Not only did he find the cause but was able to prescribe a treatment guaranteed to cure. Just a matter of fitting new batteries in the smoke alarm.

Early one morning in 1980, London GP Stephen Hirst sat in an armchair by Mr B's bedside, waiting for an ambulance and writing a letter to accompany his patient to hospital.

He'd been called by Mr B's wife who was worried because her husband had had bad pain in his chest for an hour and 'had gone a funny colour'. When the doctor arrived, he confirmed what he suspected from the message. Mr B had had a coronary thrombosis.

By the time Dr Hirst sat writing the letter, the intravenous injection of heroin he had given his patient had worked wonders. Mr B was no longer pale and sweaty and his pain had disappeared. His doctor had been able to distract him with talk about his work and family and he was now at peace with the world.

In the distance, Dr Hirst could hear Mrs B talking to the neighbour she'd aroused by knocking on her door. 'John's very ill. When the ambulance comes, I'm off to hospital with him. I don't want to leave the flat empty without telling anyone.'

The two women then intruded upon the carefully nurtured calm in the bedroom: Mrs B with a coat over her nightdress, the neighbour in curlers, one hand clutching her pyjama trousers, the other covering her mouth.

'This is Mrs Williams,' said Mrs B. 'She lost *her* husband last week.'

One of Dr John Lewis's patients in Manchester in 1938 was a lively theatrical landlady who prided herself on accommodating only the crème of music-hall artistes. Late one evening, Dr Lewis was called by one of her lodgers, who thought he had acute appendicitis. When the doctor arrived at the house, he opened the door to the kitchen to ask the landlady the number of the invalid's room and found her on the floor in *flagrante delicto* with one of her lodgers. She looked up and giggled at the GP over the shoulder of her heaving lover. 'Oh doctor,' she said, 'you must think me a terrible flirt.'

AN EPIDEMIC THAT THE WORLD FORGOT

BOSTON, USA, 1941

In the 1960s, the thalidomide disaster shocked the world. A sleeping pill that women took during pregnancy caused 8,000 children to be born deformed. Twenty years before, a similarly untested medical treatment administered with uncritical enthusiasm had blinded some 12,000 babies. If we had learned the lessons of that earlier catastrophe, the thalidomide tragedy might never have happened.

On St Valentine's Day 1941, Dr Stewart Clifford, a paediatrician, called at a young rabbi's home in the Roxbury district of Boston, making a routine visit to a baby girl born prematurely the previous November. When he examined her, he was shocked to discover that she was blind. He called in Dr Paul Chandler, an ophthalmologist, who found she had a condition he had never seen before. A grey membrane, rich in blood vessels, covered the back of the lens in both her eyes.

Later in the same week, Dr Clifford saw another baby, seven months old, with the same condition. The two babies were the forerunners of an epidemic that, over the next twelve years, would blind more than 12,000 children around the world.

Retrolental fibroplasia (RLF) had been seen only rarely before 1941, yet by 1950 was the commonest cause of infant blindness. During those nine years, more than fifty 'causes' of RLF had been identified, only to be discarded when no evidence could be found to sustain them. And a series of 'cures',

113

including the miracle drug of the moment, cortisone, had raised hopes that were all too quickly deflated. As the epidemic spread, patterns began to emerge. RLF seemed to be linked to affluence. The outbreak in the United States had been followed by outbreaks in other developed countries – Britain, France, Sweden, Holland and Australia.

In 1951, two British doctors working in Birmingham, Mary Crosse and Phillip Jameson Evans, suggested that oxygen might be the cause. Most cases occurred in the United States, where oxygen was used freely, and the disease had appeared in Britain only with the coming of the National Health Service, when hospitals installed modern incubators. Dr Evans even detected a political evil. The coming of the welfare state had brought 'well-intentioned but misguided change'. A return to 'less indulgent care of the premature infant' would prevent RLF.

Two years later, a pathologist at the Institute of Ophthalmology in London showed that young animals subjected to high oxygen levels developed changes in their eyes that could lead to RLF. By then, 7,000 of the 10,000 babies blinded by RLF had been born in the United States. American paediatricians, weary of chasing false leads, decided to set up a scientific study to determine whether the disease was linked to the oxygen that premature babies received during the first days of their lives. After a great deal of argument over the ethics of depriving some babies of what might be life-saving levels of oxygen, eighteen hospitals joined in a co-operative trial in which premature infants were allocated to a 'routine oxygen' group or a 'curtailed oxygen' group.

The trial lasted a year and the results, announced at a New York medical congress on 19 September 1954, showed that the babies in the 'routine oxygen' group ran a much greater risk of getting RLF than those in the 'curtailed' group. Premature baby units reduced the level of oxygen in incubators and the RLF epidemic came to a halt.

Twenty years later, the epidemic was largely forgotten, save by those who had been blinded by it, and medicine seemed not to have learned the lessons that it taught. One man who never forgot was William A Silverman, who at the time was professor of paediatrics at Columbia University in New York and regarded as the 'father' of neonatal intensive care. He spent twelve depressing years at the centre of the epidemic and, when he and his colleagues set up the eighteen-hospital study, they were accused of practising 'experimental medicine' and of depriving the 'curtailed' babies of life-saving treatment. When he retired, he joined an organisation providing services for the blind and, with the help of one of the victims, the musician Stevie Wonder, set about raising money for victims of the epidemic.

Sixty years later, Silverman was still angered by the way paediatric textbooks dismissed RLF as a curiosity. He believed it taught 'essential lessons about medicine'. We are completely irresponsible, he said, if we don't try to understand how 12,000 babies were blinded by a relatively minor change in paediatric practice: 'I became convinced that the unpleasant memory of the most dramatic episode of infantile blindness in recorded history was being repressed from the collective consciousness of medicine because it was too painful to recall.' One of Silverman's 'essential lessons' was the need for clinical trials to determine the efficacy of new treatments by comparing their results with those achieved in similar patients receiving a different treatment or an inactive substance. Yet those who conduct such trials today still face the criticism Bill Silverman faced all those years ago. Many people are repelled by the idea of allocating patients randomly to treatment, despite the evidence that guessing in medicine carries horrific risks. To maim or kill with well-meaning guesswork is acceptable because it is not perceived as 'human experimentation', while scientific trials, carried out under controlled conditions, still draw pejorative headlines.

Bill Silverman likes to quote a notice displayed in a firework factory: 'It is better to curse the darkness than to light the wrong candle.'

BRIEF ENCOUNTER: REAL-LIFE VERSION

CUMBRIA, 1940s

In the days when communities were more self-contained than they are now, and before televised soap operas usurped the influence that Hollywood had on popular culture, GPs often claimed that their daily rounds offered real-life versions of the stories that their patients watched on the local silver screens. In 1977, Dr G M Jolly, a general practitioner in Cumbria, committed one of those stories to print.

During the 1940s, he had looked after an unmarried teenager during her pregnancy and had then delivered her son. After much heart-searching, the young mother decided to let her baby go for adoption. In truth, says Dr Jolly, she had little choice. She was an only child and both her parents were invalids. Even as a child, she had looked after them with great devotion and continued to do so long after her baby was adopted. Only when they were both dead did she get married. Her husband was much older than her and she greatly regretted that she had no more children. Her regret was shared by Dr Jolly. She was a fine young woman, he wrote, 'who had much to give'.

In those days, family doctors often played an active role in adoptions, particularly in recommending suitable adoptive parents, and Dr Jolly was involved in the adoption of the young mother's baby. He didn't tell her that the couple who adopted her child were also his patients, and he watched the boy grow up through childhood and adolescence until he became 'a bearded young man of large proportions and friendly nature' with two children of his own. By then, Dr Jolly suspected that he was the only person still alive who knew of the link between mother and son. Neither of them had ever asked, or even spoken to him, about the other.

Then in the spring of 1977, the woman who Dr Jolly called 'the heroine of this little story' came to see him in his evening surgery. At the end of the consultation, as she said goodnight, he rang the bell for the next patient and, as was his custom, walked with her to the top of the stairs. A bearded young man who was climbing the stairs stopped on the landing and smiled at her. She stood aside and waited for him to finish the climb. 'It isn't lucky to pass on stairs,' she said. They again exchanged smiles as he passed, then she went down the stairs and out into the night.

When the young man had gone, Dr Jolly finished his surgery 'in a mood of reflective sadness'. Hollywood in its golden days would have arranged things differently. 'From the book by Fannie Hirst, directed by Frank Borzage', the film would have broken records at the box office. Dr Jolly was unsure how the moment of recognition would strike – maybe a look, a gesture, a birthmark, even telepathy – but strike it certainly would. And, in the scene on his stairs, Barbara Stanwyck would have had cinema audiences around the world drowning in tears.

At which point, the good doctor reverted to his professional role and re-entered the 1970s.

'Goodbye, romance,' he wrote. 'The only dramatic thing in Cumbria nowadays is the scenery.'

ALBERT HOFMANN'S PROBLEM CHILD

BASLE, SWITZERLAND, 1943

On Friday, 16 April 1943, a quiet, cautious but imaginative Swiss was in his research laboratory at the Sandoz pharmaceutical company in Basle. Albert Hofmann, then aged 37, was working, as he had been for years, on synthetic chemicals he had derived from ergot, a poisonous fungus that grows on rye.

Suddenly, in mid-afternoon, he was afflicted by uncontrollable restlessness and a slight dizziness. He went home, lay on a couch, and slipped into a pleasant semi-intoxicated state. Yet his imagination seemed to have been set afire. When he closed his eyes, he saw a stream of fantastic pictures and extraordinary shapes bathed in a kaleidoscopic play of colours.

When, after two hours, this dream-like state faded away, he decided it must have been provoked by the substance he'd been working on. But how had he absorbed it? Because of the known toxicity of ergot, he had always maintained what he called 'meticulously neat work habits'. Maybe a drop of solution had got onto his skin and been absorbed. If that were so, he was dealing with a chemical of extraordinary potency. The only way to unravel what had happened was to experiment on himself.

Three days later at 4.20 in the afternoon, he swallowed a minute and much diluted dose of the chemical. By five o'clock, he was having feelings of dizziness and anxiety, was suffering visual distortions, and had a strong desire to laugh. He had proved to his own meticulous satisfaction that the chemical had

118

caused the previous Friday's strange experience: the altered perceptions were much the same, only more intense.

The experiment, however, refused to stop. By six o'clock, he felt so uneasy that he wanted to go home. He had to struggle to speak intelligibly, but was able to ask his laboratory assistant, who knew of the experiment, to escort him. As the pair of them cycled through the sedate streets of Basle, Hofmann's condition grew vaguely threatening. Everything in his field of vision was distorted as if seen in a curved mirror. Yet he kept cycling and, when he got home, asked his companion to call the family doctor.

He was later able to write a punctilious account of his experience:

> The dizziness and sensation of fainting became so strong at times that I could no longer hold myself erect, and had to lie down on a sofa. My surroundings had now transformed themselves in more terrifying ways. Everything in the room spun around, and the familiar objects and pieces of furniture assumed grotesque, threatening forms. The lady next door, whom I scarcely recognized, was no longer Mrs R, but rather a malevolent, insidious witch with a coloured mask.

Even worse than the transformations of the outer world were the changes that Hofmann perceived within himself.

> Every exertion of my will, every attempt to put an end to the disintegration of the outer world and the dissolution of my ego, seemed to be wasted effort. A demon had invaded me, had taken possession of my body, mind, and soul.

He jumped from the sofa and screamed, trying to free himself from his demon, but sank down again and lay there helpless. The chemical, with which he had dared to experiment, had vanquished him. The scornful demon had triumphed over his will. He was seized by a dreadful fear of going insane. Or was he dying? Could this be the transition into death? For a time, he was an observer outside his body, watching the tragedy he had created. He had not taken leave of his wife and their three children, who had gone on a visit to Lucerne.

Would they understand that I had not experimented thoughtlessly, irresponsibly, but rather with the utmost caution, and that such a result was in no way foreseeable?

Not only was a young family losing its father, he was leaving his research unfinished, research that meant so much to him, research about to bear fruit. His bitterness was tinged with irony. He was being driven from the world by a substance he had brought into it.

When the Hofmann family doctor arrived, the laboratory assistant told him about the experiment. The doctor carefully examined his patient but the only abnormalities he found were widely dilated pupils. He stayed by the bed perplexed and awaiting developments. Hofmann remembers the doctor standing there, watching over him as he himself drifted back from a threatening world to reassuring reality. Slowly the horror softened into feelings of good fortune and gratitude. He grew more confident and lost the fear that he was going insane.

Little by little I could begin to enjoy the unprecedented colours and plays of shapes that persisted behind my closed eyes . . . Every sound generated a vividly changing image, with its own consistent form and colour.

Late in the evening, Hofmann's wife returned from Lucerne. She'd been told by telephone that her husband was suffering a mysterious breakdown, but when she arrived, he had recovered sufficiently to tell her what had happened. That night, he felt exhausted and slept soundly. Next morning he awoke refreshed and with a clear head.

A sensation of well-being and renewed life flowed through me. Breakfast tasted delicious and gave me extraordinary pleasure. When I later walked out into the garden, in which the sun shone now after a spring rain, everything glistened and sparkled in a fresh light. The world was as if newly created.

Hofmann realised that he had created a unique psychoactive substance. No other substance was known to provoke psychic effects of such profundity in such a minute dose. Even more significantly, he could remember the experience in every detail. The conscious recording function of his mind had not been interrupted. Throughout the experience, he'd been aware that he was participating in an experiment yet, despite this insight, could not escape from the fantasy world he'd entered. Another surprising property of the substance was its ability to produce such a far-reaching, powerful state of inebriation without leaving a hangover.

Hofmann had created LSD, and his immediate expectation was that it would prove valuable in psychiatric research and treatment. In 1943, he never contemplated it being used outside medical science. Having experienced LSD's terrifying, demonic aspect, the last thing he expected was that it could be used as a pleasure drug. Only thirty years later in the era of Timothy Leary and psychedelia did this quiet, cautious and kindly Swiss start referring to LSD as his 'problem child'.

THE LAST OF THE ITINERANT SURGEONS

LONDON, 1945

In a stately room in the Royal College of Surgeons in Dublin hang the portraits of former presidents. All but one radiate a decorous solemnity. The odd one out portrays a lean and elegant man in a pinstriped suit, legs crossed as if posing for a 1930s illustration in the *Strand Magazine*. The subject is Terence Millin, a surgeon who trained in Dublin but made his name in London, a name which, in the 1950s, was linked with an operation performed in every major hospital in the world. He was also the perpetrator of the strangest case presentation ever made at the Royal Society of Medicine.

The operation he devised was posted on operation lists as the 'Millin prostatectomy'. Until he introduced it, the removal of the prostate was a two-stage operation and, during the gap between the two surgical assaults, the poor patient was left with a partly open wound and rubber drainage tubes connected to devices designed to deal with his urine. As one of Millin's contemporaries said: 'If he'd done nothing else, we'd be grateful to him for improving the smell of urological wards.'

Though Millin won admiration, indeed reverence, from American and non-British European surgeons during his working life, the British surgical establishment was slow to give him the credit that history has shown was his due. He was regarded as an outsider because, though recognised as a brilliant operator, he wasn't on the staff of a teaching hospital. Only after he retired did London, and indeed Dublin, grudgingly recognise the contribution he'd made to his craft.

Not that Millin minded. He was a lively, entertaining man unlikely to hit it off with any establishment. 'I was born to be awkward,' he said, 'and I have a great suspicion of orthodoxy. There's always a better way of doing things if you can be bothered to look.' His suspicion of orthodoxy wasn't confined to medicine. As a medical student, he captained the Trinity College rugby XV, and devised a new team formation using only seven forwards and eight backs. That year, Trinity beat every team it played – including what some reckoned was the strongest ever Oxford University side 26–3 at Oxford – and Millin won himself an Irish international cap.

He started his surgical training as an orthopaedic surgeon but turned to urology because he found it more interesting. 'I began as a hewer of wood,' he would say, 'and ended as a drawer of water.' He performed the first Millin prostatectomy in August 1945 and gave an account of twenty cases to the French Urological Congress in Paris in October that year. He was invited to present a case to the Royal Society of Medicine in November and knew that, as an outsider, he would have to do something special to engage the attention of the great and the good of London urological society.

On the evening of 30 November, on his way to the presentation, he stopped off in Oxford Street and bought one of the large ewers which, in those days, many people still had on wash-stands in their bedrooms. He then collected his patient, took him into a pub off Cavendish Square and for 45 minutes plied him with as much beer as he could consume. The pair of them then walked round the corner to the lecture theatre at the Royal Society of Medicine.

Millin's presentation was not only strange but brief. He introduced himself to the audience, then introduced the patient. 'How long is it since I removed your prostate?' he asked.

'Eight days, sir,' mumbled the patient, dropping his trousers, raising his shirt, and proudly showing his scar.

'Please pee into this,' said Millin, holding out the ewer. The patient obliged with such enthusiasm that Millin later confessed he feared that he'd overdone it in the pub and one ewer would not be enough.

When the impressive stream finally dried up, Millin turned to the audience and savoured the bewilderment that had settled on most faces.

'Now, gentlemen,' he said. 'If you want to know what I did to this man you can read a detailed description in the *Lancet* tomorrow morning.'

He then ushered the patient out and resumed his seat. Despite cajolement, he declined to give further details of the operation but was happy to engage the audience in amiable conversation on any other subject.

The *Lancet* paper appeared on 1 December 1945 and established Millin's international reputation. American and European surgeons visited London to see him operate, and he toured surgical centres in Europe and North America demonstrating his technique. Twenty years later, a London surgeon pointed out that Millin's was the last major advance in surgery to be made by an individual; later advances were made by teams.

Millin had always said surgeons should give up operating before they were sixty, when they would no longer be doing their best work, and he followed his own advice. After he retired, the Royal College of Surgeons in Ireland, rather belatedly, elected him as its president, and he made occasional forays to the USA to accept awards and to deliver provocative and entertaining lectures.

He wasn't a great one for honours. When I first met him in 1967, he told me, 'Honours are enjoyable, of course, but memories are more important, memories of patients and memories of barnstorming, bearding the Americans in their den, operating with fewer instruments than they were used to. And memories of adventures. Arriving to examine the President of Turkey in a bullet-proof car and operating on him in the presence of the entire Turkish cabinet, all gowned up. A bit like the birth of a royal baby, yet all I was delivering was a presidential prostate.'

He also described a style of surgical life that dissolved into history sometime in the 1950s. He was one of the last of the itinerant surgeons, travelling the world to visit his patients rather than expecting them to come to him. Among the mementoes dotted around his home was a photograph of Millin and his 'operating team' – theatre nurses and an anaesthetist – posed on the steps of an aircraft at Croydon airport before they set off to pluck the prostate from yet another distant potentate. The Dublin portrait captures not just the man but the era.

THERE IS NO DOUBT IN MY MIND ...

BRITAIN, 1945–63

Medicine has never been short of moralising doctors eager to find medical reasons for condemning evils as diverse as masturbation, kissing or bicycle riding.

Just after the Second World War, when science took a stronger hold on medicine and doctors began to be more influenced by evidence than by dogmatic assertion, many hoped they had seen the end of an era defined by the phrase 'doctor knows best'. But addictions can be difficult to kick – none more so than addiction to authority and power – and recent evidence suggests that the all-knowing doctor of the 1920s and '30s lingered on into the 1940s and '50s, and even into the 1960s.

The evidence is tucked away in patients' notes. In one folder, for instance, Dr K R Clarkson, a GP in Cheltenham, found a letter written by a gynaecologist at Cheltenham General, Eye and Children's Hospital in 1958.

> There is no doubt in my mind that this patient should have termination of pregnancy and sterilisation, not only in her own interests because she is depressed and is unable to cope, but also on eugenic grounds. Continual breeding from such stock is one way of committing racial suicide.

And in 1995, when Dr Chris Scott, a GP in Exmouth, was searching through a patient's notes, he found this letter written by a consultant in 1945.

Poor little Miss L! I quite agree with you that although she is only 39 she looks much more; but then she looks bereft of all attributes both physical and mental with which a stable person is endowed.

Physically she is underweight, flat-bosomed and tight-lipped with a large cross on her chest. Mentally, she has always been a weakling ever since she can remember, and has never been quite as strong 'in her nerves' as other people.

She represents very typically what is known as a constitutional inferior.

At this age you will be able to do nothing for it whatever, except to give her encouragement and persuasion. I put her on to a simple routine treatment and gave her as much encouragement as possible.

Try, if you can, to keep her off all active treatment, as it is only trying to convert her into something she can never be.

Luckily Nature has a way of dealing with these judgements – the passage of time. Fifty years later 'poor little Miss L', said Dr Scott, was 'hale and hearty', lived independently at home, and had seen her GP only three times in the past five years.

Another dogmatic opinion came the way of a Preston GP, Dr Mike Ebdy, when he was browsing through the notes of a patient whom he describes as 'a respectable elderly lady'. In 1963, a hospital consultant had written of her:

I saw this couple last Friday and I must say I am very sorry for the husband. He seems an incredibly charitable person who is prepared to let his wife have a two-year fling, in order to sow a few wild oats and then, he hopes, settle down happily to married life. I think, in actual fact, that once she has tasted the Christine Keeler type of existence she will want to go on with it, and I told him this.

I do not think that there is anything wrong with this girl, she is just a nymphomaniac who wants a damned good spanking and I gather he is taking her up next week to live with her father. The one hope is that she has a sister-in-law up there, whom she both respects and fears, and I have told the husband to go and see this sister-in-law, tell her the whole story and get her to give this girl absolute hell. It is just possible that being really ticked off by somebody whom she respects might make her realise what a cheap little hussy she is.

Since reading the letter, says Dr Ebdy, he has treated his elderly patient with greater respect, even with awe.

THE UPS AND DOWNS OF COMPOUND E

ROCHESTER, MINNESOTA, USA, 1948

On 28 September 1948, a woman became the subject of newspaper headlines across the world just because she went shopping.

The woman was a patient at the Mayo Clinic in Rochester, Minnesota, and, a week before, had been bedridden, crippled by rheumatoid arthritis for four-and-a-half years. On 22 September, Dr Philip S Hench had injected her with a drug called Compound E. When she awoke the following morning, her joints were less painful and she could roll over in bed, something she hadn't done for years. One day later, she had lost much of the painful inflammation in her joints and she could get up and walk with only a slight limp. Four days after that, she went on her triumphal shopping trip, which lasted three hours and left her 'feeling tired thereafter, but not sore or stiff'.

At a news conference, Dr Hench and his colleagues at the Mayo Clinic described the seemingly miraculous effect that Compound E had had on the symptoms of fourteen people with severe rheumatoid arthritis, and showed motion pictures that displayed their patients' new sprightliness. When reporters telegraphed the news across the world, tens of millions of sufferers from the disease anticipated their release from purgatory. Doctors and hospitals, newspapers and magazines, were besieged by people seeking the drug, and pharmacies sold out of vitamin E, the only thing they stocked that sounded like it.

The new 'miracle drug' was a hormone that occurs naturally in the body. Compound E, later renamed cortisone, is produced by the outer layer of the adrenal glands, which sit one on top of each kidney. (The core of the gland produces adrenaline, a substance quite different in its nature and effects.) Edward Kendall, a scientist at the Mayo Clinic, had discovered Compound E in 1935 and physicians had used it to treat Addison's Disease, a condition linked to cortisone deficiency.

In 1941, Dr Hench had written in his notebook, 'Try Compound E in rheumatoid arthritis.' He had noticed that when patients with that disease suffered from jaundice or were pregnant, or had a surgical operation, the pain of their arthritis would often decrease or even disappear. Because the adrenal glands are particularly active in women during childbirth and in patients with jaundice or surgical shock, Dr Hench suspected that the glands might be producing a substance that relieved pain by reducing inflammation in the joints.

Because he was away in the army during World War Two, seven years passed before he took up the suggestion he had written in his notebook. When he did, and published the spectacular results, there was a huge demand for cortisone. The Compound E used on the Mayo Clinic patients had come from the adrenal glands of cows, but this source could never meet the new worldwide demand. Edward Kendall had, however, discovered how to synthesise it, so now the hunt was on for raw materials from which it could be made in bulk. President Truman announced, 'This will be to chemistry what the atomic bomb was to physics,' and despatched a government expedition to Africa to examine the plant strophanthus, thought to be a likely source.

Yet three years later when, thanks to frenetic chemical research and development, a ready supply of cortisone seemed guaranteed, doctors and their patients had lost their interest in it. The near-delirious optimism about the treatment of rheumatoid arthritis had turned to disillusion. Cortisone plays a complex role in the body's chemistry and the dose used as an anti-inflammation drug is much greater than its normal level in the body, so all its other effects become exaggerated. As many doctors had feared during those heady early days, its value in the treatment of arthritis proved to be outweighed by its other, undesirable effects. Even worse, an investigation by the Medical Research Council had suggested that the long-term results with cortisone were no better than those that could be achieved with aspirin.

The extraordinary rise and fall of Compound E marked the moment in history when people realised that the post-war 'pharmaceutical revolution' was not what they thought it was. Penicillin had conditioned the world to the idea of 'miracle' drugs, and miracles were assumed to be irreversible. Now the world discovered that miracles had to be paid for, and the level of public excitement over cortisone's arrival was matched by the level of public disillusion as its less than miraculous effects became known.

It was the first example of a progression that was to become familiar. A new drug is launched with trumpeted publicity and high expectations; there follows a spell in which doctors try to evaluate it while under pressure to supply it from patients who have read hyped accounts of its efficacy; then comes disappointment, maybe resentment, over dangerous side-effects.

Sometimes, however, this depressing ritual can have a happy ending. Careful assessment of all the effects of a new drug, and of ways of monitoring and controlling them, may eventually determine its real value in treatment. And while that monitoring is going on, the original drug may be refined and improved. That is what happened with cortisone. By the time it found its niche in treatment, the original hormone had been largely replaced by related compounds that were free of many of the unwanted effects. The best known of these compounds was hydrocortisone – cortisone with two extra hydrogen atoms – which could be injected into inflamed joints and, in many conditions, was more effective than the original hormone.

By 1955, 'Compound E' – in all its improved manifestations – had been rehabilitated as a valuable anti-inflammation treatment in eye diseases, skin diseases, asthma, some bowel diseases and as an emergency treatment in severe infection or of collapse during major surgery. In the end, the world had good reason to be grateful to Drs Philip S Hench and Edward Kendall.

THE BARON'S PROGENY

WEST LONDON, 1948

On 13 June 1948, Margaret Coke, aged 29, was admitted to the Central Middlesex Hospital in West London after telling the casualty officer that she'd had bad stomach pains for three days. Though admitted from an Edgware address, she explained that her home was in Houston, Texas, where she'd had the operations that had left her abdomen covered with scars. Some of these operations, she said, had been done by a 'horse doctor'. The surgeons at the Central Middlesex decided she probably had partial blockage of her intestine, gave her the approved treatment of the day, including morphine, and kept her under observation. Against their advice, she discharged herself six days later.

The following month, Elsie Silverborough, whose home was in Lancashire, was admitted to another ward at the hospital after the police had found her collapsed in the street. Earlier that day, she had discharged herself from Wembley Hospital, where an ambulance had taken her after she had been found collapsed in an alley. Elsie explained that the scars on her abdomen were relics of operations she'd had at the Manchester Royal Infirmary. One of the surgeons who examined her on the ward recognised the scars as the putative work of a Texas horse doctor and their possessor as Margaret Coke.

Hoping to unravel the story, the surgeons at the Central Middlesex rang the Manchester Royal Infirmary, but the administrators there could find no record of Margaret Coke or of Elsie Silverborough. Yet, even as they scoured their archives, a young house surgeon walking through the ward recognised the woman as Elsie Packoma, whom he had encountered twice the previous year when he worked as a casualty officer at the Royal Northern Hospital. Both times she had arrived in casualty smelling of drink and complaining that she couldn't pass water. On her first visit she was catheterised, but refused to be admitted for further treatment. She also refused to give an address and said she was going to a hotel to call in her private doctor. On her second visit, as soon as she saw that the casualty officer had recognised her, she made off before he had time to examine her.

The Central Middlesex surgeons rang the Manchester Royal Infirmary again and discovered that an Elsie Packoma, with a scarred abdomen and a Manchester address, had been admitted with partial blockage of her intestine seven months before – two days after she had discharged herself from the Royal Northern Hospital. She had not had an operation but had been given medical treatment, including morphine, before discharging herself against medical advice two days later.

Meanwhile, back at the Central Middlesex, the unholy trinity of Margaret Coke, Elsie Silverborough and Elsie Packoma had once again discharged herself. No doubt using other names, she continued to hoodwink doctors but nothing more was heard of her until February 1951 when a London physician, Richard Asher, used her case history, and those of two other chronic hoodwinkers, to illustrate his description of 'a common syndrome which most doctors have seen but about which little has been written'.

Asher called the condition Munchausen's Syndrome, after the notorious Baron von Munchausen, because those affected by it, like the Baron, travelled widely and told tales that were dramatic and untruthful. Yet their tales were always plausible enough for them to be admitted to hospital with apparent acute illness. They managed to attend, and deceive, an astonishing number of hospitals, and they nearly always discharged themselves against advice after quarrelling violently with both doctors and nurses. A particular characteristic of the condition was the large number of scars on their abdomens, which became scoreboards recording the number of surgeons they had deceived.

Their deception was resistant to intensive clinical and laboratory investigation, and they were usually unmasked by a passing doctor or nurse who recognised the patient and the performance. Often the diagnosis was made in the hospital dining room, when one of the older residents would say, 'Good heavens, you haven't got Luella Priskins in again, surely? Why, she's been in here three times before and in Bart's, Mary's and Guy's as well. She sometimes comes in with a different name, but always says she's coughed up pints of blood and tells a story about being an ex-opera singer and helping in the French resistance.'

Once Asher had defined the condition – 'as a group they show such a constant pattern of behaviour that it is worth considering them together' – and, more significantly, given it a memorable name, doctors grew more adept at recognising Munchausen patients and hospitals started to keep and exchange lists of patients they had rumbled, complete with aliases and favourite symptoms.

Though Asher defined Munchausen patients as a group with common characteristics, they differ in their motives for embarking on their voyages of deception. Asher listed a few: a desire to be the centre of interest and attention, a Walter Mitty fantasy in which, instead of playing the surgeon, they assume the equally dramatic role of patient; a grudge against doctors and hospitals which they satisfy by frustrating or deceiving them; a way to get drugs; a need to escape from the police, which leads many to swallow strange objects like nails and chains, to try to enlarge or infect their wounds, or to warm up their thermometers; a desire to get free board and lodgings for the night, despite the risk of investigations and treatment.

Yet because the group shares so many characteristics, Asher suspected that these scanty motives were probably supplemented by some strange twist of personality. Fifty years after his definitive description, we are no nearer to explaining what that 'psychological kink' might be.

A VERY BRITISH ILLNESS

SOMEWHERE IN BRITAIN, 1950

An ancient and endearing national tradition is the pride that the British take in their control over their bowels. When, in 1995, a surgeon wrote to Dr A M McEwen, a GP in Buckhurst Hill, and, thanks to a misprint, described a patient as 'a keen player in her local bowels team', he defined a social group that can be found in every corner of the kingdom. A character in Alan Bennett's 1984 play *A Private Function* described a typical member when he said, 'My wife has two topics of conversation: the royal family and her bowels.'

For generations, Britain led the world in its consumption of laxatives – or, as aficionados now prefer, 'bowel regulators' – and few doctors have escaped the proud Briton who, no matter how depressed he may seem when discussing other bodily functions during a consultation, will respond to the diffident inquiry 'Bowels?' with a triumphant smile and a defiant, 'Regular as clockwork, doc.'

This strange fixation can affect people's interpretation of straightforward events. In June 1985, for instance, when a BBC correspondent, reporting on *The World at One,* described the trouble erupting on the streets of Tehran, he underestimated the power of a transitive verb used intransitively. Yet, back at home, he sounded as if he were describing an admirable example of British stoicism.

'Although the situation is stressful,' he said, 'British citizens have been advised not to evacuate.' He then compounded his syntactical offence – and enhanced his audience's chauvinistic pride – by adding: 'The French have already evacuated and the Germans are threatening to do so.'

The strangest case of bowel fixation was described in 1993 by Dr Kerr Donald, a retired GP who lived in Lutterworth in Leicestershire. Some years before, during the 1950s, he and his wife had spent a holiday in a Northern guest-house. On their first evening, when the guests assembled for dinner, they were introduced to Auntie, an 80-year-old former nurse, demure and neatly dressed. The hostess announced that Auntie would say grace. All heads were reverently bowed and the silence broken by a clear, authoritative voice: 'O, Lord. What we are about to receive, may it pass through us peacefully.'

CELEBRATING THE VERNACULAR

SOUTH LONDON, 1950

Even when doctors strip their conversation of professional jargon, they and their patients can speak in different tongues. The difference is most marked when patients express their interpretation of the way their bodies work, mixing common-sensical observation with a form of malapropism imposed by attempts to explain things to the doctor in the doctor's own language.

GPs find it difficult to describe the vernacular they hear in their surgeries without sounding patronising or, worse, seeming to laugh at their patients. Dr Tom Madden, who practised in South London in the 1950s, tried to avoid those traps when he kept a notebook in which he recorded, with affection, some of the observations that patients made, and questions they raised, in his surgery:

- I'm glad I've got somebody to console my troubles to.
- I said to myself, 'What's that snapped in my inside?' and it went all round my belly like a needle and then settled in the shoulder.
- *Sister of a man who was admitted to hospital in a confused state and ended up being examined with a sigmoidoscope (a rigid telescope inserted into the lower bowel through the anus):* The doctor used this instrument to blow all the dust off his brains and he's back to his old self again.

138

- My husband wears a protective but sometimes he forgets himself.
- Can I have some more supporters for my back passage? *(Madden wrote in the margin: 'Up the Arsenal.')*
- I've brought the baby to be humanised.
- When you're young, they say it's growing pains. What is it when you're old? Shortening pains?
- Bowels are all right now. I've been taking some aperitifs.
- I said to him, 'Are you on a diet?' and he said, 'Yes.' I said, 'What is it?' and he said, 'Food.' I thought, that's funny.
- Could you tell me what this container is for? They say they want a sample of my emotions.
- *Retirement:* They've given me a nice clock to see my time pass away.
- I've had two servile smears.
- *Long-sightedness:* When I thread a needle, I have to look outside of my eye.
- I can't conceive. I've been serialised.
- My daughter's just had a baby. The hospital asked me to bring her to the doctor for a post-mortem.
- *GP to a woman in a retirement home:* Why don't you sit outside in the sunshine on one of the benches? *Woman:* Oh, I wouldn't risk it. I don't want to be a poppy show. There's only one from here who does. They call her the *News of the World*.

Since Madden's day, other GPs have recorded examples of the language:

- An elderly patient told Dr A N Hill of Holt in Norfolk: 'Doctor, my bowels have become erotic.'
- A patient of Dr Eric Webb of Milton Keynes explained: 'I've just put in for my infidelity allowance.'
- A Tottenham family, looked after by local GP Dr John Nixon, was suing the council because of its failure to re-house them. When Dr Nixon was invited to inspect the children's bedroom, he was told: 'Just look at all that compensation on the walls.'

• And Stansted GP Brian Hamilton knew that summer had arrived when an 80-year-old lady asked him to prescribe her old treatment, 'phenobarbecue tablets'.

THE MAN IN THE NON-IRON MASK

ST THOMAS'S HOSPITAL, LONDON, 1950

For most medical students, their first encounter with the concept of professional anonymity comes when they enter the operating theatre and discover that the clothes they have to wear – boots, gowns, masks and hats – leave only one indicator of their individuality on show: their eyes. In those first visits to the theatre, they often have little to do but hang around and watch, so the men often spice the hours with a form of mild flirtation with the nurses that involves significant eye work above the surgical masks. That's when they learn one lesson medical students never forget: eyes that enchant above a mask can disenchant at the unmasking.

In 1950, the anonymity of the operating theatre was the source of a strange happening at St Thomas's Hospital in London. The post-war generation of students then in training was an unusual one. Most were what would now be called mature students, having returned from serving in the armed forces during the war; only a minority had come straight from school. And there were even older students than the returned warriors because St Thomas's rather prided itself on taking on 'late vocations'. In 1950, the oldest medical student at St Thomas's was 'Pop' Manley, a retired Indian judge who'd taken up medicine in his late sixties to become a missionary and was so deaf that rumour had it that he didn't pass his finals till he got a case that didn't require him to hear anything through a stethoscope.

When Pop made his first appearance in the operating theatre, he shuffled in as part of the group of new students assigned to the surgeon Bob Nevin, a plump, kindly man who, because of the reverence accorded to surgeons at that time, had lost insight into the pomposity that often affected his utterance. While Nevin lectured his new students on surgical etiquette, and hinted how lucky they were to be apprenticed to a man of his calibre, Pop stood quietly in the back row, his cap and mask obscuring his grey hair and facial wrinkles.

As always, he couldn't hear a word that Nevin spoke. So when the great man finished his remarks, turned towards the operating table on which his anaesthetised patient lay and demanded a scalpel, one of his students stepped forward and said: 'Now, young man, perhaps you could tell us exactly what you're going to try to do.'

KEEPING UP APPEARANCES

DUBLIN, 1952

In the early 1950s when Richard Gordon published *Doctor in the House,* medical students and young doctors recognised the world that he described. Nearly every medical school had its share of autocratic surgeons and physicians with an occasional *Carry On* matron, eccentric professor or formidable ward sister thrown in. Not only had them, in fact, but boasted of them. Students tended to revere these hospital 'characters' and eagerly passed on their latest doings and sayings, even though most were distinguished less by wit than by offensiveness. In those post-war years, deference was still a virtue; the virtuous knew 'their place' and were not 'too big for their boots'. So laughing at feeble jokes made by your superiors was a mark of respect, as it still is in hierarchical institutions.

Yet, though hierarchies encourage deference, they also promote subversion, and the stories most cherished by the medical other ranks of the 1950s were those in which patients got their own back on the 'characters'. One such was reported from Dublin by Dr Seamus Cahalane who, like Richard Gordon, was an anaesthetist, and therefore handily placed to observe the antics of surgeons.

In the 1950s, according to Cahalane, Dublin could easily match London in autocratic surgeons. One of the most notorious confined his preoperative contact with patients to entering the ward with his acolytes on the day before operating, then striding down the aisle between the beds, pointing at each patient in turn, and announcing his intention in a single word: 'Cholecystectomy . . . appendicectomy . . . laparotomy.'

The patients, better known then as 'teaching material', were expected to respond with a quick tug at the forelock and a humble, 'Thank you, sir.'

In those days, elderly men with prostatic cancer were offered treatment by physical rather than chemical castration, so one day the surgeon's list went, 'Laparotomy . . . castration . . . appendicectomy . . .'

'Hang on a second, sir,' piped up the little man in the second bed with unforgivable impertinence. The surgeon and his retinue had already moved on, but they now paused in mid-stride. The patient, encouraged, continued: 'This castration business, sir? What exactly would that involve?'

The surgeon, perplexed rather than offended, moved to the patient's bedside.

'A simple matter, my man,' he said. 'We'll just remove your testicles. At your age, they're no use to you.'

'Oh, I know that, sir,' said the patient. 'But they are kind of . . . dressy.'

THE CASE OF THE WORRIED MINER

EDLINGTON, 1953

Doctors who hope to treat patients successfully need to study the performance arts and, like actors, learn to recognise and respond to the reactions of their audience. It was a lesson I learned many times when I was a GP, and my learning of it allows me to indulge myself by adding a strange case all my own to this collection – my own, that is, not because I played the principal role but the least commendable one.

My father was a GP in the village of Edlington in what was then the West Riding of Yorkshire. The village had a double identity. Old Edlington had been a small rural hamlet for centuries; New Edlington was a much larger sprawl of terrace houses that had grown up around Yorkshire Main colliery, for which the shaft was sunk in 1912. When I qualified as a doctor, my father had been in practice there for thirty years, and it was he who first taught me why doctors need to be performers – the subject had not appeared on the curriculum at my medical school – and though I had to re-learn the lesson many times, the first time, as is the case with more pleasurable activities, is usually the most memorable, if not necessarily the most enjoyable.

A year or so after I qualified, I acted as a deputy in my father's practice for the two weeks his partner was on holiday, and was called one day to see a miner who'd taken to his bed because he was 'sick to his stomach'. I can see him now: thin face, high forehead, watching anxiously while I examined and

145

re-examined him, did lots of investigations, yet detected nothing abnormal. I was so worried about him that I took to visiting him every day, and watched him daily grow more ill. Because I was insensitive to audience reaction, I couldn't see that the more I worried about him, the more he worried about himself.

In desperation, I called in my father for a second opinion and, again, I can see him bursting into the patient's bedroom radiating good cheer. 'Now, George, what the hell have you been doing to my son?' he said. 'You should be ashamed of yourself, worrying him out of his wits.' Then he sat on the side of the bed engaging in cheery conversation with my patient who, for the first time since I'd seen him, allowed that drawn face to melt into a smile. My father then examined him as thoroughly as I had, chatting away merrily as he did so, and extracting the news that George was having problems with his foreman, who seemed to have it in for him.

When he'd finished his examination, my father prescribed the treatment. 'You'd best get out of bed,' he said. 'Lying there is doing you no good. I think you've let this worry at work get to your stomach but you need to be up and about. I'll give you a note to Ernie Thompson to help you get on a different shift. In the meantime, don't start putting the fear of God into well-meaning young doctors.'

As we left the room, I turned and saw that the thin worried face that I'd visited daily had fattened out into a broad, expansive grin.

A DOG'S LIFE IN BEVERLY HILLS

LOS ANGELES, USA, 1955

Citizens of Los Angeles would rather admit their true age than label any form of human behaviour as extraordinary. So in 1955, they thought it only natural that their city should be the site of the world's first combined human and canine psychiatric service.

Dr Dare Miller, chief of psychology at the Canine Behavior Institute in California, put up his plate on a modern Tudor-style residence on the outskirts of Beverly Hills and, within a few years, had established a flourishing practice among Californian dogs in the higher income bracket who were having a difficult relationship with their owners. A red carpet led from the pavement to his front door, and his panelled consulting room, with framed diplomas on the wall, was furnished with a thick-piled, rich gold carpet – which must have been a grave temptation to his canine patients – a more practical legless desk and, of course, a black plastic-covered psychoanalytical couch.

To Dr Miller, the 'owner-pet situation' was a 'parent-child relationship', but he didn't allow the dogs to stretch out on his couch. This was reserved for the 'parents' to help them 'familiarise me with the child's problem'.

'The child's environment is the most important thing,' said Dr Miller, 'and the parent is the most important factor in the environment. Change the parent, change the environment, and you have a happy, blooming child.'

Dr Miller's most effective therapy was his 'concentrated

course', made up of six 45-minute sessions at $250 dollars a time – though the occasional Concentrated Course needed reinforcement with additional 'touch-ups' at $50 a go. Additional touch-ups were needed, for example, by a beagle, the 'child' of a 'major star', to cure him of his 'postman's syndrome'.

Film stars and their dogs often trod Dr Miller's rich gold carpet. He treated Kirk Douglas's apricot-coloured poodle, Teddy, for 'severe regression', and Katharine Hepburn's dog, Lobo, was the subject of one of his greatest triumphs. The athletic Miss Hepburn enjoyed running, but Lobo could run even faster and regularly outdistanced her. 'It is necessary for the child's happiness that the parent be the dominant personality in his life,' said Dr Miller. So he set up a harmonious non-competitive relationship between Lobo and Miss Hepburn, but declined to specify the nature of the relationship for fear of breaching Lobo's right to confidentiality.

Dr Miller attributed his success to an ingenious device, developed at a cost of some $30,000 – a jeweller's chain that incorporated a tuning fork which, when struck or thrown, vibrated at 34,000 cycles per second, the uppermost range of a dog's hearing. Dr Miller named the device Hi-Fido and used it, in Pavlovian style, to establish new behaviour patterns in dogs. The sound emitted by the chain, he claimed, dominated any idle thoughts wandering through a dog's mind. The Hi-Fido sound combined with a spoken word ordered the dog to 'do'; Hi-Fido without a word ordered 'don't'. The device was also, he said, a useful repellent when 'hurled at a dog'.

As a sideline, Dr Miller marketed a do-it-yourself Hi-Fido kit. As well as the magic chain and its book of instructions, the kit included Dr Miller's major work *The Secret of Canine Communication*, widely regarded at the time as the Dr Spock of the dog owner's world. Its central theme, he explained, was that, 'Dogs, like children, are shaped by the emotions of the parents. Any emotional scene leaves its mark.'

Although married, Dr Miller had no children. Nor did he have a dog.

THE MYSTERIOUS SMITHERS
AFFAIR

EAST GRINSTEAD, 1955

This case was reported to a Royal Army Medical Corps (RAMC) meeting held at the Royal Victoria Hospital in East Grinstead in the summer of 1955. The subject of the meeting was 'Malingering', a topic of great interest at the time because those were the days of national service, and young men forced unwillingly to spend two years in the army showed great ingenuity in devising ways to 'work their ticket' back to Civvy Street.

I made detailed notes of the case at the time, but when I read them recently, I wondered if I had been hoodwinked by what we would now call an urban myth. The argument against it being one is that nobody has ever described it to me as something that happened to a relative or friend. Indeed, I have heard it only once and, because the RAMC major who presented it was a serious and straightforward man, I'm happy to pass on his story much as I heard it that bright summer morning nearly half a century ago – though it may have developed embellishments during the years it has lain marinating in my imagination.

The name of the patient was Private Smithers – in those days, and maybe still, non-officers had no first names, only ranks – and the Smithers Syndrome, as I've grown to think of it, struck suddenly one morning on the parade ground, its arrival heralded by an agonised roar from the sergeant major.

'Number three in the rear rank, what the hell do you think you're doing?'

'Marching, sir,' said Smithers.

'Marching! Come out here, lad,' cried the sergeant major and out came Smithers, moving for all the world like a man whose left leg is six inches shorter than his right.

'Now, son, what are you doing on parade with a limp like that?'

'What limp?' asked Smithers.

'What limp? You're walking like a man with one foot in the gutter, boy. Fall out and go sick in the morning.'

And that's where the RAMC became involved in the person of the regimental medical officer (RMO). It was a big sick parade; it always was on the mornings of ceremonial parades, and the RMO, himself a national serviceman, had dealt peremptorily with a multitude of symptoms that would have bemused a consultant physician but were as routine to a garrison doctor as kicking the adjutant's dog out of the treatment room. He looked up from his desk and there was Smithers.

'Good morning,' said the RMO. 'What can I do for you?'

'Nothing, sir. Thank you very much for asking.'

'I beg your pardon?'

'I'm very well, thank you, sir.'

'Then what the devil are you doing here?'

'The RSM sent me, sir. He says I walk funny.'

'And do you walk funny?'

'No, sir.'

'Well, we'd better see, hadn't we? Just walk up and down in front of me.'

And Smithers started to walk with a limp so exaggerated that any sick parade regular would be ashamed to try it on a raw young medical orderly.

'You see, sir, I walk quite normal.'

The challenge had been sounded. The RMO swept Smithers onto the couch and exercised the craft and guile he had acquired in his clinical apprenticeship. He could detect not one minor abnormality.

Smithers looked up at him anxiously. 'There's nothing wrong is there, doc?'

'Nothing I can find,' said the RMO.

'I'm so glad. For a minute you had me worried.'

The RMO wrote across the sick report. 'I agree with this man that he is perfectly fit.'

An hour later, the RMO's telephone rang. It was the adjutant. 'Sorry to bother you, old boy. CO would like a word with you. Fifteen minutes. In the office. Splendid.'

Fifteen minutes later, the RMO stood before the regiment's commanding officer.

'Afternoon, doc. Sit yourself down. Know anything about a fellow called Smithers?'

'A little, sir,' replied the RMO, truthfully.

'His company commander's been on to me. Some story of a limp. Now, doc, you know I don't like to interfere in your department, but do you think it would be a good idea if he saw a specialist?'

'Of course, sir, if you . . .'

'Fair enough, doc. I was sure you'd see it that way. Thank you for calling and don't slam the door.' Smithers had been pitched, head first, into the usual channels.

First, as a gesture, the RMO sent Smithers to see an army surgeon, a gallant colonel who twenty years before, had made his name by halving the VD rate somewhere or other. Since then, his skill had gone into a decline and now existed only as the subject of his every conversation. He enumerated 27 conditions that could have caused the limp and concluded by saying that none of these was present. His only positive finding was that the RMO had applied for his opinion on the wrong form.

The RMO next tried the medical specialist, a quiet, dry, cagey Scot. Surely he had the sort of cunning required in this case. He had. His report read: 'This man does not suffer from a limp, he just walks in a peculiar way.'

At this stage, the local assistant director of medical services (ADMS) suggested that Smithers be sent to a psychiatrist. The visit produced only a telephone call. 'This chap, Smithers,' said the psychiatrist. 'Fascinating. Quite agree about his intelligence grading. Should be much higher.'

'But what about his limp?' groaned the RMO.

'Limp?' (The psychiatrist rustled some papers.) 'Oh, he said he hadn't got one, so we didn't bother to look.'

The RMO attended the final scene in the CO's office.

'It's no good, George,' said the ADMS. 'We all find him fit and you'll have to put up with him.'

'To hell with that, Paddy,' said the CO. 'He's no use to us. We can't train him and we certainly can't have him walking round the camp like that.'

'All right,' said the ADMS. 'We'll board him out.'

He turned to the RMO.

'Board him out,' he said.

So that's what the RMO did.

He happened to be passing the main gate as Smithers left on his demob leave. He was smiling happily and he walked quite normally. He had no limp.

But then he'd never claimed he had.

THE TRIALS OF THE LEGACY DOCTOR

EASTBOURNE, 1956

In the 1940s and '50s, Dr John Bodkin Adams, a respected pillar of his local church, was a fashionable Eastbourne general practitioner – fashionable, that is, among superior persons who didn't wish to be seen as patients of a National Health GP. As the years went by, he began to figure so often in the wills of his patients, many of them elderly widows who had inherited fortunes, that he became known locally as 'the legacy doctor'.

Rumours of his activities attracted the attention of the police and, in December 1956, he was arrested and charged with the murder of an eighty-year-old woman. Four months later, an Old Bailey jury took only forty minutes to find him not guilty. Though he had benefited from the wills of elderly patients, the jury found no evidence that he had murdered them.

The Bodkin Adams case had a couple of strange sequels. The prosecution's allegations received such fulsome newspaper coverage that readers were left with the impression that Adams had preyed on lonely widows and, once he'd got himself into their wills, polished them off with an overdose of morphine. The story was so convincing that it persisted after his acquittal, and up till his death in 1983, the good doctor got a regular income by suing lazy journalists who, without checking the facts, wrote of him as if he'd been found guilty.

One journalist, however, benefited from the incongruity between the publicised evidence and the actual verdict. When

Bodkin Adams died, Percy Hoskins, former chief crime reporter of the *Daily Express,* was named as a beneficiary in the doctor's will. The reason was that, during the inventive speculation that flourished before, during, and after the trial, he was the only Fleet Street crime reporter at all sympathetic to the doctor's own version of events.

Lord Beaverbrook, proprietor of the *Daily Express,* allowed his man to pursue his independent line but, as he read the lurid coverage of the evidence in his competitors' papers, he grew increasingly worried that the *Express* was taking the wrong line. When the jury announced its verdict, Beaverbrook sent Hoskins a telegram addressed, the story goes, to El Vino's, the Fleet Street wine bar: 'Two men have been acquitted today.'

The trial itself was notable for a witness's description of one of those magic moments when people unwittingly reveal something about themselves that they've long kept hidden – a moment which the prosecuting counsel, Melford Stevenson, who later became a judge, took great pleasure in recounting long into his retirement.

Adams, who was not short on sanctimony, had found that one way to impress the lonely ladies of Eastbourne was to put on a show of piety. Sometimes when he entered a house he would dramatically drop to his knees in the hall and pray for the recovery of the patient he was about to see.

The younger sister of one of his patients described at his trial what happened one day after she had admitted him at the front door and started to lead him upstairs to the patient. She was less than halfway up the stairs when she heard the doctor call out behind her and there was a loud crash. When she turned, she saw him lying on the floor of the hall. He had knelt on a mat to pray for the sick woman's recovery and the mat had slipped from under him on the polished floor.

Counsel: 'Could you hear what Dr Adams called out as he fell?'

Witness: 'Yes I could.'

Counsel: 'What did he say?'

Witness: 'He shouted, "Oh fuck."'

LUCY'S DISEASE

LONDON, 1956; DOVEDALE, 1800

Patients will sometimes describe a doctor as a good 'healer', a doctor whom they feel better for seeing irrespective of the treatment they receive. One attribute of 'healers' is that they have learned to treat illness rather than disease. The two are not synonymous. Diseases can be defined, their causes sought, organisms or mechanical defects identified; an illness is an individual event, the possession of one person whose physical condition and emotional state determine the way the disease affects that individual life.

Even with diseases where there is compelling evidence about their nature and the most effective treatment, doctors have to weigh the generality of the evidence against the particular needs of the individual, and seek to understand the feelings of regret, betrayal, fear, loneliness – indeed, all the perplexing emotions – that can turn the same disease into a different illness in different people.

There exists, however, a small group of illnesses that need the label of disease. The London physician Richard Asher defined one in a lecture that he gave in 1956. He described a condition that every general practitioner in his audience recognised, though many, before they heard Asher, had not linked cause with effect. The condition afflicted proud, lonely, often elderly people, and Asher suggested we should call it Lucy's Disease because William Wordsworth had described the sort of person who suffered from it in his lines about Lucy:

155

> She dwelt among the untrodden ways
> Beside the springs of Dove,
> A maid whom there were none to praise
> And very few to love.

We should never forget, said Asher, how great an event a medical consultation could be in the lives of lonely old people, satisfying the need we all have to be noticed. Doctors should remember that someone who might be too proud to complain of loneliness suffered no loss of pride in complaining of symptoms.

A child cries, 'Look at my sand castle'; a lonely old person, said Asher, cries, 'Look at my stomach.' A child says, 'I got two goals this afternoon'; a Lucy says, 'I got two giddy turns this afternoon.'

Consultations with lonely elderly people are often acts of deception practised in private between consenting adults. Both doctor and patient sustain the illusion that what is being sought is medical advice, when the true substance of the transaction is companionship. Sufferers from Lucy's Disease miss not just the warmth of companionship, but the advice and criticism that go with it. Under the guise of seeking advice about health, an elderly woman may be seeking advice about family affairs. 'Ostensibly, she is asking for advice about her bad heart,' said Asher, 'but *au fond* she seeks advice about her bad nephew.'

Lucy's Disease is a misnomer, a flag of convenience for both patient and doctor, for it is, of course, an illness. At a time when politicians talk about the NHS almost exclusively in terms of hip replacements, intensive care, heart surgery and so on, they need to be reminded of the existence of illness. As recently as 1999, a survey revealed that 'some 40 per cent of new disorders seen by GPs do not evolve into conditions that meet accepted criteria for a diagnosis'. Illness is far more prevalent than disease, and Lucy is as deserving of NHS care as anyone else.

THE CHANGING FACE OF FAMILY MEDICINE

BRITAIN, 1957–98

Textbooks define 'family medicine' as 'treating patients within the context of the patient's family'. The phrase can also be used to describe a less rewarding, though no less entertaining, activity: treating patients within the context of the doctor's family.

Medicine has an awkward habit of encroaching on the most intimate of family moments. In 1998, a medical journal suggested that the presence of telephones in bedrooms meant that GPs were the only people in the country who thought that premature ejaculation was an asset.

A classic case of family medicine was that reported by Dr John Oldroyd who, before his retirement, was not just a distinguished GP but a much-respected secretary of the Inner London Medical Committees. Oldroyd was renowned for his common-sensical shrewdness yet, in the mid-1950s, in the innocence of his youth, he made the mistake of practising on the doorstep of the West Riding community in which he had grown up. One aspect of the job that he particularly enjoyed was working for a few sessions each week as an anaesthetist at a local hospital.

On one of his hospital days, he was giving an anaesthetic to a woman whom he hadn't seen before and, as he prepared to inject the anaesthetising Pentothal into one of her veins, she asked:

'Did I hear the nurse call you Dr Oldroyd?'

'Yes,' said John.

'So was Mr Oldroyd the manufacturer your father?'

'Yes.'

The woman smiled wistfully and, before she slipped into oblivion, muttered, 'You know, if I had played my cards right I could have been your mother.'

Forty years later, the character of family medicine began to change as more women took up the craft and found they had to cope with the competing demands of their own and their patients' young families.

In 1998, when a medical journal published excerpts from the diaries of women GPs, one anonymous contributor described what happened on a morning her childminder went missing and she had to take her daughter Joanna with her to the surgery. Because of the fuss over the missing childminder, she arrived late and dashed into the health centre hoping, in a rather pathetic way, that she could hide the fact that she had a child with her. Luckily, the surgery was reasonably uneventful and Joanna sat on the floor scribbling on anything she could find, including the patients' notes. No matter what she did, however, her mother kept smiling sweetly in her direction in a desperate attempt to prevent her antics interrupting the patients.

Eventually, there entered a man who had come for an opinion about a rash on his penis. Already embarrassed by the idea of having to show it to a woman doctor, he turned a sickly shade of pale at the prospect of displaying it in the presence of her daughter. Before he could beat a retreat, the GP ushered him behind a screen. Then, after he'd slipped down his trousers, she set about examining the rash in a resolutely matter-of-fact way.

As she did so, Joanna stuck her head around the screen and shouted, 'Mummy, what *are* you doing?'

DANGEROUS BEND

CARDIFF, 1958

Surgical instruments are often named after the person who invented them or first used them. Thus, the Foley catheter is named after a nineteenth-century American urologist and the Drew Smyth catheter after a twentieth-century British gynaecologist. These eponyms were sometimes used – maybe still are – by examiners who seek to relieve the tedium of oral sessions by asking candidates who, for instance, Foley was. Mischievous examiners examining in partnership with Drew Smyth were known to ask candidates who were Drew and Smyth. Even more mischievous examiners would ask for details about the inventor of the Coudé catheter – a trick question because the catheter, invented in France, got its name because it had a bend in it. (The adjective *coudé* means bent.) It was, in fact, invented in 1836 by the Parisian urologist Louis Mercier, who later invented the double-bended bi-coude catheter.

Yet, though the trick question about Coudé had long been used by English-speaking medical teachers to tease their students – indeed, was such a chestnut that Cardiff students published a spoof biography of Coudé in their medical school magazine – it had somehow eluded one of the twentieth-century's most prolific authors of surgical textbooks. His name was Hamilton Bailey and his texts were remarkable for their lavish use of illustration and their authoritative footnotes. His discovery of the true meaning of Coudé in 1958 provoked a letter to the *British Medical Journal* of memorable pomposity.

Sir – In volume 6 of the winter number of *The Leech* – the journal of the Cardiff Medical Students' Club – there appeared an article on Emile? Coudé, 1800-70, a surgeon of Niort, France, who, it was alleged, invented, and in 1835 published an account of, the Coudé catheter. This biography was written in a serious and restrained vein, and was replete with two references, one to the autobiography of Emile Coudé, and another to *Le Mois Medical* for a description of the invention. In addition, the article contained a reproduction of a woodcut purporting to be a likeness of the inventor.

We have been able to prove that the whole of this article is a fabrication and the references are fictitious. To expose this deception is of practical importance. As a result of the hoax, a number of pages of the 11th edition of *A Short Practice of Surgery* that were passed for press have had to be reset in as far as the capital 'C of Coudé is concerned, and biographical footnotes to Emile Coudé deleted.

To save others from falling into this mire, we hope that you will publish this letter.

The letter was signed not just by Hamilton Bailey but, probably at his behest, by the editor of *Medical History* and the president of the Société Internationale d'Urologie, who that year happened to be an Englishman.

Bailey might have fared better if he'd just smiled and owned up to being had. His pompous, and rather sad, attempt to excuse a minor ignorance that examiners were happy to exploit in students got its reward the following month when, in a letter describing what could have been a scene from Richard Gordon's *Doctor in the House,* Dr Stephen Power wrote to the *British Medical Journal.*

Sir – The scene is a surgical ward of the London Hospital in the early twenties. Russell Howard is taking a teaching round, and is on the warpath.
RUSSELL HOWARD: What is the name of this catheter, you?

STUDENT: A Coudé, sir.
RUSSELL HOWARD: Why is it called Coudé?
STUDENT: After a French surgeon, sir.
RUSSELL HOWARD (*with the well-known leer*):Yes, and I suppose his brother Bi Coudé invented the other one. *Collapse of student.*
Mr Hamilton Bailey must have missed this particular round.

A BMA BOOK BURNING

LONDON, 1959

During the 1950s and '60s, the British Medical Association (BMA) published a successful monthly consumer magazine called *Family Doctor* that made a handsome contribution to the BMA's income. It was well-informed and entertaining and breathed life into the arid BMA brief that it deal with 'matters of health of interest to the lay public'.

The reason for its success was that it was edited by an ebullient man called Harvey Flack who was not only a talented editor but had the one qualification deemed essential by the BMA – a medical degree. Sadly, his worth was never really appreciated by his masters – a fate often suffered by the talented mavericks the BMA occasionally employs through inadvertence rather than through choice. As one journalist wrote when Flack died: 'He did more to win friends for the BMA than they ever knew, and probably more than they deserved.'

In 1959, Flack's editorial flair got him involved in a BMA happening that was strange even by the standards of an organisation that specialises in the strange and hilarious. In the spring of every year, *Family Doctor* published a highly profitable paperback *Getting Married,* addressed to the audience specified in its title. For the 1959 edition, Flack commissioned a piece from Dr Eustace Chesser, a psychiatrist of liberal views who could write well and was often asked by newspaper and magazine editors for authoritative trips around territory mapped by the titles of his books: *Love Without Fear, Marriage and Freedom, Unwanted Child* and *How to Make a Success of Your Marriage.*

Chesser responded with a lively yet essentially serious consideration of a question often asked in spring, when young people's fancy turns to thoughts that have never really left their minds during the winter: do we really need to wait till the wedding night? The piece started with a double-page spread, across which ran the headline 'Is Chastity Outmoded? Outdated? Out?' and a photograph of a boy and girl sitting side by side in long grass and engaged in nothing more adventurous than conversation. For those who read the article through to the end – and events were to show that few people did – Chesser answered the questions posed in the title with an emphatic 'no'. Chastity, he suggested, was still in.

Yet when advance copies were distributed to members of the BMA council, blood pressures rose and gaskets began to blow. The journalist Paul Vaughan, who was an assistant BMA press officer at the time, later wrote: 'Even to ask the questions in Chesser's title was considered by certain councillors to be grossly indecent, and to ask them in a publication adorned with the august name of the British Medical Association – well, no doubt about it, this time Flack had gone too far, and as for this Chesser fellow . . .'

The next meeting of the council was consumed by tempestuous debate. One councillor declared that Chesser deserved to be imprisoned for writing one sentence that suggested that pre-marital intercourse was not only common but could be 'more than ordinarily pleasant'. At the end of the debate, indignant councillors demanded the destruction of the entire 1959 edition, a quarter of a million copies of Flack's profitable annual. According to Paul Vaughan, one of the arguments that clinched the decision was the observation by a distinguished member of the Central Ethical Committee that if you carefully examined the couple in the photograph, you could just see that the girl in the long grass wore no stockings. When Chesser died in 1973, the *British Medical Journal's* obituary acknowledged his championship of reform of the laws on abortion and on homosexual behaviour, but made no reference to you know what.

BODY AND SOUL IN STOCKBROKER COUNTRY

THE STOCKBROKER BELT, 1959

Baffling the doctors is not as rare an accomplishment as some would have you believe. In the late 1950s, Mary Wellings – the name is false but the story, slightly disguised, is true – was enjoying life in comfortable middle age. Happily married to a high-voltage businessman and the mother of two teenage children, she lived on the very buckle of the stockbroker belt.

In 1959, she started to get an itchy rash on her left hand every four or five months. Usually it affected only one finger and it always started as a small patch around her wedding ring. Occasionally it became a nasty, raw and peeling rash that spread over her whole hand, but it usually faded after a few weeks.

She saw a skin specialist, who tested her ring for impurities to which she might be allergic, a move which didn't please her husband, who could still remember the price he'd paid for what he'd been told was pure platinum. The tests showed no impurities but the specialist advised her not to wear the ring for a spell. Yet she still got the rash and it always started at the place on her finger where the ring would have been.

As often happens when doctors are baffled, the patient came up with the answer. She noticed she got the rash whenever her husband was due to fly abroad on business. She herself was so terrified of flying that her family had once had to cancel a holiday after they had arrived at the airport because she could not get on the plane.

Discovering the link between her anxiety about her husband and her rash did not cure it but gave it a name. Skin specialists recognise 'wedding ring dermatitis' as a rare affliction. Most cases, unlike Mary's, occur when a marriage is under strain or about to break up, and are dramatic examples of the way that mind and body are irretrievably linked in illness.

The GP who reported the case of Mary Wellings also looked after a man who suddenly developed asthma in his late forties. A battery of physicians who investigated his heart and lungs and tested him for allergy to all sorts of dusts and pollens could identify no cause for his illness. Then his wife, a formidable and overpowering lady, died and he had no more asthma attacks. The man had clearly been 'allergic' to his wife.

Most people now accept that anxiety can cause headaches or indigestion, even skin rashes. But many are disturbed by the idea that it can cause a rash, like Mary's, that is linked to something that is only a symbol. Even the intelligent and sophisticated find it hard to prise themselves away from the cosy seventeenth-century philosophy that mind and body are separate entities. They recognise that anxiety can produce physical symptoms – as in the student who has to keep dashing to the lavatory on the eve of an exam – but if a doctor suggests, no matter how delicately, that anxiety might be the cause of some of their own symptoms, they feel they're being told that they are 'imagining' their troubles. They have real physical symptoms, so they want a real physical disease.

The doctor, of course, isn't suggesting they're imagining anything. The diarrhoea a student gets before an exam is no less severe or uncomfortable than that produced by an infection. The symptoms are exactly the same; only the cause is different.

Nor is illness always something dramatic that patients switch on and doctors switch off. It's often an intermittent niggle that accompanies us through life. Mary Wellings didn't try to get her husband to change his job because she knew he was happy doing it. She decided to put up with the rash and not let it get between her and the many pleasures that came her way. By that decision, her rash lost the status of a disease and became instead a nuisance that was only a minor part of a life that she thoroughly enjoyed.

THE PATHOLOGIST'S TALE

SOMEWHERE IN BRITAIN, 1960s

Pathologists are medical voyeurs who spend most of their time monitoring the bodily performance of patients and the professional performance of doctors. While we are alive, they judge us by reading what is written in the bits that surgeons cut from us, the fluids that nurses and doctors draw from us, and the specimens that we willingly render unto them. Then when we die they chop us up to reveal any secrets that our bodies have withheld.

Small wonder that pathologists have good tales to tell, and none told them better than Professor William St Clair Symmers, who served his time as a pathologist at Charing Cross Hospital in London and who, on his retirement, published two books, *Curiosa* and *Exotica,* recording some of his 'pathological experiences'. He took great care to protect the privacy of those of whom he wrote, so he never placed his tales in time or space. Internal evidence suggests, however, that the central events in this tale took place in the early 1960s.

It concerns a student who was a passenger in a sports car driven by her sister, 'a lively and successful member of a learned profession'. The driver wore a seat belt; her younger sister did not. They had not seen one another for some time and, as they swapped gossip, the driver kept her car irritatingly close behind a lorry. The lorry driver grew increasingly angry and decided to teach this 'woman driver' a lesson. He accelerated to top speed then slammed on his brakes. The young woman braked, swerved and avoided running into him, but her sister pitched forward into the windscreen, which shattered and cut her scalp and one side of her neck.

She was taken to a local hospital, where the casualty officer found that her wounds were clean and stitched them up. Once she got over the shock and the blood had been wiped away, she discovered she had lost a pearl earring, and the loop from which it had been suspended had cut itself though her ear lobe. Police later found the gold mount amid the glass on the floor of the car, but the pearl had gone missing.

The girl's parents assumed that because the casualty officer was an overseas graduate, he must be incompetent, so they called in a Harley Street surgeon for an opinion. To their surprise, the great man praised the casualty officer's work and, sure enough, when the wounds healed, there were no unsightly traces of the wounds except for the split in the ear lobe, which the casualty officer had left for later repair – a decision applauded by the London surgeon.

Some months later, the student grew aware of a lump in her neck that seemed to be getting bigger and was sometimes painful. It was some six centimetres from the nearest of the healed scars, and a surgeon she consulted thought it unlikely that the lump had anything to do with the original injury. He feared it might be cancerous, so he decided to operate, and carefully dissected out what, to his naked eye, was just an anonymous tumour which he sent for examination in the pathologist's laboratory.

The tumour turned out to be lump of fibrous tissue but, when the pathologist tried to cut a section from it to put under his microscope, something hard shot from it onto the floor, then disappeared through a grid covering a drain. The pathologist was not greatly concerned. He assumed it was a piece of calcified tissue or, more likely, a piece of glass or some other foreign body that had lodged under the skin at the time of the accident. His young assistant, surprised by his lack of concern, reminded him that regulations forbade the disposal of tissue down the laboratory drains, but the pathologist was disinclined to let her lift the grill.

'How do you know it wasn't a pearl?' she said. 'It looked just like one to me.'

At the time, neither of them knew about the patient's earring. All the pathologist had been told was that the young woman had a lump in her neck, that the surgeon suspected it was a cancer, and that, some time before, her neck had been badly cut by glass. Whatever had popped from the specimen, the least likely possibility was a pearl. He thought the suggestion stupid and said so.

The assistant was not pleased and, later that day, returned to the room with a colleague. They lifted the grill over the drain and removed the skull of a mouse, countless cockroaches – most but not all of them dead – a few bottle tops, the cap of the pathologist's Parker pen, which he'd assumed had gone forever . . . and a large pearl.

The patient's jeweller identified the pearl as twin to the one in her other earring and restored it, unblemished by its adventures, to its mount. A plastic surgeon had already repaired the divided ear lobe and had even re-pierced it so the young woman was able to re-hang her earrings.

The incident produced a string of sequels.

The two laboratory assistants were ticked off for opening the drain without authority, without the knowledge of the safety officer, without wearing protective clothing, and in contravention of agreements between staff and management as to who does what.

A hospital directive declared the laboratory a restricted area and a notice was posted on the door: 'The Pathology Laboratory is not Treasure Island.'

A legal action for damages against the casualty officer and the hospital for failing to find the pearl at the time of the repair of the lacerations was withdrawn when the defendants refused to settle out of court.

The lively and successful member of a learned profession was advised by the police to drive more carefully in future.

The lorry driver was fined fifty shillings. When, after hearing the sentence, he offered the court his views on women drivers, the police, magistrates and inequality under the law, the fine was doubled. He opted for a month in jail.

IN THE EYE OF THE BEHOLDER

BRITAIN, 1961

I'm sure we all agree that many people – excluding, of course, ourselves – see only what they want to see. Not all of them suffer from politically selective vision; as the science writer Colin Tudge pointed out in 1974, the human necessity to see a little and infer the rest can make even the clearest message open to misunderstanding.

Tudge suggested that if you hung a notice on a tap saying 'Please do not drink water from this tap' or one saying 'Do not drink this water', or even 'FOR GOD'S SAKE STAY AWAY FROM THIS WATER AND DO NOT DRINK IT' someone would eventually drink it, not because he wanted to commit suicide but because he was thirsty and saw the words 'water' and 'drink'. It's an evolutionary thing, said Tudge, based on the need to jump when you see a red blur and not wait to work out whether it is a bus.

This evolved need for quick interpretation is also the origin of oculogenic confusion, a condition often encountered by doctors and a rich source of strange cases. In 1989, for instance, the *Lancet* published a report from a professor of medicine who, when walking from hospital to university with the chest piece of his stethoscope dangling from his hip pocket, was stopped by a respectful boy scout who said, 'Excuse me, sir, but your catheter is hanging out.' And, in 1996, when Dr Robert Walton was testing a patient's vision in his Southampton surgery and asked her to read the chart on the wall, she started off: 'U . . . N . . . I . . . V . . .' Only when he checked to see which line she was on did he realise that she was reading one of his medical diplomas.

An equally odd case was described by Dr David Tomlins who, when he was a GP inWeybridge in 1961, was visiting an elderly woman in her home and sought to make conversation by asking what television programmes she enjoyed. 'I *quite* like the boxing,' she replied, 'but I'd like it even better if they didn't take their teeth out at the end of every round.'

The strangest case of this interpretive disorder must be that of Dr Margaret Barker, a consultant paediatrician in Dorchester, who, as she browsed through the March 1996 edition of *The Sarum Link,* found a page dominated by the headline, 'Harvest of the Sewers'. She read the article beneath expecting to learn of some new biological method of reclaiming valuable essences from effluent. Instead, she found a story about a group of dedicated embroiderers who were replacing shabby hassocks in Salisbury Cathedral.

GOTTERDAMMERUNG DOWN UNDER

SYDNEY, AUSTRALIA, 1961 AND 1981

On 16 December 1961, the *Lancet* published a letter from a 32-year-old obstetrician and gynaecologist working at Crown Street Women's Hospital in Sydney. In it Dr William McBride suggested that thalidomide, a sleeping pill that women often took during pregnancy, could be responsible for their babies being born with deformed limbs. When further research confirmed that McBride was right, he won international acclaim and, during the years of litigation that followed, his growing international celebrity turned him into an Australian hero. He was the 1962 Australian of the Year and later listed as one of the hundred most influential Australians of the twentieth century. His fame enabled him to drum up the resources to found his own research centre, Foundation 41, at the Women's Hospital.

Twenty years later McBride issued another warning, this time about the drug Debendox, which was given to pregnant women to prevent severe nausea and vomiting in pregnancy. He and two of his scientific associates at Foundation 41 published an article in the *Australian Journal of Biological Sciences* describing how eight rabbits had been born with deformed limbs after their mothers had been given the drug. Yet, when one of the associates, Phil Vardy, read the article, he got a nasty shock. He had done much of the research and saw immediately that the data in the article were not those he had recorded. He rechecked his notes and found that dosages and the rate of malformations had been falsified and that data from two extra, non-existent rabbits had been added. He realised to his horror that he was leafing through a fraudulent article with his name on it and, when he talked to the other junior author, Jill French, they realised there was only one person who could have altered the data.

It was a traumatic moment for Phil Vardy, who hero-worshipped McBride. Vardy was confined to a wheelchair after breaking his back in a motorcycle accident, and claimed he had never been prouder than on the day McBride offered him a job. He and Jill French decided to confront their boss, and went to see him together. McBride refused to admit to fraud, just muttered phrases like, 'Look, I'm very disappointed in this,' and 'I'm sure you're mistaken.'

Within a week, Vardy and French were sacked. Seven other junior researchers wrote to the Foundation's research advisory committee about the allegations but their complaints were rejected. And when Vardy and French wrote to the *Australian Journal of Biological Sciences,* which had published the article, the journal didn't print their letter. Vardy found it impossible to get another job locally and, when he eventually found one in Tasmania, the separation from his wife contributed to the foundering of his marriage.

Vardy, an impoverished PhD student, had neither the muscle nor the resources to tackle the might of Foundation 41, and McBride's fraud remained concealed for another five years. Then Vardy telephoned someone at the Australian Broadcasting Commission (ABC) about another matter and, by chance, the phone was answered by Dr Norman Swan, one of the first medically qualified journalists in Australia.

Swan, who graduated in Aberdeen, had worked as a paediatrician in the United Kingdom before emigrating to Australia and had heard insiders' gossip about McBride. When he heard Vardy's name, he remembered his connection with Foundation 41. They arranged to meet and Vardy found he had a sympathetic listener who wasn't overawed by McBride's reputation. Yet he didn't want to 'go public' with his tale. He had no desire to topple an idol he had once revered. Nor did he want to damage the reputation of Australian science.

Swan spent many months trying to persuade Vardy that staying silent was more damaging to Australian science than speaking out. Meanwhile, he checked the details of Vardy's story and used a handwriting expert to confirm that McBride had altered laboratory test results. But only when he was sure that Vardy would appear in court if needed did he go on air to announce: 'This is a programme about the conduct of science and how misconduct can escape detection, be covered up or just ignored. It's also about the way unscientific research can be accepted by lay people . . .'

That programme is now regarded as a milestone in Australian broadcasting. Some newspapers rushed to defend 'the lion of Australian medicine' with stories that hinted Vardy was after money or enviously trying to 'knock down the tall poppy'. But most journalists, once they tempered their immediate disbelief, started to ask awkward questions about McBride. A book about him, written by journalist Bill Nicol and including evidence about the Debenox incident, had been denied publication for years because of the risk of defamation. Now, with Swan's help, Nicol found a publisher.

The publicity eventually forced Foundation 41 to set up an internal inquiry, headed by former chief justice Sir Harry Gibbs. Later a medical disciplinary body, the New South Wales Medical Tribunal, after a protracted hearing alleged to have cost seven million dollars, announced the end of what it called 'a sorry saga' by finding McBride guilty of scientific fraud. (He had to resign from the board of the foundation but, once 'a decent interval' had elapsed, he rejoined it.)

The makers of Debendox were not the only victims of McBride's deceit; they at least had the resources to survive the loss of a valuable drug. The most tragic victims were the parents who thought that the drug had damaged their babies. McBride had often been used by American and Australian lawyers as an expert witness for families suing the manufacturers and, over the course of thirteen years, some 30 per cent of plaintiffs had won their cases. After the exposure of the fraud, most of the cases were thrown out on appeal and the families lost everything.

Other losers were women who suffered from severe nausea in pregnancy. The search for legal evidence had spawned over forty research studies, so Debendox ended up with a clearer bill of health than most drugs ever get. Yet, because of the initial publicity, many women believed Debendox *did* cause defects and stopped taking it. Falling sales and the costs of litigation eventually led the manufacturers to withdraw the drug, abandoning the women who benefited from it.

Meanwhile, Phil Vardy had turned his back on the past. He helped to establish sailing for the disabled in Australia and laid the groundwork for his country's success in the Paralympics. Norman Swan was named Australian Radio Producer of the Year, and was given Australia's top prize for science journalism and a string of broadcasting and journalism awards. As for McBride, in 1991 he admitted that he had changed some data 'in the long-term interests of humanity' and had allowed himself to depart from 'proper scientific practices'.

The case of William McBride may exemplify a phenomenon defined nearly thirty years before by the Nobel laureate Irving Langmuir, who used the phrase 'wishful science' to describe cases in which 'perfectly honest' scientists who have a great enthusiasm for their work grow blind to the way that subjective judgement and wishful thinking are leading them astray, and trick themselves into recording false results.

DOING FREDDIE PROUD

LONDON, 1963

One charming medical tradition is the civility with which
doctors deal with one another in public. Off stage, they can be
as bitchy as those who practise the other performing arts, but
their traditional public relationship is one of deference and
exaggerated *politesse*. Things now may not be quite what they
were, but in the sixties, doctors were still introduced at meetings
in terms that would sound extravagant in their obituaries.
Medical audiences which heard, 'Tonight we are privileged to
be in the presence of someone who has made a significant
contribution to contemporary thought and practice,' would
recognise the routine introduction of a consultant from a local
hospital.

And the obituaries themselves were products of a process that
John Rowan Wilson, surgeon, journalist and novelist, described
as 'doing old Freddie proud'. Wilson was, at the time, in charge
of the obituary pages of the *British Medical Journal (BMJ)*, a
useful post for writers in need of the sustenance of a regular
cheque until they establish themselves as authors. A previous
incumbent, Richard Gordon, distinguished himself by
publishing the obituary of a prominent doctor who was still
alive. When a doctor of music of the same name perished,
Gordon rang a few friends of the putative corpse and persuaded
them to supply a few kindly words. The subject of the obituary
was not at all put out, indeed was amused. The people who were
really cross were his friends, who had said flattering things

178

about him that they would never have uttered if they'd known he were still alive.

When Wilson took the job, the *BMJ*s editor, Hugh Clegg, assured him that though he might find the work a little boring, he was performing a vital function. 'Obituaries are the very stuff of medical history,' he would say whenever he felt Wilson was looking down in the mouth. Every doctor over fifty, said Clegg, turned to the obituary column in eager expectation. If he saw that one of his friends or rivals had finally hung up his stethoscope, he would rub his hands in triumph and his step that morning would have an extra spring. 'Did you read about old Freddie?' he would ask his friends, wagging a copy of the journal. 'They did him proud. His wife will be pleased about that.'

Doing Freddie proud, said Wilson, was largely a matter of length. The content was of less concern than the column inches. Whenever he was rapped over the knuckles about an obituary, it was always for giving someone more or less space than he or she was considered to deserve. Judgement on delicate matters of this kind, he claimed, was what separated the men from the boys in medical journalism.

In 1963, Wilson compiled a glossary of words and phrases plucked from obituaries submitted to the journal, adding a note of the truth that lay behind each cliché. Much of his glossary has survived, augmented down the years with phrases diagnosed by others. Thanks to the lingering tradition of medical politeness, some would say it is as useful a code-breaker today as it was when Wilson first created it.

A character:	A tiresome old man.
A perfectionist:	An obsessional neurotic.
Assertive:	A bully.
Plain spoken:	Offensive.
Did not suffer fools gladly:	Damnably offensive.
Not easy to get to know:	Morbidly suspicious.
Mercurial:	Paranoid.
A man of strong opinions:	A bigot.

Charming:	Dim but smiled a lot.
Respected:	Feared.
One of the old school:	Hopelessly out of date.
Widely travelled:	Left his juniors to do his work.
Many interests outside medicine:	His juniors did all his work.
A popular after-dinner speaker:	An eminent old bore.
Fond of the good things of life:	A drunk.
Lived life to the full:	A drunk.
Popular patron of the student rugby club:	A drunk.
Had all the irresistible charm of the Celt:	A talkative drunk.

After he left the *BMJ*, John Rowan Wilson would occasionally amuse himself by rewriting a published obituary, substituting the truth for the cliches. It is still a rewarding game to play.

THE GP'S REVENGE

SOMEWHERE IN BRITAIN, 1964

Few GPs who write about their craft manage to convey its inconsequentiality. An exception is Dr Bev Daily who, after sampling general practice in different parts of the country, settled at Burnham in Buckinghamshire, whence he published a series of case reports that recorded the reality of his experience.

One of Daily's stranger cases featured a family he looked after in 1964. The 'Pilkingtons' – father, mother and son – were patients whom GPs would classify as 'frequent callers'. They all worked at the same factory on the same shift and their favourite time to call the doctor was when they arrived home at the end of their working day. So regular were they in this habit that Daily dreaded the weeks when they were on the 6 p.m. to 2 a.m. shift.

Early one morning, around half past three, the bedside telephone summoned the doctor from his sleep. 'I would like you to come and see Mr Pilkington, doctor. He's not at all well. He's got a very nasty cough and he's very tight across the chest.'

'Has he been to work?'

'Yes. But he's felt very poorly.'

'Well, Mrs Pilkington, I'm sure if you give him some cough medicine he'll be all right. I'll come and see him in the morning.'

'All right, doctor. But he does look a little bit blue.'

And with that adjective she had Daily hooked. Words like 'blue', 'breathless' and 'cold and sweaty', he said, were flies that made him leap like a trout even though he knew that they were probably made of feathers.

And so it proved that morning. Mr Pilkington sat in bed reading yesterday's *Sun,* coughing occasionally, smoking a cigarette and 'as blue as his rose-coloured candlewick bedspread'.

Daily refused to get cross. There was no point. Yet he knew that when he got home he'd be too wide awake to get any sleep before morning surgery, so he decided to take revenge. The following morning at 10 a.m., the middle of the Pilkingtons' night, he went to their house and kept ringing the bell and banging the door till it opened to reveal bleary-eyed Pilkington Junior.

'Mum, it's the doctor.'

Mrs P shuffled into the hall in dressing gown, slippers and curlers.

'Hello, Mrs Pilkington,' said Daily, 'I thought I'd drop in to see how your husband is this morning.'

'Much better, thank you, doctor.'

'I'd better have a look,' said Daily, marching into the bedroom.

'Good morning, Mr Pilkington,' he bellowed. 'Let's have a look at you.' He then performed a rigorous examination, with much stethoscope play and chest tapping until his patient was fully awake.

An unexpected voice came from behind him. 'Would you like a cup of tea, doctor?'

He turned. 'I'd love one, Mrs Pilkington.'

When it arrived they all sat on the bed, drank tea and chatted for half an hour. There would be no more sleep that day for the Pilkingtons. Daily's resentment dissolved and was replaced by righteous satisfaction.

The following day, while Daily was out on his rounds, Mrs Pilkington arrived at his house and handed Mrs Daily a large box of chocolates. 'I wonder could you give this to the doctor. We don't really like to call him but it was so kind of him to come and see my husband again the next day. Really thoughtful. We do appreciate it.'

Every year after that, Daily got a Christmas card from the Pilkingtons: 'Thanking you for all your kindness.'

As Dr Cameron said to Finlay – or was it the other way round? – general practice is never quite what you think it's going to be.

BREAKTHROUGH

THE WORLD OF MEDICAL SCIENCE, 1964–95

While GPs and hospital consultants spend much of their time dealing with life's mundanities, medical scientists continue their unremitting exploration of the great unknown. Many of their finest achievements lie buried in medical journals and never achieve the publicity they deserve. Here are a few of the stranger cases buried in medical archives:

- Investigators at the Hospital del Salvador, Santiago, Chile, reported in the *British Medical Journal* in 1980 that when 54 normal, healthy people had one hand immersed in warm water, the skin wrinkled in 38 subjects but did not in the other 16. After due consideration, they concluded that this was 'probably within the bounds of normal biological variation'.
- In 1989, three psychologists at the University of Wisconsin – Dennis Middlemist, Eric Knowles and Charles Mather – investigated events at a men's public lavatory equipped with three urinals, to each of which they had attached a flowmeter. Keeping secret watch through a periscope, they discovered that micturition varied in speed, volume and length of time according to whether one, two or all three urinals were occupied.
- In 1995, Dr James A Heathcote reported a study that addressed the question of why old men have big ears. He studied 206 patients aged from 30 to 93 years and reported

in the *British Medical Journal* that the mean ear length was 675mm. [For those interested in this sort of thing, he added that 'the linear regression equation was: ear length = 55.9 + (0.22 x patient's age) (95% confidence intervals for B coefficient 0.17 to 0.27)] His paper included a 'scatter plot' of the relationship between ear length and age which suggested that, as men get older, their ears get bigger by an average of 0.22mm each year. Sadly, after this intense and rigorous study, he had to conclude: 'Why ears get bigger when the rest of the body stops growing is not answered by this research.'

- In May 1980 the *Lancet* published a paper entitled 'Ability to lie on bed of nails not due to endogenous opioids.' The author acknowledged the help received from Esther Rantzen.
- After their seminal 1994 investigation 'Handedness and longevity: archival study of cricketers', J P Aggleton et al. were able to report in the *British Medical Journal* that 'left-handedness is not, in general, associated with an increase in mortality'.
- A research report in the *Practitioner* in May 1964 concluded with the sentence: 'Surprisingly, 36 per cent were stated to be alive up to one hour before death.'

Other dramatic breaches of the frontiers of science – also known as 'breakthroughs' – include:

- Effect of ale, garlic and soured cream on the appetite of leeches. AB, HS, *British Medical Journal*, 1994
- Masturbation using metal washers for the treatment of impotence: painful consequences. AR, NS, *British Journal of Urology*, June 1994
- Copulation as a possible mechanism to maintain monogamy in porcupines. ZS, HM, *Animal Behaviour*, No. 5, 1988

ESSENTIAL GASMANSHIP

LONDON, MID-1960s

In the mid-1960s, an Australian anaesthetist, regarded by his colleagues as something of a philosopher, defined the three essentials of modern anaesthetic practice:

- Always check the oxygen supply
- Always identify the patient and the operation
- Hate all surgeons and hate the slow bastards most

At around the same time, British anaesthetist Brian Lewis, who was to become a considerable figure in medical politics and who usually introduced himself to audiences as 'Lewis the Gas', was in the early days of his career. One night, he was on call to deliver anaesthetics in the casualty department of a hospital which he coyly declined to name and, in the early hours, was summoned from comfortable sleep by a casualty officer who needed his assistance. A patient who had tripped over when leaving a pub at closing time had broken his wrist.

The casualty doctor wanted to reduce the fracture under an anaesthetic and, because it was a busy night, asked Lewis to 'get the patient under' while he went into another room to finish sewing up the scalp of another customer from the same pub who'd been hit over the head with a bottle. The patient with the broken wrist, he told Lewis, was Polish and his name was Slobachanski, or at least that was the pseudonym Lewis chose for him when he described the incident.

Lewis found the patient next door, sitting on a bench clutching his right arm. Patient and anaesthetist were joined by a nurse who'd just returned from her early morning 'lunch' in the canteen, and she and Lewis confirmed that the patient was Mr Slobachanski and that he had a signed consent form in his notes. Lewis checked that the spare oxygen cylinder was full before they eased the patient out of his shirt and into a gown. They then removed his teeth and helped him onto the table. As Lewis started the anaesthetic, he completed the Australian triad of anaesthetic 'essentials' by directing a few hateful thoughts at the surgeon who had got him out of bed.

Mr Slobachanski was well anaesthetised when the casualty officer arrived. Yet when he picked up the patient's right arm he discovered that the wrist was perfectly normal. He and Lewis put the X-ray up on the viewing box and it clearly showed a fractured wrist. Their puzzlement turned to concern when they examined the left wrist and found that that too was normal. Their concern dissolved into panic when a man closely resembling the patient who lay anaesthetised on the table walked into the room. He was more than slightly inebriated and his right arm was in a sling. He'd just returned from the lavatory, he said, and wondered what they were doing to his brother, who had come to take him home.

The man's perception was so blunted by alcohol that doctors and nurse were able to persuade him that his brother had fallen asleep before they whisked him into another room, anaesthetised him, and reduced his fracture. Both brothers were later despatched by prepaid taxi to North London with a carefully worded letter for the patient's GP.

At nine o'clock the following morning, Brian Lewis rang his medical defence society for advice, but he never heard a word of complaint from the patient, his brother or the family lawyer. He later, however, got many complaints from patients who thought he took the process of identification to obsessional lengths. That night, he had added a fourth 'essential' to the Australian triad: always check whether the patient has similar-looking relatives on the premises.

DOCTOR IN THE HOUSE

HOUSE OF COMMONS, LONDON, 1966

When young Dr David Owen was elected as MP for Plymouth Sutton in 1966, he was determined to continue his day job as a doctor at St Thomas's Hospital directly across the Thames from the Houses of Parliament. Indeed, he harboured an ambition to become a professor of psychiatry, and may well have thought that attendance at the House of Commons would provide some useful field work.

He also discovered that he was unable to shrug off his medical identity during the short walk across Westminster Bridge from one place of employment to the other. The Palace of Westminster had no 'company doctor', and MPs struck down suddenly by illness had to rely on the often rusty skills of their medically qualified colleagues. In an emergency, the choice of doctor was made by the police and, as Owen points out in his autobiography *Time to Declare,* they first called the doctors whom they judged to have the greatest knowledge. 'In my early years, I was near the top of their list,' Owen recalls. 'As the years passed they wisely dropped me to the bottom.'

He soon discovered that dealing with an emergency north of the Thames posed problems unencountered by doctors working in the well-equipped hospital to the south. In the Palace of Westminster, the doctor had no skilled and experienced colleagues near at hand and had to conduct a medical examination in a tiny room that contained an examination couch and little else. Owen's response to the challenge was pragmatic.

If he was certain of the diagnosis, he sent the ailing MP to St Thomas's; if he was uncertain, he sent the patient to Westminster Hospital and so protected himself from the mockery of his colleagues.

The strangest case he had to deal with revealed that one thing that didn't cross the river with him was the trust that St Thomas's patients and their relatives had in the medical authority of their doctors. He was called to see an MP who had collapsed in the Chamber and arranged for him to be carried to the medical emergency room and placed on the couch. Owen stayed with him for a while until, confident his patient was stable, he slipped out for half an hour, asking the young policeman on duty to keep an eye on the sick MP till he returned. As he'd promised, he was back within thirty minutes and returned at regular intervals over the next few hours.

Sadly, the young policeman lacked the trust in doctors that was expected at St Thomas's and grew so concerned that a comatose MP was being left untreated in the room that he called his superintendent. When Owen arrived on his next routine visit, both policemen enquired politely whether it might not be wise to call an ambulance and get the MP admitted to hospital. Owen replied, equally politely, that it would not and continued his regular visits until the MP was well enough to go home. As Owen writes in his autobiography: 'I am not sure the young policeman ever realised the diagnosis. The MP was, quite simply, drunk.'

THE DOCTOR WHO WAS TOO
GOOD TO BE TRUE

GROVETON, TEXAS, 1966

Freddie Brant was born in 1925 into a poor family in Louisiana. Like many who grew up during the economic depression that afflicted the USA in the 1930s, he had to leave school early but was rescued from poverty by World War Two. He spent four years in the army only to discover when he was discharged after the war, that there were few jobs for men with his lack of education. He rejoined the paratroops but, in 1949, he and another bored soldier robbed a bank and were given a seven-year prison sentence. While serving his sentence, he worked in the prison hospital and had his first contact with the rituals of medical practice. He so enjoyed it that, when he was released, he took a job as a laboratory and X-ray technician with Dr Reid L Brown of Chattanooga, Tennessee, with whom he stayed for four years, learning something of the science of medicine and a lot about the behaviour of doctors.

When he left Chattanooga, he took copies of Dr Brown's diplomas with him and, assuming his employer's identity, moved to Texas, got a licence to practise medicine in that state, and worked for three years on the staff of the state hospital at Terrell. When he resigned, he took his wife on a motoring holiday and, when they stopped for a meal in the small village of Groveton, Texas, he treated a local boy who had injured his leg. The boy's parents told him that Groveton had lost its town doctor some years before and its citizens were eager to find

190

another. So 'Dr Reid L Brown' put up his shingle, established a thriving practice, and became a respected and popular community leader.

His success derived not just from his engaging personality and his willingness to devote a lot of time to listening to his patients; he was respected for the way in which he referred all potentially serious cases to doctors in nearby towns. This defensive move was seen by his patients as a sign of commendable humility and, in the end, he was unmasked not by a medical error but by a company clerk. By a strange mischance, he ordered drugs for his practice from a pharmaceutical firm in Louisiana that was also used by the real Dr Reid L Brown, and one day a clerk discovered she was processing orders from physicians in Groveton and Chattanooga who appeared to have identical names. After a police investigation, Freddie Brant, alias Dr Reid L Brown Mark II, was charged with forgery and with making a fraudulent claim to be a doctor.

The strangest aspect of this case was the reaction of the people of Groveton. They grew angry not with Freddie Brant but with the authorities who sought to deprive them of their doctor. Newspapers were inundated with testimonials to his skill. One paper reported how his patients had included 'some of Groveton's leading citizens as well as miners, loggers and welfare patients'. The local pharmacist claimed that the arrest of Freddie had caused many cases of hardship, and a local farmer offered compelling evidence not just of his skill but of his economic value: 'My wife has been sick for fourteen years. We've been to doctors in Lufkin, Crockett and Trinity, and he did her more good than any of 'em. She was all drawed up, bent over, you ought to have seen her. He's brought her up and now she's milking cows and everything.'

The people of Groveton stood by their man. A grand jury refused to prosecute him and when the authorities put him on trial for perjury and moved the hearing to another county, the case ended with a hung jury, eight members voting for acquittal.

One newspaper, *Chicago's American,* reported that justice was thwarted because of a 'lava flow of testimonials from Groveton and Terrell to the effect that Freddie Brant was a prince of a medical man, license or no license'. The paper also suggested that the people of Groveton should have known that he was not a doctor because he did too many undoctorly things. He made house calls for only five dollars and charged only three dollars for an office visit. He approved of Medicare – then under fierce attack from the American Medical Association as a form of 'socialised medicine' – and would drive for miles to visit a patient, often without fee if the patient was poor. Besides, his handwriting was legible.

Though acquitted by the court, Brant was unable to resume practice and disappeared into the vast hiding place of 1960s America. Today, of course, he could have set up as an 'alternative practitioner' and stayed on as the hero of Groveton.

IRONMONGERY

RHODESIA (NOW ZIMBABWE), 1966

In January 1966, a 26-year-old prisoner in a Rhodesian prison was admitted to hospital after swallowing nine bedsprings. He passed two of them into a bedpan but the others had to be removed by operation. He had swallowed the springs, he said, to keep his friend company.

His friend was his 28-year-old cellmate who between 1964 and 1965 had been admitted to hospital seven times after swallowing what were generically described as 'foreign bodies'. These, later put on display at the museum in Westminster Hospital Medical School in London, included nails and screws of various shapes and sizes, and razor blades, broken and intact. The nails and razor blades had signalled a change in diet. The young man had previously had a taste for bedsprings. In December 1965, he was admitted to hospital after swallowing eighteen of them.

Soon after that episode, the prison governor received an ingenuous letter from Her Majesty's Government instructing him 'to withhold all types of edible foreign materials from this prisoner'. Though it read like an order to deprive him of imported foodstuffs, it was, of course, an instruction that no one could implement. With this young man, who could define what was 'foreign' and what was 'edible'? The prisoner immediately demonstrated the fatuity of the instruction by devouring another fourteen bedsprings.

When HM Government demanded more information, the

prison doctor reported that 'the patient appears in no way to be unbalanced in mind'. The diagnosis was well founded. The man's mind was healthily well balanced. After serving his sentence in Rhodesia, he was due to be repatriated to the Republic of South Africa, where he was wanted on gun-running charges and, if found guilty, would face a sentence of 25 years' hard labour. His iron diet was designed to encourage the Rhodesian doctors to certify him as insane and thus unfit for extradition.

While in hospital, he described his technique for swallowing bedsprings: 'I wrap each article in toilet paper, then throw my head back, press the handle of a knife to the back of my throat and slide the spring along the knife.'

Unlike his friend, he was unable to pass any of the items he'd ingested, and the accumulating ironmongery had to be removed in a series of operations. While he was in hospital recovering from one of them, his doctors discovered that he was suffering from another disease that he had not inflicted on himself. Blood tests revealed that he was anaemic. And the cause of the anaemia was 'iron deficiency'. An ironic diagnosis.

MEDICINE'S FIRST INSTANT CELEBRITY

CAPETOWN, SOUTH AFRICA, 1967

When the South African surgeon Christiaan Barnard performed the first human heart transplant on 3 December 1967 at Groote Schuur Hospital in Cape Town, he won an immediate international fame never before granted to a doctor. Before the coming of Barnard, doctors occasionally got their pictures on showbiz pages if they were photographed with well-known actors; after Barnard, lesser-known actors, and especially actresses, could get themselves noticed by being photographed with him.

The strange thing about this episode was that Barnard won his celebrity by performing an unsuccessful operation. The first patient to receive a transplanted heart, 53-year-old Louis Washkansky, died of pneumonia eighteen days later. And when his condition started to deteriorate, as many experienced transplant surgeons had predicted it would, Barnard was out of the country, jetting round the world on a publicity tour, described by one of his fellow consultants at Groote Schuur as 'a rather impetuous, flamboyant and undignified global lap of honour'.

Dr Donald Gould, then editor of *New Scientist,* always treasured an issue of the *South African Medical Journal* that appeared soon after the operation and was devoted wholly to the miracle that had taken place at Groote Schuur. One of the articles, signed by Barnard and his team, was headed 'successful human heart transplant', while the front page, edged in black, regretfully announced the death of Louis Washkansky. As Gould said, it breathed life into the old joke that the operation was successful but the patient died.

Significantly, as one of Barnard's fellow consultants pointed out, the journal contained 'no mention of the ethical or even legal issues surrounding removal of the heart from the donor and no suggestion that she might have been regarded as living when she was taken into the theatre for the removal of her heart'.

The condition of the donor was not the only source of ethical and legal concern. Any surgeon wanting to transplant a human heart in the 1960s faced a technical barrier that had nothing to do with the surgical techniques that were given much publicity at the time. These were within the competence of any experienced heart surgeon. A more serious problem, amply demonstrated in animals, was that the body's defences would reject and destroy the tissue of the 'alien' heart.

When Barnard chose to go ahead, that problem had not been solved. Yet the instant fame accorded to him spurred other surgeons, no nearer than the South African team to solving the rejection problems, to go ahead with hazardous operations in which science appeared to run second place to hype. Within 48 hours of the South African operation, two heart transplants had taken place in America, soon followed by one in India and three in quick succession in France.

When Frederick West became Britain's first heart transplant patient, British newspapers carried pictures of the transplant team from the London Heart Hospital grinning at the camera and proudly displaying Union Jacks overprinted with 'We're Backing Britain'. Mr West died 46 days later. Two months later, Gordon Ford became Britain's second heart transplant patient and the world's 24th. When he died 57 hours later, only six of the remaining 23 were still alive, most having died within days or hours.

During this spell of media frenzy, surgeons in Houston, Texas, put a sheep's heart into a 47-year-old man, who died on the spot, the British team attempted to implant pigs' hearts into two dying patients, and Barnard prepared to transplant a baboon heart into a five-year-old boy. Once he'd opened the boy's chest, however, he decided that a valve replacement would suffice.

After the early death of Britain's third heart transplant patient, the Department of Health, on the advice of the government's chief medical officer, Sir George Godber, made it clear that the operation was unacceptable in NHS hospitals. Yet Barnard continued to radiate the glow of celebrity. He was lionised in Washington and appeared on coast-to-coast American television. *France-Soir* named him Man of the Year, and the French nation voted him the third most popular man in the world – after President de Gaulle and Pope John Paul II.

Yet, though the world awarded Barnard a grade-A celebrity rating, the man who established heart transplantation as an acceptable and effective treatment was the American surgeon Norman Shumway. He and Richard Lower, his colleague at the Stanford Medical Center in California, had been the first people to transplant a dog's heart successfully. They then embarked on eight years' intensive research into ways of preventing, detecting and treating tissue rejection. Shumway decided his team would not operate on a human until a dog with a transplanted heart had survived for at least a year. Barnard came to Stanford during their experimental programme and learned the operative technique, which makes no great demands on a surgeon. Observers at Stanford think he then went back to South Africa and 'jumped the gun' knowing the rejection problems hadn't been solved.

Because Shumway, a cool, laid-back Westerner, didn't want contentious publicity to get in the way of his scientific work, he was reluctant to criticise Barnard at the time of the disastrous South African operation. Even nine years later, the nearest he got to criticism came when I asked him to define the best way to determine whether a surgical team was ready to perform a human heart transplant. 'You should ask them to produce an animal that has lived for six months after the operation,' he said. Then he added, 'That condition was not fulfilled in South Africa. They never had any animal that lived more than a few hours.'

Despite the setbacks caused by the precipitate action of Barnard and others, Shumway and his Stanford team eventually made heart transplantation not just an acceptable but a routine operation. When I visited them in 1976, they were offering patients for whom the only alternative was an early death a greater than 70 per cent chance of surviving the hazardous six months after the operation. And the survivors were able to resume active lives, returning to school or to the work they were doing before they became ill, or moving into a comfortable retirement. The team's objective, enunciated by Shumway, was to offer additional life rather than extend the process of dying.

Meanwhile, in his book *Heart Attack:You Don't Have to Die*, published in 1972, Christiaan Barnard had written:

> Where controversy exists, we should seek and act upon the advice of the established corps of top rate scientists, and we should give less weight to what the amateurs have to say. [He made quite a thing of dividing his colleagues into amateurs and professionals.] The traditional values of conservative or orthodox science have been toppled by tuppenny-ha'penny hicks with big mouths, a slick line on television, and a fantastic ability for diverting the scientific issue into irrelevant polemic territory where emotionalism takes over from rational argument.

Some who read that paragraph asked themselves who on earth he had in mind. The obvious answer was too strange for belief.

THE INSCRUTABLE WORLD OF CHINESE MEDICINE

YANGTSE RIVER, CHINA, 1967

When the *Chinese Medical Journal,* official organ of the Chinese Medical Association, appeared in English translation in London in 1967, British doctors had their first chance to judge the current state of Chinese medicine. A glance at the contents page revealed that this learned journal highlighted areas of medicine sadly neglected by Britain's reactionary health service:

- Chairman Mao stands on the deck of the launch reviewing the swimmers battling the waves of the Yangtse.
- Chairman Mao has a good swim in the Yangtse, braving the wind and waves.
- Chairman Mao swims in the Yangtse.
- Swimming – to the melody *Shui Tiao Keh Tou* (Mao Tse-tung).
- Follow Chairman Mao and Advance in the Teeth of the Great Storms and Waves.
- Long live the Great Proletarian Cultural Revolution.
- Raise high the Great Red Banner of Mao Tse-tung's Thought and carry the Great Proletarian Cultural Revolution through to the End: Essential Points for Propaganda and Education in Connection with the Great Cultural Revolution.
- A New Stage of the Socialist Revolution in China.
- Subacute Endocarditis due to Brucella Melitensis.

The same sense of proportion pervaded the case reports at the back of the journal. All but the most superficial detail was omitted to preserve the pure line of thought. Here is an extract from an account of a neurosurgical operation:

> The medical staff attending him regard the operation as another triumph of Marxism-Leninism and Mao Tse-tung's thought. Before the operation, the Party committee of the hospital arranged for the surgeons and nurses to undertake a thorough study of the relevant parts of Chairman Mao's works; in particular they concentrated on the idea of whole-hearted service to the people and the dialectical method of analysis.
>
> On the eve of the operation, a meeting was called by the hospital's Party committee, at which the Party secretary read out to all the medical workers concerned a letter from the political department of the Canton garrison. It encouraged them to live up to the expectations of the Party and Chairman Mao and of the people of the whole country, to hold high the great red banner of Mao Tse-tung's thought and to make the operation an outstanding success.

That detailed account of preoperative preparation was tucked away in a short 'case-note' and offered but a pale reflection of the intensity that went into the main articles in Chinese medicine's only learned journal.

> With steady steps, Chairman Mao walked down the gangway and dipped himself in the water for a while before stretching out his arms and beginning to swim. It was exactly 11 o'clock.
>
> Nieh Chang-hsin, a swimmer from the Militia of the Hankow Thermal Power Plant, became so excited when he saw Chairman Mao that he forgot he was in the water. Raising both hands he shouted: 'Long live Chairman Mao! Long live Chairman Mao!' and sank into the river. He gulped several mouthfuls, but the water tasted especially sweet to him.

The Chinese Medical Association underlined its individuality by offering significant poetry in its official journal.

Swimming by Mao Tse-Tung

> I have just drunk the waters of Changsha,
> And eaten the fish of Wuchang;
> Now I am crossing the thousand-mile long river,
> Looking afar to the open sky of Chu.
> I care not that the wind blows and the waves beat;
> It is better than idly strolling in a courtyard.

When they heard the line about the courtyard, reported the journal, the Chinese people were overjoyed and danced in the streets, crying 'Long live Chairman Mao!' Some visitors from Indonesia were so overcome 'that they cheered on and on and then broke into revolutionary songs in powerful voices'.

When the journal arrived in London, a British doctor, inspired by his first direct contact with Chinese medicine, threw off his imperialist shackles and composed a poem to be sung by the then Prime Minister, Harold Wilson, as he led his people in a processional swim through the turbulent waters of the Yellow River that flowed through his parliamentary constituency.

Leading the People up the River

> As I cleave my way
> Through the scented waters of the Mersea,
> A thought strikes me.
> Chairman Mao must be a better swimmer
> Than am I.
> Suddenly I am drowning.
> Help.
> Glug
>   Glug
>   Glug

SMILE, PLEASE

BRITISH HOSPITALS, 1968

In the second half of the twentieth century, hospitals shed their reputation as places of sanctuary and threw open their wards to unwelcome intruders. The reason? Politicians discovered they were ideal sites for photo opportunities.

It's difficult to pinpoint the exact year of capitulation. It may well have been 1968. That was the year when David Ennals, then a junior minister with a distinctly earnest approach to politics, entered a children's ward, brandished a baby at the television cameras and intoned, 'The future lies with this six-week-old baby,' while an aide scuttling in his wake rasped in none-too-muted tones: 'It's six *months* old, minister.'

An unintended benefit of photo opportunities is that they can act as a healthy diversion for hard-pressed doctors and nurses, particularly those who see them being set up. By definition, a contrived 'opportunity' involves deception, and even those who work hardest at it cannot sustain deception all the time. The moment that medically trained watchers cherish comes when the 'opportunity' is over and the tutored smile of the performer relaxes for a second or two into an expression they can read. Doctors learn early in their careers that the world is easier to understand if you ignore the words that drop from the lips and read the message in the face; even party political broadcasts grow informative when you turn the sound down.

All photo opportunities are intrinsically strange, so it's difficult to pick the strangest of the genre. A close runner-up would be the one described in a reader's letter published in the *Surrey Advertiser* on 4 February 1995.

> Readers of your Godalming editions saw our MP Mrs Bottomley pictured with my father pulling a Christmas cracker when he was a patient at Milford hospital. Although described as one of her constituents, he is not her greatest fan (who is?) but nevertheless went along with the photograph.
>
> What wasn't told was that it was Mrs Bottomley who insisted on having a 'prop'. Nursing staff spent more than 20 minutes touring the hospital to locate a cracker.

Ironically, despite the industrious use of hospitals by politicians, the motive behind the strangest photo opportunity of all was commercial rather than political. Indeed, the occasion had the makings of what marketing men would consider a five-star promotional wheeze. Just before Christmas 1991, the makers of Cabbage Patch dolls donated one of their products to a hospital in Guildford. The big idea was that a grand press opportunity would provide not just pictures of a little girl, condemned to spend Christmas in hospital, cuddling the doll, but of doctors demonstrating the alleged reason for the gift by using it to show the children where their incisions, bandages and drips would go.

Come the day, when the journalists and photographers turned up, the organisers discovered that all the children in the ward were boys. Never mind, the doll could be used for the demonstrations. Or could it? According to the local paper, the doll was undeniably female and the boys had all been admitted for circumcision.

DUBLIN'S LONELY OUTPOST

DUBLIN, 1969

Dublin's Merrion Square is decidedly top drawer – late eighteenth-century Georgian houses, the birthplace of Wellington and the sometime residence of Castlereagh, Daniel O'Connell and Oscar Wilde. On 5 February 1969, those who lurked behind its elegant façades – foreign diplomats, ancient firms of solicitors, expensive doctors and government commissions – were joined by an impertinent intruder at number ten: the Republic of Ireland's first full-blown family planning clinic.

Its opening was impudent and courageous. Only six months before, the Pope had declared that 'artificial' contraception was contrary to God's law and, at the time, the Republic of Ireland, in which the Roman Catholic Church wielded great power, had the most stringent anti-contraception laws in the world. Anyone who advertised, imported or sold contraceptives, or even mentioned the word 'contraception' in print, laid themselves open to legal action. One of the attractions of the Merrion Square house to those who worked in the clinic was that it had an 'emergency exit' through the back garden into a lane if it were raided.

In 1969, the Republic of Ireland indulged in self-deception on a grand scale. The Pill, shamelessly described as a 'cycle regulator', was advertised in Irish medical journals; magazines with advertisements offering contraceptives 'under plain wrapper' were on sale in Dublin, and chemists in the Republic sold 20,000 packs of the Pill each month. Doctors refused family planning advice in their hospital clinics but prescribed the Pill in their private practices; priests, depending on how their consciences were affected by the social tragedies in crowded city slums, made wildly different interpretations of the Pope's instructions on contraception; and Catholic women went on shopping trips for contraceptives across the Irish Sea or to the north. The chemists' shops in Newry, just across the border, had more customers from the south than from their own home town and, a few months before the Merrion Square clinic opened, a group of women travelled to the north, had themselves fitted with contraceptive diaphragms and, when returning home across the border, declared they were carrying illegal imports and challenged embarrassed customs men to remove them.

The drive for improved family planning facilities came mainly from Catholics – many of them priests and doctors – but, with a few brave exceptions, supporters of a change in the law were afraid to declare their support in public. The clinic in Merrion Square – founded by three Catholics, three Protestants and a Jew – blew a hole in the hypocrisy. But the founders had to tread carefully. The brass plate outside the door proclaimed it as a fertility guidance clinic, a name they detested. Choosing a politic name had consumed more committee time than any other decision and, when they sent out letters under their new letterhead seeking subscriptions, one woman wrote back: 'I thought fertility was one thing we had enough of in this country.'

The clinic got more support from Irish doctors than it might have expected. In the early 1960s, some Catholic doctors in the Republic had begun to prescribe the Pill as a contraceptive, their consciences stirred by medical and social conditions rarely seen across the Irish Sea: women with rhesus antibodies producing an annual stillborn child; women with heart disease who, if they survived a perilous labour, were condemned to sexual abstinence because of the unreliability of the rhythm method of contraception; a prematurely aged woman with a dozen children under the age of twelve leaving hospital to the traditional farewell from the sister, 'See you next year'; and large families shackled to poverty by the annual arrival of another mouth to feed.

The crunch for these doctors came with the Pope's announcement, yet a surprisingly large number, particularly in Dublin, continued to prescribe the Pill with no scruples about their own or their patients' moral propriety. One Dublin gynaecologist claimed that the Pope's language, with its heavy reliance on 'natural law', had no meaning in medical terms; a Dublin GP spoke affectionately of the Pope but claimed, 'The poor oul' fella didn't know what he was talking about.'

In the end, the emergency exit behind number ten never had to be used. Most packages addressed to the clinic from abroad were opened by customs, but the senders were shrewd enough to ensure they never contained confiscatable goods, and a number of books that were ordered never arrived. Some Catholic Dubliners made pejorative reference to 'that place in Merrion Square', but there was no picketing. Nor was there any overt action against the clinic or its directors and little noticeable reaction from Church or State. The Archbishop of Dublin, a well-known pouncer on those who strayed from the narrowest of paths, remained silent and, though Dublin's lonely outpost was only a stone's throw away from Leinster House, home of the Irish parliament, no stones were thrown.

In the late 1960s, a new Irish generation was beginning to reject restrictions imposed by de Valera's dream of a Catholic Ireland. Spurred on by imaginative businessmen and politicians (including a young senator called Mary Robinson), by a new generation of radical journalists, and above all by television, the Irish began to accept that they could no longer isolate themselves from the problems of a larger world. The strange intruder in Merrion Square was a harbinger of change that, as it accelerated in succeeding decades, released the creative energy that had been bottled up during the de Valera years.

Young Dubliners of today find it difficult to understand why the opening of a family planning clinic in their city thirty years ago was considered an extraordinary event.

MEDICAL SENTENCING POLICY

PLACCAVILLE, CALIFORNIA, 1969

A long sentence is the routine punishment imposed on doctors foolish enough to seek for information in the memoranda they receive from colleagues. The usual stretch is 73 words, a standard established in the USA in 1969 when Dr Edmund J Simpson, of Placcaville in California, wrote to the *Journal of the American Medical Association* quoting this sentence from a psychiatric report:

> Her spontaneous replies from unconscious sources within her, indicate that the therapeutic goal of reorienting a portion of herself that has been so frantically and anxiously dependent upon outside sources of support has been responding to, accepting and depending upon internal sources of wisdom and strength and that this has lessened the panic coming from this source, and has also given the self a means of internal influence upon the formerly uncontrollable anxiety.

Dr Simpson pointed out that, though the paragraph contained the standard 73 words, he wondered if it really was a sentence. 'Every time I look for a verb I get a headache,' he said.

The punishment later crossed the Atlantic and standard 73-word sentences started to be handed out in Britain, as in this letter from a specialist in community medicine at a London regional health authority:

When I have completed my enquiries with the medical and supporting services I intend to get the Authority's approval to put this on a formal basis and will then be sending copies of what I have finally decided is the best approach to the Area so that these discussions can be put on a formal basis, in order that a composite multi-disciplinary report covering all aspects of this proposed move can be prepared.

Recently, as the repetitive cycle of NHS management reform has accelerated, the sentences handed out in Britain have grown increasingly severe. The record stretch so far, 252 words, was imposed by the operational executive at the Queen's Medical Centre in Nottingham on 15 May 1995. It was passed on a doctor who had innocently inquired about the meaning of a phrase he had stumbled across in another document.

Soft Money is any money received by or payable to any employee of the Trust, anyone holding an Honorary Contract from the Trust, (or the agent of either of them) or any Trust Fund which is used or intended to be used for the benefit of the Trust, University Hospital or any of the Trust's employees, honorary contract holders, patients or any undergraduate or postgraduate student at University Hospital, which has been received in good faith and not stolen from the Trust, and which is not held in an account opened by the Trust in accordance with Standing Financial Instructions (Section 7) and reported in the Trust's Annual Accounts, nor held in an account opened by the Special Trustees for Nottingham University Hospitals in accordance with their Standing Financial Instructions and reported in their Annual Accounts nor in the case of an honorary contract holder paid into an account in the name of his or her employer and which has been received by or is payable to, such person or Trust fund as a result of that employee or Honorary Contract Holder acting (actually or ostensibly) under or in connection with his or her Contract of Employment or Honorary Contract with the Trust and which has been given or is paid or payable in return for service rendered or to be rendered by the Trust or that person in his or her capacity as such employee or Honorary Contract holder or for the benefit of the Trust, its patients, staff, trainees or students.

Recent developments suggest that this will soon be seen as a relatively light sentence.

THE DAY IT RAINED CATS

SARAWAK, BORNEO, 1970

In 1957, the World Health Organisation (WHO) declared that it would rid the world of smallpox and malaria. The promise was in keeping with the spirit of the time and no one thought it boastful. Indeed, the WHO fulfilled its promise with smallpox and, in 1980, was able to announce that, thanks to its international programme of vaccination, the disease no longer existed.

The problem with its war against malaria was that it chose the wrong weapon. The plan was to attack not the parasite that causes malaria but the mosquitoes that carry it, and the chosen weapon was the 'new' pesticide called DDT. In truth, DDT wasn't all that new. It had first been tested in 1939 as a way of destroying Colorado beetles and, at the end of the war, had been used in the delousing of European 'displaced persons'.

Before that, DDT had proved its worth during the war in the South Pacific. When the Japanese seized the Dutch Indies, which were the world's main source of quinine – then the only reliable treatment for malaria – they reckoned that the mosquitoes in the Pacific jungles would be their most powerful allies. And, indeed, half a million American soldiers were taken out of action by malaria between 1942 and 1945. Thanks, however, to the liberal spraying of mosquito breeding grounds with DDT, and the development of a new anti-malarial drug, the Americans were eventually able to defeat the mosquitoes and the Japanese.

When the WHO opened its war against malaria, DDT's reputation, thanks to its wartime history, was riding high. Some described it as the 'atomic bomb of the insect world' and, in 1966, a WHO consultant, appearing on a BBC World Service programme, heralded it as the greatest medical development of all time, ahead of antibiotics or anaesthesia. His enthusiasm captured the spirit of the moment, and the DDT onslaught on mosquitoes proceeded with unquestioning passion. During the 1960s, the WHO sprayed or dropped over 76,000 tons of the stuff on 76 countries.

As the sixties drew to a close, enthusiasm was already being eroded by disillusion. DDT had killed mosquitoes with spectacular efficiency, but it had also encouraged the growth of new generations of the insect that were resistant to the insecticide. Ten years later when the WHO could claim it had rid the world of smallpox, it had to admit that its war against malaria had produced some sixty varieties of mosquito which, if they felt inclined, could shower and bathe in DDT without suffering ill effects.

Resistance wasn't the only health hazard bequeathed by random spraying. One of its oddest effects occurred in 1970 in Sarawak in Borneo, where peasants living in isolated villages were temporarily moved from their homes during the spraying. The DDT killed not only mosquitoes but cockroaches and, when the families returned, the village cats ate the poisoned cockroaches and died. As a result, the local Malaysian field rats, no longer hunted by their cat predators, began to thrive, and the villages, though free of mosquitoes, became infested with animals that were notorious carriers of plague and typhus.

The threat of plague was so great that the WHO sought help from the Royal Air Force and, one bizarre morning, RAF planes flew over Sarawak dropping cats by parachute into the isolated villages. Luckily for the villagers, Operation Cat Drop, as it was inevitably called, helped avert an epidemic of plague caused by the very best of good intentions.

A CHEKHOVIAN MOMENT

SOMEWHERE IN BRITAIN, 1970S

Many a GP has discovered that a good way to empathise with the ills of others is to adopt a bemused attitude to the mysteries of existence loosely based on Gustav Mahler's observation that 'humour is the only antidote to the poison of life'. Indeed, Vladimir Nabokov could have been describing a wise GP when he wrote of Anton Chekhov: 'Things for him were funny and sad at the same time, but you would not see their sadness if you would not see their fun.'

But then, of all the writers who were also practising doctors, Chekhov is the one who most clearly reveals how close the art of a writer is to that of a clinician. In his short stories and his plays, the observant doctor and the gifted writer become one.

In general practice, tragedy often enters hand in hand with comedy, and one GP who regularly reported their conjunction was Dr Bev Daily who, until he retired, practised at Burnham in Buckinghamshire. He had been in general practice in other places before moving there, so we can never be sure of the location of many of the encounters he described in medical journals. The obfuscation was intentional because he wanted to protect the privacy of his patients.

At one stage in his career, his list of patients included an odd couple: a middle-aged man and his elderly father who lived together in an isolated house and were as dependent on one another – and as argumentative – as Steptoe and Son.

One day, Daily was called to the house and when he arrived

he found the son busy in the kitchen. He explained to Daily that he was worried because his father had been 'a little bit quiet' all morning. When Daily went up to the father's bedroom, he found that the old man was dead – indeed, had been dead for some time. Daily spent a minute or two trying to assemble the right words to break the news to the son, whom he could hear whistling cheerily in the kitchen below – a son whom, he knew, loved his father more than he loved any other creature on earth. Yet when Daily went downstairs he found, as so often happens, that he lapsed straight into platitude.

'I'm sorry to say,' he muttered, 'that your father has passed away.'

'Bloody hell,' said the son. 'I've just made him a big plate of stew.'

But you would not see their sadness if you would not see their fun.

PUTTING THE FEAR OF GOD INTO DOCTORS

FOUR MARKS, 1971

The Hampshire village of Four Marks, population 1,616, straddles the A31 between Alton and Winchester. In March 1971 one of the village's better-known residents, the author George Beardmore, wrote to his MP.

> You will have read in the press, I daresay, that a Four Marks doctor, Richard Barker, has been suspended for nine months by the Disciplinary Committee of the General Medical Council (GMC) for alleged adultery with a married patient, Mrs Kerr. This is a more flagrant example than most of the 'private tribunal' working outside standard legal procedure and by its findings ruining, or going far to ruin, the life of a professional man for an offence which at law is no crime at all – is in fact a commonplace. Agreed that doctors are a special case and that their code must be more stringent than that of most, the sentence in this case is so blatantly unjust that I recommend it to your attention. The facts are as follows:
>
> Mrs Kerr was an unhappily married woman and Dr Barker an unhappily married man. (I knew both parties socially before the affair came about.) Mrs Kerr felt herself attracted to Dr Barker and he to her, and she removed her name from his list of patients.
>
> The attraction resulted in their associating with each

other – greatly, I must add, to the health and advantage of both and to the practice. There was no abuse of professional privilege. Both were mature people, knowing what they were about. There wasn't even folly. The man himself is a conscientious doctor, and I am certain that he was conscientious in associating with Mrs Kerr only when she had ceased to be his patient. The story, in short, is a very human and very common one. Yet, in this case, a private tribunal (chaired, I am told, by a man of 71) condemns him to withdraw from practice for nine months.

Most of the facts presented at Dr Barker's 'trial' were undisputed by both sides. Richard Barker had been in practice at Four Marks since 1961. He had looked after the Kerr family and once, when his receptionist was on holiday for three weeks, Mrs Kerr had acted as a replacement. No evidence was produced of their relationship at that time being anything other than employer and employee.

Later that year, Mrs Kerr changed to the list of another doctor, from whom she received treatment. A month or so later, Dr Barker took her out to dinner. Both said that it was not until that evening that they realised that they were becoming attached to one another, and early in November, they started to have sex. In December, Mrs Kerr's husband left home after she told him she was in love with another man, and the following year, Mrs Barker divorced her husband on the grounds of his adultery with Mrs Kerr. In September 1969, Mrs Kerr moved into Dr Barker's house and changed her name to his. They planned to marry as soon as she was free to do so.

On 25 June 1970, a year and eight months after he had started his relationship with Mrs Kerr, Dr Barker received a letter from the GMC asking for an explanation of his 'association' with Mrs Kerr. He was not told then, nor later, who had provided information against him. (Suspicious people pointed out that a member of the GMC was in practice just six miles from Four Marks and could be regarded as one of Dr Barker's competitors.) Barker was summoned to appear before the GMC's disciplinary committee in November 1970, but after he had waited at the Council's offices for a day, his case was postponed until February 1971.

He didn't realise the seriousness of his plight. He assumed he would be accused of a specific offence, and thought there would be no case to answer because at the time he committed adultery with Mrs Kerr, she was not on his list of patients. He didn't realise that the GMC accused everyone of the same offence, 'serious professional misconduct', and serious professional misconduct was what members of the disciplinary committee decided it was on the day.

When the Barkers arrived for the disciplinary hearing, they both believed it would be a formality. Dr Barker's confidence even survived his entry to the council chamber, where he had to sit in the dock facing a raised magisterial bench behind which sat the president and the legal assessor. 'Behind the president,' he told me later, 'was a tall stained-glass window. At ground level, members of the disciplinary committee sat flopped behind desks. The chair in the dock was low and uncomfortable with no arms, so you spent the first few minutes wondering where to put your hands and elbows. You realise they've put you in the lowliest place in the room. I tried not to cringe, though the way the proceedings were run, I got the feeling that cringing was what was expected of me.'

As the morning wore on and the GMC went through its ponderous routine, Dr Barker's confidence began to seep away. 'I came out at lunchtime pale and shattered. And after lunch, things got worse. The lawyers, president and committee members – except for the two who'd dozed off – started playing petty legal games that seemed to have little to do with whether I was a fit person to continue as a doctor. It was hard to believe it was me and my future that were at stake. They gave the impression they would continue their games even if I wasn't there. And not once throughout the proceedings did the president look at me.'

Then the committee went into camera to make its decision.

'As we all trooped out,' said Dr Barker, 'I reckoned I was for it.' Not that he had much time to contemplate his plight. While they were outside, the GMC's counsel who'd laid the case against him wanted to talk about cricket. 'I hear you were Percy Chapman's doctor. A very fine cricketer. A very fine cricketer indeed.' He heard another lawyer discussing what he described as the 'juicy cases' and realised that he was probably one of them. 'The lawyers talked as if it were another game, like Percy Chapman's cricket. And I suppose it was, for everybody except me. A bell rang and I had to return to the council chamber and stand before the president, who still didn't look at me. He just read at me from a bit of paper.'

The disciplinary committee found him guilty of serious professional misconduct and sentenced him to nine months' suspension from practice. The following morning, he had 37 patients in his surgery. Every one had heard or read about the case. No one was critical. Some were outraged. Dr Barker's appeal was turned down by the privy council which is traditionally averse to challenging the GMC's interpretation of professional misconduct and usually restricts itself to ensuring that the legal niceties have been observed.

The GMC's disciplinary power derives from its responsibility to protect the public and a medical journal that, much to the GMC's anger, published the details of the case, posed the question: 'Do the citizens of Four Marks sleep any more soundly in their beds because Dr Barker is to be suspended from the Register?' And if he were a danger to the public, asked the journal, why was he allowed to continue practising until the suspension took effect? Between February, when the case was heard and publicised, and July, when Dr Barker had to cease practice, the number of patients on his list actually increased.

After Dr Barker's suspension, I spent five days listening to the opinions of people in the village and failed to unearth one resident who thought the community's interests had been protected. Many villagers were angered by the GMC's action, and Dr Barker's patients claimed they'd been unjustly deprived of a skilled and conscientious doctor.

The suspension had come into operation six weeks after the appeal, and Richard Barker did not know which day he would have to give up practice until it actually dawned. The suspension legally began at the moment the Queen signed the order, and there was no way of predicting when that moment might be. In the event, Dr Barker learned he had to stop work when he got a telephone call from a clerk at the local NHS committee.

There followed a bizarre episode in the history of healthcare in Four Marks. The local NHS committee decided to run the practice. They hired a seventy-year-old locum, who lodged with the Barkers. They also paid Mrs Barker as receptionist and dispenser, and Dr Barker an agreed rent for his surgery premises. So, living in one house in the village, were a locum who knew little about the patients but was officially looking after them, Dr Barker, who knew a lot about the patients but was not allowed to look after them, and Mrs Barker, who was party to Dr Barker's 'offence' but was permitted to deal with patients and give the locum the sort of details that Dr Barker could have provided were he allowed.

The incongruity was accentuated nine months later when, on a date again determined arbitrarily by the Queen's having time to sign a document, Dr Barker was assumed to have suffered a sudden change in character, intellectual stature or moral fibre that made him no longer a threat to the health of the local citizenry.

The debate sparked by the Barker case, and others of similar ilk, led eventually to a government inquiry and reform of the GMC. Yet until a new medical act reached the statute books seven years later, the disciplinary committee continued to serve a purpose defined by the journalist Paul Ferris as 'putting the fear of God into doctors'.

A RICHLY DECORATED CASE

SOMEWHERE IN THE MIDDLE EAST, 1973

In the 1970s, Dr Philip Evans was one of the most respected paediatricians in the UK. A consultant at London's Guy's Hospital and at the Hospital for Sick Children in Great Ormond Street, he also, from 1972 to 1976, looked after Prince Charles and Princess Anne in his official role as physician-paediatrician to the Queen. He was an erudite and kindly man who was as popular with his juniors as he was with his patients. Indeed, in the 1960s he sometimes stayed on duty for extra hours at Guy's covering for one of his juniors, James Appleyard, when he was out making political speeches about the way senior doctors exploited their juniors.

In 1973, Evans was invited to act as an external examiner at a Middle Eastern medical school. The invitation offered an opportunity for exotic travel and he was delighted to accept it, especially when he learned that, during the exams, he and a second external examiner, another distinguished British physician, would be lodged in a hotel renowned for its luxury.

On the evening before the viva voce exams, Evans was visited in his room by a rich and distinguished local potentate who, in the course of a delicately constructed conversation, revealed that his nephew would be confronting the examiners the following day. Then, merely as a token of his esteem for Philip's great wisdom, he offered him 'a little gift' – a gold cigarette case encrusted with precious stones.

Philip, exercising the diplomatic skill you would expect from someone who had to deal with royal children, declined the gift politely. Yet, scrupulous man that he was, he began to worry that, if the nephew did appear before him next morning, he might be biased against him because of the uncle's attempted bribe or, alternatively, might be too generous for fear of being prejudiced.

Luckily, he never saw the nephew; and the following evening was able to relax alongside his fellow examiner in the first class cabin of the plane back to London. As the attendant brought them their drinks, his colleague turned to him and said: 'I can't remember Philip, do you smoke?' And from his pocket he produced a gold cigarette case encrusted with precious stones.

OUR HONOURED GUEST

TWIXT THE THAMES AND THE TWEED, 1974

From the age of Galen to that of Richard Gordon, medical teaching was recognised as one of the performing arts, and the lecture theatre proved as dramatic a stage as the anatomy or operating theatre. Even in the age of the internet, the set-piece lecture remains deeply entrenched in medical culture, and 'visiting lecturer' is still an honourable title in medical society.

In the second half of the twentieth century, the medical lecture began to shrug off its associations with sermons and pulpits and slowly established itself as an academic period set aside for rest and recovery or for diversionary entertainment. In medical schools, lecture theatres became the only places offering sanctuary from harassment, and one of the century's greatest medical researchers, Sir Peter Medawar, claimed that 'no sleep is so deeply refreshing as that which, during lectures, Morpheus invites us so insistently to enjoy.' Physiologists, he said, were impressed by the speed with which the ravages of a short night or a long operating session could be repaired by a nod off during a lecture.

The sort of diversionary entertainment lectures could provide was explored in 1974 by the medical journalist Philippa Pigache, who described how the students of B F Skinner, the behavioural psychologist, experimented on him during his lectures. When he moved to a certain position on the platform, they would reward him by offering rapt attention; whenever he moved away from the chosen spot, they shuffled, coughed and fidgeted. Eventually, they had the arch-conditioner pinned to a corner of the platform that they had selected.

The strangest lecture of that period, however, was one which Donald Longmore, physiologist and medical inventor, delivered to a local medical society which he delicately placed 'somewhere twixt the Thames and the Tweed'. Longmore hadn't realised that many of these local societies had become an excuse for social get-togethers where retired doctors could meet with former colleagues and rivals to indulge in gossip and consume large quantities of food and drink. Because the lecture was merely the excuse for an evening of indulgence, the more civilised societies would invite the lecturer to perform before the meal so that he could then join the members in their celebration of the true purpose of the meeting.

Sadly for Longmore, his hosts adhered to an earlier tradition. He'd been asked to talk about the engineering problems involved in designing an artificial heart and had prepared what he thought would be a challenging but lively text. When he arrived, he was a mite discomfited to discover that the membership consisted entirely of elderly men, and even more discomfited when he learned that he was expected to dine with the members before getting up to speak. He then had to sit through a five-course meal, sipping water and trying to concentrate on what he was going to say, while all around him the members joyfully demolished vast quantities of food and downed an impressive litreage of wine. During the meal, the sound of gossip rose in a Rossini-like crescendo until, after the port had circulated and the cognac had been served, it suddenly faded away and Longmore was invited to do his stuff.

During the lecture, by Longmore's own account, each member of the audience nodded off in turn and, when he finished, the silence was so deafening that it woke the chairman, who immediately rose to his feet and, still nodding his head to clear it, said: 'I'm sure you'll all join me in expressing our thanks in the usual manner to Dr Barnes Wallis for his fascinating talk on the dam-busting bomb.' Whereupon Longmore received polite applause and everyone went home.

HOW TO START A SOCIAL
REVOLUTION: BLOW UP A CONDOM

THAILAND, 1976

In February 1976, a smartly dressed Thai man approached five European businessmen sipping coffee in a Bangkok hotel. 'My name is Mechai,' he said. 'Have one of my cards.' He handed each a brightly coloured condom.

He then moved on to a couple of Thai men at a nearby table. Their condoms were attached to cards on which were printed a graph showing how much an extra child would cost them, a strip cartoon showing how the condom should be used – the last panel showed a penis smiling gratefully after being enshrouded – and a message which translated roughly as: 'Plan your family with rainbow-coloured mechais. Bright colours, beautiful perfume, safe . . . and so easy to use. Reduce anxiety. No side-effects. Highly effective family planning and whisper-quiet home-delivery service.'

The young men accepted the cards with amused giggles. They knew this wasn't a personal sales pitch. They recognised Mechai Viravidya and knew of his campaign to convince a deeply conservative nation that sex was healthy and that family planning was as much a part of everyday life as eating or sleeping.

Mechai's direct assault on Thailand's population problem proved spectacularly successful. In its first two years, and using few resources, his organisation recruited between six and eight million family planning 'participants' (to use family planners'

223

jargon), a figure that staggered those accustomed to results achieved by traditional methods. And the methods he used had such an impact that the local colloquialism for a condom became a 'mechai'.

Some events were designed to generate publicity. On New Year's Day 1975, young women wandered around Bangkok offering traffic policemen free boxes of mechais and New Year calendars that carried a ticket offering a half-price vasectomy. The idea was to encourage newspapers to run the headline 'Cops and Rubbers' which, unsurprisingly, they did.

Eye-catching activities were just the outward signs of a serious approach to economic development. The true targets of Mechai's organisation, Community Based Family Planning Services (CBFPS), were the villages. Although CBFPS had been set up with help from international aid agencies, it achieved results not by sending in impressive teams of specialists backed by Western expertise and money, but by getting people to help themselves. 'It's too easy,' Mechai told me in 1976, 'to look on village people as stupid and to think they won't get on without expert help. Village people are intelligent and prepared to help themselves. How did Thailand become a rice-exporting country? Because of the villagers. It's only because of "expert help" that it's becoming a rice-importing country. I've found that if you're prepared to learn from the people, they're prepared to try and learn from you.'

The key figures in CBFPS were the village distributors – maybe a shopkeeper, dressmaker, village head man or teacher – recruited when one of Mechai's teams descended on the village and sold the idea of family planning with staggering panache. They usually picked the time of a festival, a temple fair, a wedding or a weekend market. Then, like an old-style medicine man, Mechai or one of his lieutenants would gather a crowd, unwrap a condom, stretch it to show its elasticity, extol its virtues and finally, to everyone's delight, inflate it like a balloon. Mechai would then tie it off, rip off the rubber ring at the neck, hand the balloon to a delighted child and show the crowd how the ring could be used to tie up a girl's hair or secure a parcel.

Within minutes, balloons of all colours would be being inflated everywhere in the crowd while Mechai explained how condoms had more than one use; how they could be used to store clean water or rice. 'Village society,' he said, 'is not a throw-away society, and villagers are more likely to accept a product that has many uses.'

Acceptance was the object of the performance. Once villagers accepted that condoms were just another item they could buy at the local shop, they had no inhibitions about using them. Mechai and his staff then found it relatively simple to introduce them to the Pill or IUDs or the idea of sterilisation or vasectomy.

The initial village happening was set up like a carnival, the highlight being a condom-blowing competition in which competitors raced to be the first to blow one to bursting point while a local band played the Thai equivalent of the William Tell overture. There would also be movie shows (buy three condoms to get in, give two to the doorman and keep one for yourself), roll-a-coin stalls where you tried to roll your coin onto a condom, and a stage on which you could rent a dance with a girl – price, one condom for a minute.

The sense of fun that the carnival generated broke through the villagers' natural shyness and encouraged a matter-of-fact approach to family planning. And, of course, the CBFPS team never left town before selecting and establishing a local distributor. Each district had a supervisor to keep an eye on the distributors and to help and encourage them but, just as the organisers of Tupperware parties had learned in the West, the local distributors were the key figures.

CBFPS supplied the contraceptives but insisted that the local people be the providers and motivators. 'Once their credibility is established,' said Mechai, 'we're able to move into a series of health and development programmes. We regard the family planning programme as only the first step in a long war. It teaches people that if they participate, it works and is to their benefit.'

Mechai, an economics graduate who went to school and university in Australia, had previously been head of the

225

government's Development Evaluation Division, and had travelled around Thailand reporting on development programmes. He found that all of them – in education, agriculture, transportation and power – were failing, and failing because the people they were aimed at had no part in them. 'They were looked on as recipients instead of as part of the executing agency.' He came to two conclusions: development could not work without participation, and it would never work if the country could not regulate its fertility. He sought ways of getting people to take part without needing too much training, and decided sex was a good place to begin. As he said, 'You don't need a PhD to understand it.'

STRANGE TALES FROM MEDIAWORLD

BRITAIN, 1976–97

Some of the oddest medical cases are those reported in a world that runs parallel with our own. In Mediaworld, people may be misquoted, and events misrepresented or invented, yet it is an altogether more entertaining place than that in which most of us live. Which is, of course, its point.

Mediaworld draws on two main sources of strange medical cases.

1. Medical newsflashes

These are the sparks that fly when journalists under pressure reach for the medical dictionary. As in the *Oxford Times* in May 1996:

A psychiatrist for the defendant said that he was suffering from a psychiatric condition known as ambivalence.

Some journalists don't need a dictionary to add a new dimension to an otherwise mundane story. In 1977, for instance, *New Scientist* used a headline to turn a row over the shortage of kidneys for transplantation into a painful political experience:

Minister rapped over organs.

227

This sort of enhancement can be difficult to resist. On 10 November 1976, the *Journalist,* official organ of the National Union of Journalists, reported:

> KIRWAN RECOVERS. National Organiser Lawrence Kirwan is now recuperating from an operation for hernia and hopes to be back in harness in early November.

2. Mediaquotes

These are penetrating insights into current events provided by media medical correspondents.

On 24 September 1997, when *The Times* reported that a Saudi Arabian court had sentenced a British nurse to repetitive flogging, it called on its medical correspondent for a comment. The kindly Dr Thomas Stuttaford was happy to oblige.

> The punishment will be as much psychological as physical. She will know that, even after she has lived through any particular session, the whole process will be repeated again many times. The sentence will inevitably bring on severe depression.

Years of medical training go into the honing of that level of perception.

The only person to outmatch Dr Stuttaford was the anonymous Dr A N Expert who, in 1990, told Radio Four's *Today* programme:

> They are suffering from starvation due to lack of food.

Sometimes, the experts are too shy to show off their erudition in public and arrange for someone to do it on their behalf. Hence, in June 1996, a Radio Two newsreader had to announce:

> The grass pollen count issued by the Asthma Research Council at 10 a.m. today was nil – which Dr Anderson says is very low.

TUNING IN WITH A CAT'S WHISKER

BOURNEMOUTH, 1977

In 1910, Dr Albert Abrams, an American who had returned to the land of his birth after getting a medical degree in Heidelberg, produced the first of a series of machines that he claimed could detect 'the electronic reactions of Abrams' or, as he preferred, ERA.

Abrams claimed that all parts of the body vibrate and emit electrical impulses of different frequency, and that the frequencies from diseased organs differ from those from healthy ones. To diagnose illness, he 'tuned in' a specimen of the patient's blood on an Abrams ERA machine, which measured abnormal vibrations and pinpointed the nature of the illness. He could then administer the 'cure' by feeding 'proper' vibrations into the body with another Abrams machine.

In a series of court cases, scientists and technicians queued up to condemn Abrams as a charlatan, his machines as technically meaningless, and his theory of 'radionics' as balderdash. Yet, far from deterring quackery, the court cases, by revealing how much money Abrams was making, encouraged a host of others to set themselves up as 'radionics practitioners'. New machines appeared, and practitioners started to use body tissues other than blood. Some claimed that their machines could transmit treatment and cures over long distances, thus sparing them the trouble of having to see the patients.

In 1977, long after Albert Abrams had departed this planet, Dr David Delvin, a medical journalist, discovered there were some fifty radionics practitioners in Britain. Using a pseudonym, he wrote to one who practised in Bournemouth and who described himself as a doctor.

> Dear Dr C,
> I have obtained your address from the Radionics Association. Would you be able to help if I sent you a specimen of hair?
> Yours sincerely,
> K Sears (Miss)

Dr C replied promptly, enclosing two small packets for the hair and a request for a 'complete statement of present condition and symptoms'. Delvin composed a case history which he hoped that a practitioner of radionics, or of anything else for that matter, would recognise as symptoms of diabetes. He then sent it off with some hairs from the family cat, which he'd cast in the role of 'Miss Sears'.

> Dear Dr C,
> Thank you for your letter. I enclose the two packets, each containing some hair. My problem is that for quite a while I have been feeling weak and listless. I am sure I am losing weight. I drink a lot more than I used to and I never seem to have any energy. If you will forgive my mentioning it, I also have to go to the toilet rather a lot.
> I do hope you can help me. Please let me know your fee.
> Yours sincerely,
> K Sears (Miss)

Dr C was not grasping. When he replied, he didn't mention his fee. But nor did he warn Miss Sears that she might have diabetes and should see a doctor. He just sent a brief note saying that he had started 'general (non-specific, harmonising) broadcast', a statement that was as meaningless to Dr Delvin as it was to his cat.

A week or so later, Dr C wrote again:

I am commencing detailed treatment today. The nervous system seems radionically quite disturbed, and I shall be treating it. How (sic) you experienced a period of anxiety?

The glandular system, in conjunction with the nervous system, also requires attention, and I shall be applying broadcast to assist it.

There is disturbance in the small and large intestines, partly associated with the nervous disturbance, but also from deranged microbial activity, which will also be treated.

My fees are: £5 for analysis, and £2 per week for broadcast treatment. Both unfortunately plus VAT. With kind regards.

Delvin didn't know what most of that meant. All that was clear was that Dr C had failed to recognise the symptoms of diabetes – though maybe he could claim in his defence that the radionic emanations from the cat's hairs gave no indication of that disease. On the other hand, he hadn't diagnosed the one thing that Delvin knew the cat was suffering from – worms. Unless, of course, they were covered by 'disturbance in the small and large intestines'.

Delvin sent Dr C his fee and, at the same time, dropped an even broader hint about diabetes:

I still feel very thirsty and am losing weight. However, I hope that your broadcast will help. Do I have to be in the same place to receive it each time? Would it help if I faced Bournemouth at the times you are transmitting?

Dr C replied:

The projected patterns and energies are considered to operate in the ether, which is universal, and I find that time and distance do not seem to exist as regards the broadcast treatments.

The direction in which you are facing is not important in this respect.

231

I carry out the work required in your case regularly, conscientiously and with great concentration as I sit at my instruments. You are also much in my thoughts at other times. The analysis indicates that some patience will be necessary for proper results to develop with the treatment.

At this point, Delvin decided it was time to bring the patient to the brink of diabetic coma.

Dear Dr C,
Thank you for your letter. It is good to know that you are concentrating on my case. Apart from the thirst and loss of weight, I have been going to the toilet a lot. I've also had a lot of boils and this week have been feeling rather sick.

As I write, I am feeling very drowsy. So must close now, looking forward to hearing from you.

Yours sincerely,
K Sears (Miss)

This letter implied that the life of Miss Sears was under threat and that she needed urgent treatment. Yet Dr C did not respond. Delvin had virtually given up on him when, two weeks later, another report arrived.

Dear Miss Sears,
I worry regarding you. Your progress seems slow – so far about 25 per cent in general terms – and I feel the need of interim reports from you. I gain the impression that you are very overstrained.

Your treatment follows through a number of stages and is not static. A new treatment has been applied this evening. As I expected and indicated to you, results may be slow in developing. I enclose my account for broadcast treatment so far.

With this letter came a bill for a further £8, plus VAT.

Delvin decided things had gone far enough and wrote back under his own name.

Dear Dr C

Re: K Sears

Thank you for your bill for the broadcast treatment up to 9 March. In fact, when there was no reply to our letter of February 22, the patient was placed in more orthodox medical care. [Quite true. Miss Sears was in fact a tom cat and had been taken to the vet to be 'doctored'.]

However, in fairness to you, I enclose a cheque in settlement of your bill.

Yours sincerely,

D Delvin

Despite the radionically disturbed nervous and glandular systems, Miss Sears remained healthy, though Delvin later admitted he was a bit worried when two bald patches appeared under 'her' chin.

Maybe he should have faced her/him towards Bournemouth after all.

CALIFORNIAN BABES

SOUTHERN CALIFORNIA, 1977

Some thirty years ago, many of the strangest cases in American medicine – strange to European eyes, that is – regularly put themselves on display at cocktail parties in southern California. During the 1970s, plastic surgeons took over from psychiatrists as purveyors of the American Dream, as many Americans decided that what was holding them back were not inhibitions but baggy eyelids, baldness or sagging boobs. Suddenly, physical image became as important as mental cleanliness, and personal fulfilment was not so much a matter of letting it all hang out as having it all tucked in.

The parties were the surgical equivalent of Tupperware parties. In southern California, a woman who'd had a face job, a nose job, a chin job or a boob job would give a cocktail party for her plastic surgeon just as soon as the scars had healed and invite her friends round so they could see what he had done for her. The women had no inhibitions about their operations. Damn it all, the surgery was so expensive you wanted folks to know you could afford it.

The surgeons, whose role hovered uneasily between doctor and gigolo, were delighted to attend, because the show-off parties were where they recruited most of their future customers. In October 1977, when I visited the annual convention of American cosmetic surgeons, the high serious-ness of the scientific programme was undermined by the whispered observations in the corridors. 'Guess whose nose he just got . . . There goes the boob king of San Diego . . . That guy's reslung half the asses in Beverly Hills.' The length of the limousines that queued to collect their owners at the end of each day fuelled the suspicion expressed by other American physicians that cosmetic surgeons were doctors who trained to do good, then learned to do well.

The stands in the exhibition hall did a brisk trade in aids to self-advertisement. One offered 'customised visiting cards'. (What on earth is a non-customised visiting card?) On the back of his cards – the surgeons were all men – the purchaser could have a cartoon of an ape-faced man saying, 'Don't envy a good complexion, buy one', or of a woman – blonde, of course – sitting *en negligee* before her dressing table saying, 'Mirror, mirror on the wall . . . lie to me.'

The convention hotels offered plentiful evidence of cosmetic overkill. One evening, I happened upon a hotel lobby filled with tuxedoed surgeons and their wives and girlfriends. The women looked stunning, and I realised that when a girl hitches up to a cosmetic surgeon, she becomes a walking, talking advertisement of his skill. There wasn't a wrinkle in sight, not even on the petite blonde whose ball-gown seemed fashioned from a fisherman's net of none too narrow a mesh, presumably to show off her guy's overall competence. Yet the scene was surprisingly unarousing, as unarousing indeed as those aloof ladies who, when I was an adolescent, posed in their underwear on London Underground posters and whose breasts and thighs seemed sculpted from ice.

In 1977, it wasn't just breasts and thighs. When I got into conversation with a couple of the surgeons' 'accompanying persons', I discovered that their faces were also frozen, hoisted into place so often that, like Nancy Reagan ten years later, they were stuck with the same expression whether they confronted tragedy or comedy. Their faces, thanks to their surgeon boyfriends, had become closed books.

The carefree Californian attitude to cosmetic surgery derived naturally from the cult of youth that then prevailed in the southern end of the state. In Santa Monica, for instance, you qualified for a senior citizen's pass at the age of fifty, but few citizens applied. On my way home, I discovered that the cult didn't travel well. One of the more depressing features of New York evenings in 1977 was the sight of men in Manhattan mid-town bars, weary after a day in the office, striving dangerously to live up – or, more accurately, down – to the age of their hair transplants. Strange cases indeed.

RURAL EMERGENCY

SUFFOLK, 1979

Patrick came from Ireland to work as a labourer at a sugar beet factory in Suffolk. He lived on his own in a caravan on an isolated farm. 'A nicer man you could never meet,' said his GP, Dr Edward Cockayne, in a case report he published in 1980. 'He was eternally cheerful, as befits a man who has remained unmarried up to the age of 45.'

Patrick never bothered the doctor much, so when the milkman telephoned early one morning to tell Dr Cockayne that Patrick wasn't well, the doctor wasted no time in visiting him. He expected to find an ill patient and, sure enough, he did. Patrick had had a nasty pain in his chest all night and showed all the signs of having suffered a coronary thrombosis.

Cockayne offered the euphemism 'I think you've had a slight heart attack' – more reassuring, he said, to a man on his own than 'I think you've had a massive coronary thrombosis' – then gave Patrick an injection of heroin, a treatment commonly used because it was the best drug to relieve the pain and defuse the anxiety that aggravates the condition. 'Just you lie here,' said the doctor, 'and I'll get the ambulance.'

The caravan was in a meadow at the back of the farm. Rain had been falling for hours and Cockayne, equipped like every rural GP with a pair of stout wellies, trudged through the mud to the farmhouse, where he made a couple of phone calls, to get a hospital bed for Patrick and to order an ambulance. When he got back to the caravan, he found his patient feeling a lot better.

237

Thanks to the heroin, the pain in his chest had virtually disappeared, and Cockayne sensed that Patrick thought that the doctor was making too much of a fuss.

In a calculated breezy way, Cockayne tried to emphasise the seriousness of the illness without painting too black a picture. He also explained he'd have to leave Patrick alone for another short spell. He had patients waiting for him in his surgery, but the ambulance would be along in a few minutes. 'Just you stay in bed until it comes. Don't try to pack any clothes or anything. That can all be sorted out later.'

Cockayne had parked his car in the meadow alongside the caravan. It was still raining heavily and when he got into the car, he found all the windows misted up. He started the engine, engaged first gear and let out the clutch. The car moved not an inch – the back wheels just spun in the mud. He cursed and tried a higher gear, but the same thing happened. So he put the car into reverse and slowly edged it out of the ruts he had created. He selected first gear again, moved the steering wheel a quarter of a turn to the left, and accelerated as hard as he could. This time the car sailed through the mud onto firm ground. As he congratulated himself on his driving skill, he glanced in the wing mirror and saw why he'd succeeded. Patrick had been pushing with all his might from the rear.

Patrick, Dr Cockayne was relieved to add, made it safely to the hospital whence, after treatment, he eventually made it out again to restart his solitary life.

TRAVELLING IN STYLE

DAWLISH, 1979

The ambulance strike that was part of the 1979 'winter of discontent' posed John Andrews, a GP at Dawlish in Devon, with a difficult problem. It also encouraged him to devise an imaginative solution.

One of Dr Andrews's patients, who had slipped a disc in his back, developed worrying neurological signs in his leg, suggesting that the disc was pressing on a spinal nerve. When Dr Andrews discussed his patient's condition over the phone with a consultant surgeon, the surgeon wanted the man admitted urgently to hospital for a spinal operation that would relieve the pressure on the nerve.

The only safe way for the man to travel was lying flat on his back; even if he could be got into a car, which was doubtful, a journey with his hips bent would be not only painful but dangerous. Yet, when Dr Andrews telephoned the ambulance headquarters in Exeter, the managers there decided that this wasn't the sort of emergency that could be exempted from the strictures of the strike. The more vigorously Dr Andrews argued his patient's case, the more adamant grew the refusal.

Soon after he had put down the phone in disgust, Dr Andrews displayed the talent for improvisation that denotes a GP of quality. He remembered there was one member of the community who had long experience of transporting people lying flat. So he rang the local undertaker who, said Dr Andrews, was most obliging as always, and delighted to handle a live body for a change.

Within the hour, a hearse had glided impressively up to the patient's front door and GP and undertaker gathered up a mattress and blankets from the spare room and made up a bed in the hearse's palatial rear compartment. Dr Andrews then gave his patient an injection of morphia, and while they waited for it to work, he and the undertaker shared cups of coffee and local gossip with the patient's wife. When the man seemed adequately sedated, doctor and undertaker manoeuvred him gingerly into the back of the hearse. There were no flowers or prayers, said Dr Andrews, though the victim, despite the morphia, did manage a few imprecations.

The hearse purred off sedately and, to protect the patient from any jolts or judders, the undertaker kept the speed down to 15mph. The road to Exeter's orthopaedic hospital passed the crematorium and, as they approached it, other cars refrained from hooting or overtaking, so the hearse was soon at the head of a procession. As people on the pavement noticed the procession passing by, a few turned inwards and stood still, bowing their heads, the men among them doffing their hats.

At this stage, the undertaker started to twitch a little and Dr Andrews decided that the poor man had probably never driven past the crematorium before and was fighting off the temptation to put on his black topper and turn left. The hearse even started to pull to the left like a hound picking up a scent. But hearse and driver were encouraged to avoid temptation by the increasingly impious exhortations coming from the man in the back.

Soon, the orthopaedic hospital was treated to the rare sight of a hearse driving proudly up to the front door rather than slipping discreetly round to the back, and the porters managed – just – to keep straight faces while they transferred the patient to a trolley and thence to a hospital bed.

The operation was a success. The patient lost his pain and recovered his mobility – almost as quickly, said Dr Andrews, as he and the undertaker recovered their mobility after downing large quantities of celebratory whisky.

EUROPE'S MEDICAL NORTH-SOUTH DIVIDE

EUROPE, 1980

Can a country's religious history affect the way it licenses modern prescription drugs and monitors their safety? The question is not as strange as it might sound, and two doctors who asked it in 1980 suggested that the answer could be 'yes'. They claimed that the Reformation, particularly the teachings of Luther and Calvin, had both reflected and affected Europeans' attitudes to medicine.

Doctors Graham Dukes and Inga Lunde had experience of licensing new drugs – Dukes in Holland and Lunde in Norway – and, for the purpose of their argument, defined two areas of Europe based on the religions that had divided or united them over the previous four centuries: a northern, predominantly Protestant area – the Nordic countries and the northern and eastern part of what was then the EEC – and a southern, predominantly Roman Catholic area, in the south and west.

North European man, they claimed, was a sober, even sombre, individual, who acknowledged the need for law and authority and tended to be frugal in his ways. If he had a heavy cold, he would tell himself it must run its course and maybe take some camomile tea, aware of the adverse effects of anything more potent. South European man, suffering the same symptoms, might visit a doctor or a pharmacist to ask for and receive a medley of antibiotics, antihistamines and analgesics.

Dukes and Lunde admitted that they could have exaggerated

the difference when it came to illness, but claimed it was more clearly defined in drug regulation. There, they said, the further you moved into the Protestant zone, the more restrictive the regulations became, though the relationship between drug manufacturer and drug regulator remained one of mutual respect. The manufacturer was likely to regard a drug regulator, like a tax inspector, as an official who could be expected to make rigid but reasoned demands in accordance with the letter of the law.

In the more relaxed atmosphere of Europe's south, the drug regulator, like the tax inspector, was treated as a sparring partner whose demands were just a starting point for sporting argument, and the law itself, however impressive it looked in the statute book, was not necessarily enforced, or even enforceable.

Both the regulators were northern Europeans – Dr Dukes educated in England before becoming a Dutch national and Inga Lunde a Norwegian – so they were punctilious in pointing out that a country's religious history was not the only determinant of national identity. Their real point, they stressed, was that international legislators needed to remember just how much nations could differ in their physical needs and mental attitudes – something too often forgotten when officials meet beneath fluorescent light in sterile conference rooms.

AFTER THE BALL

WHITBY, 1981

Accidents, by their nature, can occur in bizarre circumstances. Yet there can have been few more bizarre than those recorded in a case report that Dr J O'Donnell published in November 1981. Dr O'Donnell was a GP in Whitby, and he described how two of his patients, a husband and wife, had attended a wedding reception held at the house of one of their friends. They both had too much to drink and the woman, feeling distinctly queasy, went upstairs to a guest bedroom and lay on a bed, hoping to sleep off the effects of the drink. Her husband fell asleep on a couch downstairs.

The other guests were soon, as Dr O'Donnell discreetly puts it, 'feeling very cheerful' and decided it was time for a practical joke. Roast turkey had been served at the reception, so they went to the kitchen and retrieved the discarded neck of the bird. Then, with the air of conspirators perpetrating the wittiest jape the world had ever seen, they partially inserted the turkey neck into the fly of the husband's trousers while he lay deep in trusting sleep.

The joke was soon forgotten as the party proceeded along its predetermined route. Soon, all the guests were in much the same state as the sleeping couple and, by two o'clock in the morning, all had either staggered off home or staggered upstairs to their beds. A few remembered the joke they had played and hoped to have a giggle with its victim the following day.

At three o'clock in the morning, the wife woke suddenly, as

is the way with people who anaesthetise themselves with alcohol, and found herself alone in a silent house. Feeling none too well, she went in search of her husband. Most of the lights were still on and, when she got to the top of the stairs, she saw her husband lying on the couch with the family cat on top of him, gnawing cheerfully at the tasty morsel protruding from his flies. The sight so affected her, wrote Dr O'Donnell, that she fainted, fell downstairs, and 'sustained a Colles' fracture of her left wrist'.

I suspect that the dedicated health and safety persons who catalogue the cause of every fracture filed this one under 'miscellaneous'.

LABOURS OF LOVE

SHEERNESS, 1981

In the summer of 1981, William Bennett of Sheerness discovered he was pregnant again. At the age of 79, he found it a bit tiresome, but this was his thirtieth pregnancy and he had learned to put up with it.

Whenever one of his four daughters became pregnant, Mr Bennett's belly began to swell, and it stayed swollen until his grandchild was delivered. He never swelled when his wife was pregnant but he never missed out on any of his 26 grandchildren. Mr Bennett's GP, Dr R T Fitzgerald, told me that when three of William's daughters were pregnant at the same time, his waist measurement increased by more than thirty inches. He also spanned a generation and came out in sympathy when each of his four great-grandchildren were expected.

William Bennett's condition was one that medical textbooks call 'couvade', though it was a highly unusual example. Couvade usually occurs in expectant fathers rather than grandfathers, and the symptoms are rarely as consistent or as dramatic as Mr Bennett's.

Derived from the French *couver,* meaning 'to hatch', couvade is said to affect between 10 and 65 per cent of expectant fathers, depending on which study you read. Only a tiny few put on a dramatic display, and the symptoms range from simple weight gain to back pains during pregnancy and stomach spasms during birth. The symptoms can occur at any time during the pregnancy but most often appear around the third month or around the time of delivery and mimic the symptoms suffered by some pregnant women: nausea, weight gain, vomiting, indigestion, backache, mood swings, leg cramps and cravings for strange foods. All the symptoms disappear after the baby is born.

The term couvade was coined by nineteenth-century anthropologists to describe the custom in primitive communities of men simulating the mother's condition during childbirth. The anthropologists discovered that the custom had been practised in slightly different forms in cultures that had no historical links, suggesting that its roots lay in man's humanity rather than in cultural tradition. The ritual usually involved the man taking to his bed while his partner was giving birth and mimicking her by feigning contractions and reacting to 'birth pains' with huffs and puffs, grunts and groans that echoed hers.

Details of the ritual varied from country to country. In Papua New Guinea, as soon as a woman knew she was pregnant, the man would separate himself from the rest of his tribe, build a hut for himself and fill it with food and clothing. He would then live separated from his wife and avoid social contact with the other men of his village. As the woman's time drew nigh, he would stay in bed and mimic the pain of childbirth until eventually the woman arrived at his new hut and handed the baby to him.

Basque men would take to their beds when they heard the woman had gone into labour and start to complain noisily about their labour pains, thus ensuring they got the same attention as their partners from the village nurses.

The Mozetena Indians of north-west Bolivia did much the same as the Basques save that, as soon as the child was born, the mother would hand over the baby to the man and go off to work to make sure food would be ready that evening. Meanwhile, the man, in a reversal of roles, looked after the baby.

Anthropologists can only guess at the reasons for these customs. Those they have suggested include:

• It strengthened the bond between father and child.
• The father's simulated birth asserted his paternity.

- The man may have been seeking to protect the mother and baby from bad spirits by drawing them towards him because he was screaming louder.
- A belief that the father had stronger supernatural powers than the mother and could better guide the child into the world.
- It made the father's role in pregnancy more profound than just the sexual act nine months before.
- It was a form of anxiety catharsis for the man.

Doctors have been equally tentative in offering explanations of the medical version of couvade – the psychosomatic condition of sympathetic pregnancy in which the man suffers symptoms for which there are no physical reasons. Their guesses at the reasons include:

- A physical expression of anxiety over the birth.
- Sympathy or empathy with the mother.
- An expression of guilt for making the woman pregnant.
- An assertion of paternity.
- Jealousy of the mother's ability to carry the child and give birth.

. . . and so on and so on. The length of the list is determined by the imagination of the person doing the speculating.

Like many things in medicine couvade is just a label, not an explanation. Medical journals have reported a few cases similar to the one in Sheerness, though not so extreme, but the case reports fail to enlighten us on what actually went on in Mr Bennett's swollen belly.

THE PERKS OF OFFICE

BRISTOL, 1981

During a discussion of the privileges that come the way of doctors because of their calling, Dr Ken Heaton, reader in medicine at the University of Bristol, reported an unusual case that occurred in the early 1980s.

A young woman doctor took a job at the Bristol Royal Infirmary that involved her getting quickly from her home to the hospital on the days and evenings she was on call. The only reliable way for her to travel was by road and, when she discovered how much she was spending on taxi fares, she decided to buy a car. The snag was that she had only a provisional licence, so she went on a course at a driving school, which eventually pronounced her ready to take a driving test.

During the test, she thought the examiner seemed withdrawn as she went through the manoeuvres she'd been conditioned to perform by the school. Then, just after he had rounded off the test with the statutory questions about the Highway Code, he complained of pain in his chest, turned pale and collapsed with an acute myocardial infarction. The young woman gave him emergency resuscitation, used his car phone to call for help, and travelled with him in the ambulance to the hospital.

Over the next week or so, she faced an unusual dilemma. The lack of a full licence continued to cost her a fortune in taxi fares, but the local Department of Transport office was unable to help her. She was told that if she hadn't resuscitated her examiner and he'd expired, the office could have granted her an immediate re-take, but because she'd completed the test, it had to wait for his report before it could do anything. Yet she could hardly walk into the coronary care unit and ask a desperately ill man if she'd passed. In desperation, she petitioned the examiner's cardiologist who, after a number of postponements, eventually decided his patient was well enough for her to visit him.

The examiner greeted her effusively. He'd been told that her action had almost certainly saved his life, and he solemnly thanked her on behalf of himself and his family. She accepted his thanks with becoming modesty before moving diffidently towards the purpose of her visit.

'I'm terribly sorry to bother you,' she said, 'but I just wondered, did I pass?'

The examiner responded with a kindly smile.

'I'd like to assure you, my dear, that I had reached my decision before you saved my life. So I can tell you, quite without bias, that you failed.'

THE WORLD'S SMALLEST SURGEONS

BUCKINGHAMSHIRE, 1981

On a summer's evening in 1981, a car veered off the M40 motorway, crashed down an embankment, and ended up in a gully invisible from the main road. The young driver was thrown through the windscreen and lay beside the car seriously injured for three days before he was found. When he was taken to Wycombe Hospital, his wounds were infested with maggots. The nurses, overcoming their revulsion in the way that nurses do, removed the maggots, and when surgeon John Church examined the man, he found the wounds were 'as clean as you could make them'. He didn't have to take his patient to the operating theatre to clear dirt from the wounds; the maggots had done the job for him.

That incident made Church think about the ways maggots might be used in treatment, and when he turned to the history books, he found it was by no means a new idea. Some 400 years before, military surgeons had noted that wounded soldiers who had maggots in their wounds did better than those who hadn't – they were less likely to die of gangrene, tetanus or septicaemia. In the nineteenth century, the renowned military surgeon Baron Dominique Larrey, surgeon general to Napoleon, had promulgated the usefulness of maggots, as had twentieth-century surgeons who served in the First World War. When those surgeons returned to civilian life, many of them, particularly the Americans, had cultivated greenbottle flies in laboratories and used the larval maggots to treat the wounds of thousands of patients during the 1930s and '40s.

The treatment fell out of fashion in the late 1940s when penicillin became widely available, but John Church thought it was due for a revival. He founded an organisation that investigates the medical use of living organisms and, in the 1990s, was involved with Dr Stephen Thomas in setting up the LarvE company based at the Princess of Wales Hospital in Bridgend, where Dr Thomas is director of the surgical materials testing laboratory.

In the laboratory's 'breeding room', thousands of greenbottles live in large transparent plastic bags and while away their time feeding and laying eggs. The eggs are taken from the bags, sterilised, and allowed to hatch. Then the hungry maggots that emerge are despatched in small tubes to over 800 centres across the UK where they are used to treat all manner of wounds, from pressure sores to the infamous 'flesh-eating disease', necrosing fasciitis.

The demand for maggots continues to grow because they are remarkably effective. Dr Thomas likens their action to that of carpet shampooers – not carpet sweepers that just pick up loose dirt, but shampooers that release cleansing agent into the carpet to dissolve the dirt before sucking it out. Maggots pump out a powerful mixture of enzymes, which break down all the dead tissue in the wound and turn it into a liquid soup that they then suck back as a source of nutrient. What makes maggots so useful is that, when they clear the wound, they do so with discrimination, going only for tissue that is dead and avoiding that which is living. They also destroy any bacteria they ingest, including those that are resistant to antibiotics, including the 'superbugs' that pose such a threat in hospitals and are often harboured in chronically infected wounds.

Maggots can be used outside hospitals. David Powell treats himself with maggot dressings at his home at Porthcawl. For nearly twenty years, the raw sores on his heels failed to respond to every treatment that his doctors could devise – until he started using maggots. For many people, the very thought of the treatment conjures up the world of the medieval apothecary, but the process doesn't look medieval. The gauze and the bandages that David uses have that whiter-than-white look that you find in a modern clinic. The maggots are sealed in a dressing so they remain invisible, and the only notice they give of their activity is what David calls 'a feathery feeling'.

David is delighted with the progress that he's making, yet, when he first asked a couple of surgeons about maggot treatment, they told him it was a load of nonsense before, as he says, 'setting about me with their scalpels'. His experience confirms one odd aspect of maggot therapy: it is more acceptable to patients than to doctors. Patients continually contact the laboratory at the Princess of Wales Hospital asking if they can have the treatment but doctors, says Stephen Thomas, are suspicious of it because 'it's not sexy modern medicine'.

Prejudice has always been a stumbling block to advances in medicine. And maybe a deep-rooted aversion, born of seeing the writhing mass in a fisherman's bait box, has slowed doctors' acceptance of what seems an extraordinarily useful technique. The highest of high technology has yet to produce a treatment that can discriminate between dead and live tissue – an ability possessed only by humans and maggots. That's why Stephen Thomas calls these wriggling creatures 'the world's smallest surgeons'.

FADDY ABOUT HIS FOOD

HUESCA, SPAIN, 1983

Mercedes Gimenez, aged 31, went to see her doctor with a worry that many mothers bring to their GPs. Her three-year-old son Manuel never seemed to eat anything. The doctor wasn't too worried because the toddler seemed to be gaining weight, so he muttered the Spanish version of the platitude that children of his age could be faddy about their food. Any reassurance Mercedes drew from the platitude didn't last for long. Try as she might, she couldn't get Manuel to touch his meals, and she and her husband sought advice elsewhere. Yet none of the doctors they consulted seemed concerned. Manuel, they pointed out, must be eating something because he wasn't losing weight.

Manuel's parents grew more worried when he started to complain of stomach pains. Once again, they visited a string of doctors but none was able to offer a diagnosis or an explanation. Eventually, in January 1983, after eighteen months in which they had visited nine doctors and three hospitals, Manuel was seen by Dr Perdo Fernandez, senior surgeon at the San Jorge Hospital in Huesca, northern Spain.

Dr Fernandez sent Manuel for an X-ray, which showed a variety of strange shadows in the child's stomach. 'I decided to operate immediately,' he said. 'And when we opened his stomach, I just couldn't believe my eyes. There was object after object, and most of them had obviously been there for months.' He removed thirty pebbles, two collar studs, two buttons, two coins, one screw and two plastic gambling chips.

The weight of the objects was 6lb 3oz, which Dr Fernandez explained was three times the weight of food that a grown man has in his stomach after a heavy meal. 'How he lived with that lot in there, I just don't know.'

After Manuel had recovered from his operation, Dr Fernandez tried some gentle shock treatment: 'I showed him what we had taken out of his stomach. Then I told him he would die if he ate one more pebble. He was very impressed.' So impressed that when he got home, Manuel celebrated by tucking in to half a chicken.

Later, his mother Mercedes said: 'Now, thanks to God and the good doctor, Manuel is fine. We never saw him swallowing these things, though he once brought up a small pebble. He wouldn't touch meat or fish and we fed him mainly on soup and peas. We knew he was ill because he rarely ate anything. But he never lost weight. How could he with all that inside him? He was never completely well but, though we kept taking him to all these doctors, they just said it must be something he'd eaten.'

The doctors could claim that that was an accurate diagnosis.

JARMING THE BLUES AWAY

QUINCY, MASSACHUSETTS, USA, 1984

1984 was a bad year for joggers. In July, their guru Jim Fixx, the long-distance runner who had claimed that running would 'significantly reduce the risk of developing coronary heart disease', died suddenly of a heart attack at the age of 52. Newspapers and medical journals published articles about the hazards of jogging and an American psychiatrist suggested that much of the enthusiasm for plodding along in tracksuits was a form of hysteria. Men in saloon bars no longer felt guilty when they saw earnest figures pounding past the pub, and then started to tell jogger stories. Have you heard about the one who dropped dead in the road? His pal looked down at him proudly and said, 'What a way to go! In the peak of condition.'

Then, in an article in *Modern Medicine,* Dr Joseph D Wasserug, a family doctor in Quincy, Massachusetts, announced there was a safer form of health-promoting exercise. The group most noted for leading long and healthy lives, he said, was not joggers but orchestra conductors and concert violinists and pianists. He cited in evidence Karl Bohm, 86, Adrian Boult, 100, Arthur Fiedler, 86, Richard Strauss, 86, Arturo Toscanini, 90, Walter Damrosch, 85, Leopold Stokowski, 96, and Arthur Rubinstein, 94.

Anyone watching conductors and soloists in action could see how much aerobic exercise they took during each performance. And when elderly conductors talked about the physical exertion that their work involved, they often boasted that their efforts could not be matched by younger, untrained people. The time had come, said Dr Wasserug, to silence the advocates of jogging. Doctors should stress the value of exercising the arms instead of the legs and proclaim the health benefits of 'jogging with the arms' or, as he preferred to call it, 'jarming'.

He was puzzled by the dearth of scientific investigation into arm exercises, either as a form of treatment or as a way of measuring cardiovascular stress. Most medical articles confined themselves to work done by the legs. Almost everything written about stress-testing, for instance, involved leg exercises on a treadmill or a bicycle; no one seemed interested in measuring the effects of exercising the arms. Science, wrote Dr Wasserug, should now give at least as much attention to jarming as it had to jogging. If need be, the exercise could be made more rigorous by getting the jarmer to wear weighted gloves or to hold a dumbbell in each hand.

One great advantage of jarming was that people could indulge in it at any age and in almost any setting. Dr Wasserug had found it valuable for patients confined to their beds or to wheelchairs, and for people who, for other reasons, were unable to get outdoors. Another advantage was that jarming carried little risk of injury. Joggers were prone to foot, knee, hip and spine injuries caused by repetitive pounding of weight-bearing legs on hard pavements. Joggers who were overweight, or who didn't warm up adequately, were particularly susceptible to leg injuries. A jarmer's weight-bearing limbs were never at risk.

Like all innovators, Dr Wasserug ran into reflex opposition. The first negative response came from Dr Hans Neuman, medical director of New Haven Department of Health. 'If conducting an orchestra is an exercise of optimal duration and intensity,' he said, 'it is difficult for lesser mortals to come up with similar types of physical activity.' And, though he admitted that jarming could be helpful, he added rather sniffily, 'One cannot advise hiring an orchestra for physical training purposes.'

Dr Wasserug bounced back by pointing out that people could buy an orchestra on tape or disc: 'Almost any time you wish, you can take your Walter Mitty baton in hand, roll the tape and

stand on the podiums of Toscanini, Fiedler and Stokowski.'
Indeed, jarming's big advantage over jogging, he said, was that
it could be performed at any age, no matter how fit or unfit the
performer. Not only that but, 'like the tai-chi of the Chinese,
jarming may be a sport of beauty and grace when properly
performed. Indeed, the hand motions of leading symphony
orchestra conductors rival those of prima ballerinas.'

Sadly for Dr Wasserug, the world reacted to his imaginative
proposal with a fever of intense apathy.

MISCALCULATING THE ODDS

LULEA, SWEDEN, 1984

The laws of probability are not as simple as they seem. That's why there are a few rich bookies and a lot of poor punters. It's also why doctors who seek to bring some logic to their practice are thwarted by the fact that most people don't understand risk.

On 15 July 1992, newspapers carried front-page reports that the antihistamine Triludan had caused irregular heartbeats in six patients who had either exceeded the recommended dose or taken it with an antibiotic with which it was incompatible. On the same morning, the diary in the *Independent* reported that 'at least two US soldiers die each year as a result of kicking faulty vending machines and another 25 are injured after kicking, striking, shaking or otherwise assaulting malfunctioning vending machines which in consequence fall over.' It was a good diary piece, even worth a laugh. Yet the laughably minute risk of being killed by a vending machine was at least 200 times greater than the 'drug scare' risk presented in stark solemnity on the front page.

Ignorance breeds superstition, so the public perception of risk often owes more to fear than to the mathematics of probability. And fear is more easily triggered by one major event than by a series of minor ones. If a fully laden jumbo jet crashed at Heathrow killing all passengers, the tragedy would make headline news. If exactly the same thing happened at Heathrow the next day, there would be outrage and alarm. If it happened again the following day, the airport would probably be closed, and all jumbo jets grounded. And if the accident were repeated on a fourth day, all air travel would probably be brought to a halt, pending investigation. Yet the number of people killed would have been no greater, indeed slightly less, than Britain's unrelenting weekly death toll attributable to cigarettes – a number that the British public accepts with resignation and the British government with apparent equanimity.

One reason for this disparity of reaction is that our perception of risk involves a political quality that was neatly illustrated in a lecture given by the distinguished mathematician Sir Hermann Bondi at Wolfson College, Oxford, in the spring of 1984. He described a Swedish government plan to study the aurora borealis, the northern lights, by firing instrument-carrying rockets into it. When the rockets had done their job, the burnt-out remnants were due to fall over an area of Lapland so sparsely populated that the mathematical risk of anyone being hit was minute. Even so, the Swedish government felt it should offer protection, so it lifted out the isolated reindeer herders by helicopter to Lulea and lifted them back when the experiment was over.

Sir Hermann calculated that the mathematical probability of one of them being hit by a piece of rocket was less than one per cent of that of a helicopter accident. But he also invited his audience to look at the political implications.

If someone had been hit – or even had 'a bad fright' – the interior minister would have faced angry accusations that he had done nothing to protect people for whom he was responsible. Yet, if there had been a helicopter crash, people would have happily accepted a ministerial statement: 'We deeply sympathise with the relatives of the victims of this tragedy. We used a well-tried helicopter, recently serviced, and flown by a well-trained and experienced crew. We are appalled at what has happened but there is no other precaution we could have taken.'

Sir Hermann's argument is convincing and underlines the need, in our increasingly litigious times, for politicians to restore the concept of an act of God.

SILENT KNIGHTS

LONDON, 1985

It is a universally acknowledged truth that ambitious doctors eager to climb medicine's hierarchical tree need to acquire a strange entity that they call gravitas. Their efforts to display it lead to a defining moment in a medical career when the young turk transmutes into an old fart.

The symptoms of impending transmutation can be spotted by the aspirants' contemporaries. Men – most are men but an increasing number are women – who once were lively, witty and intelligent companions suddenly assume a public persona quite at odds with the character that previously served them well. Where once they would have enlivened conversation, they make observations of paralysing mundanity. Drawn into public discussion, they rasp on earnestly and nod wisely as if naught but weighty thoughts were granted admission to their minds. And, on the slightest of excuses, they rise to their feet to make pompous speeches. Most grievously of all, they refrain from using their private wit in public places for fear that amusing or penetrating remarks might prove politically inept.

When I was a young doctor, we used to recognise a condition in our elders that we called knight starvation, and were amused by the antics in which some senior doctors indulged in their chase after ephemeral honour. As we grew older, we recognised the damage that could be done to the careers of others, to the health service and to our own profession when intelligent persons started a ruthless hunt after symbols for their own sake.

260

An odd event in 1985 suggested that the hard-nosed pursuit of 'honour' was more common than we feared.

In July of that year, I wrote, fairly light-heartedly, in the *British Medical Journal* about the symptoms of knight starvation, and described how I found them less amusing when some of my contemporaries started to display them. 'I find it painful to recall,' I wrote, 'how one person whom I once admired achieved the honour he so coveted by an act that denied the very qualities for which he'd won respect. But then if someone wants to buy your political support, be it with a free lunch or with a knighthood, you must have something that's worth selling. Often it's your integrity.'

I didn't name the man but later I and the journal's editor, Stephen Lock, received pained complaints from three people who assumed I'd been writing about them. I had, in fact, been writing about someone else, but I still wonder what those other three had been up to.

A SAVAGE AFFAIR

LONDON, 1985

A strange, some would say sinister, incident in 1985 delivered a nasty blow to the complacency of British doctors who believed that their profession had abandoned its old oligarchical ways, and that the coming of the NHS and spectacular scientific advance had swept away the chauvinism of pre-war British medicine.

In May of that year, Mrs Wendy Savage was suspended from her job as senior lecturer at the London Hospital and consultant obstetrician to Tower Hamlets District Health Authority. The directive under which she was suspended was designed to protect patients from dangerous doctors, yet she had practised freely for a year after the incidents that were alleged to reveal the danger. As the suspicion grew that the real reason for her suspension was that other consultants at her hospital, all of them male, wanted her out, many doctors began to fear that the traditional hypocrisies of their profession were not dead but had just been hibernating in the woodwork.

Publicity given to the case in medical journals provoked a dramatic response. Over 80 per cent of the GPs practising in Tower Hamlets signed a petition calling for Mrs Savage's reinstatement; over a thousand patients marched in protest through the streets. Local GPs, less easily silenced by administrative process than hospital doctors, defended Mrs Savage's obstetric record and claimed that the case was an eruption of the chronic obstetrical dispute between the 'high-tech, interventionist, hospital-based' style of obstetrical practice and the 'community-based, woman centred' approach.

Away from the public stage, traditional medical tactics were deployed. Some doctors who complained that the public protest about the charges constituted 'trial by media' seemed to find nothing repugnant in medicine's traditional 'trial by gossip'. Two senior members of the profession were later found to have poured poisonous rumour into the ears of colleagues in private, while maintaining a discreet public profile on the grounds that the case was under judicial consideration. Other gossip included allegations about Mrs Savage's sexual and marital history which, though untrue, were passed on by some of the most senior people in medicine and accepted, unquestioned, by their peers.

There were also professional smears. One professor of obstetrics described how he was deterred from supporting Mrs Savage because he had been offered evidence of 'unforgivable surgical incompetence'. Later he discovered that the 'evidence' did not exist, though the allegation had been widely circulated among the obstetrical establishment.

Not all of Mrs Savage's supporters were prepared, or even allowed, to declare their support. The most junior doctors at the London Hospital were instructed not to talk to outsiders, nor to sign petitions, nor to go on marches. Registrars at the hospital thought it prudent to keep their sympathy for Mrs Savage under wraps lest it count against them in the highly competitive interviews they faced when seeking a consultant job. Junior consultants were disinclined to do anything that might rock the boat when they became eligible for patronage in the form of a research grant or a merit award.

Doctors in other hospitals who admitted in private that Wendy Savage was being treated unfairly didn't want their opinion publicised because they didn't want to 'get involved' or 'let the side down'. Their attitude was well summed up by he who said, 'These things are best settled between ourselves without dragging the good name of the profession through the mud.' Yet the profession was already up to its armpits in mud thanks to newspaper articles and television programmes that had examined the motives behind the case.

Despite the public protests, Mrs Savage eventually had to face a judicial enquiry set up under a procedure designed to investigate serious professional malpractice. It would judge her professional competence not by looking at her general standards of practice but by examining five cases that, after a trawl through the hospital records, those who complained about her thought she had managed least well.

Few doctors would like to have their competence judged on their conduct of their five worst cases, yet Mrs Savage's clinical reputation emerged from the ordeal in better shape than could be hoped for by most obstetricians. The evidence about four cases crumbled early in the trial, the fifth crumbled later, and anyone who reads the transcript will see that the enquiry's conclusions were inevitable. It found she was not incompetent and that her standards for safe obstetrical practice were no lower than those of anyone else at the London Hospital. Yet her suspension had lasted for eighteen months.

The issue that most worried medical observers surfaced when Ronald Taylor, professor of obstetrics and gynaecology at St Thomas's Hospital, gave evidence. He was an impressive witness because he was an old adversary of Mrs Savage in the abortion debate, yet he described how her new professor had said that one of his first jobs after his appointment would be to get rid of her. It was a cathartic moment, and the only public signal of the off-stage antics that troubled many doctors.

How did Wendy Savage win the day? Despite the rumours, she was not a tough woman; a tenacious debater, maybe, but, like many doctors whose life revolves around their work, she had a soft centre. Her case was helped by the support she won from local colleagues and from a few distinguished members of her own specialty who, appalled by what they saw going on, came to her assistance. But what tipped the balance was her decision to seek legal advice outside the magic circle of lawyers who specialise in medical matters and who many felt had too cosy a relationship with the medical establishment. Her solicitor Brian Raymond, fresh from defending Clive Ponting against charges under the Official Secrets Act, managed, after a struggle, to get her case heard in open court and, at a stroke, disarmed the rumour campaign that was being conducted off-stage. The enquiry transcript makes it clear that Mrs Savage's accusers would have preferred to make their accusations behind closed doors.

What seemed strange at the time, and seems even stranger in retrospect, were the blatantly sexist tactics used by the rumour-mongers at a time when 50 per cent of British medical students were women.

TRIAL BY GATEKEEPER

PITTSBURGH, 1986

In June 1986, two manuscripts were submitted to the *New England Journal of Medicine*. Both reported the results of the same drug trial, conducted over three years at the Otitis Media Research Center at Pittsburgh's Children's Hospital. The trial, which had involved 518 children, had been set up to determine if the antibiotic amoxicillin was of any value in the treatment of a particular type of ear infection. One of the submitted manuscripts concluded that amoxicillin was effective and should be used in treating this infection in children; the second concluded that amoxicillin was not effective.

The editor of the journal wrote to the University of Pittsburgh School of Medicine and to the Children's Hospital to ask which of the two manuscripts was the 'official' version. Both institutions replied that Dr Charles Bluestone, the principal investigator, and Dr Ellen Mandel, the lead author, were the only persons authorised to report the results. The 'official' version was then reviewed by the journal's editors and published in a slightly amended version. The maverick manuscript was returned without review.

This bizarre event had its origins in a disagreement that had begun even before the trial was over. The disagreement was between Dr Bluestone and Erdem Cantekin, a bioengineer who was director of research in the Department of Otolaryngology. The Research Center received money from pharmaceutical companies, and three years earlier, Cantekin had expressed

266

doubts about 'the scientific validity of research commissioned and funded by pharmaceutical companies seeking to prove the effectiveness of their antibiotics'.

He argued that the Center should disassociate itself from industry-sponsored studies and claimed that Dr Bluestone was publicly advocating the use of amoxicillin for the infection under investigation before the trial was over. Cantekin also alleged that Bluestone had spent substantial time travelling at the expense of the pharmaceutical company to advocate use of their product.

When the trial was finished and drafts of a manuscript were circulated, Cantekin disagreed with the conclusion about the effectiveness of the drug and bowed out as a co-author after the paper had been redrafted thirteen times. He then asked two experts in the analysis of data to join him in writing the maverick version of the report that was rejected without review by the *New England Journal of Medicine*.

In August 1986, shortly after the unauthorised paper was submitted for publication, Cantekin was discharged from his position at the Center. A board of the medical school had accused him of committing 'serious violations of research ethics'. Over the next few years, he wrote letters to the dean of the medical school, to the Food and Drug Administration, to the US Congress and to the editors of medical journals to put forward his complaints of a conflict of interest and of misrepresentation of the trial results. He also tried, without success, to get the maverick paper published.

At a series of investigations, including two hearings before a subcommittee of Congress, all parties traded charges and counter-charges. Eventually, there emerged a grudging acknowledgement that there was some substance to the criticisms levelled against the official report of the trial.

One of the many strange elements in what became known as the Cantekin Affair was the reason the editor of the *New England Journal of Medicine* gave for rejecting the maverick paper: 'The important question . . . is not whose interpretation is correct . . . but who has the right to publish.' A lawyer later wrote to the editor: 'Let me reword your statement just slightly to demonstrate its astonishing absurdity: "The important question . . . is not whether Galileo or the Pope is correct with respect to whether the sun revolves around the earth or vice versa, but rather, who, as between the Pope and Galileo, has the right to publish his opinion." '

The distinguished American paediatrician William Silverman later pointed out that this cautionary tale confirms the suspicion that temptations to circumvent the rules of evidence are particularly great when huge sums of money in drug sales depend on the outcomes of such trials. 'Moreover,' he wrote, 'the gatekeepers (department chairs, institutional review boards, editors), who control the flow of information that passes before the eyes of doctors on the front lines, seem to abhor controversy more than they love the truth. If this dour judgement about the weak safeguards to ensure integrity in present-day drug trials is correct, it suggests, among other things, that the lessons of past drug disasters, like Thalidomide, are fading from memory. Unfortunately, as Santayana observed, "Those who cannot remember the past, are condemned to relive it."'

PSEUDOLOGIA TOXOPHILUS

TORONTO, 1987

When Patrick Couwenberg applied to become a judge in the Los Angeles County superior court, he had a couple of socio-political accoutrements that impressed the board that was making the appointment. During the Vietnam War, he had worked for the CIA as an underground agent in Laos and, after being struck by stray shrapnel, had been awarded a Purple Heart.

Unsurprisingly, he got the job. Equally unsurprisingly, he lost it in the summer of 2001 when an investigative tribunal found that his military 'achievements' were fabrications and that he had lied not just when he applied for the job but during the tribunal's investigation. Judge Couwenberg claimed in his defence that he was suffering from pseudologia phantastica – a neat example of the art of 'medicalising' misdemeanour.

Describing the judge's fate in the *Guardian,* Duncan Campbell reported that a high incidence of pseudologia phantastica had been detected in the United States where 'a combination of dogged researchers, disgruntled veterans' organisations and the internet is exposing dozens of tin soldiers who have strutted at the head of their veterans' parades or used a bogus war record to parlay their way into a job or a relationship'.

Oddly, Campbell failed to mention America's most cele-brated sufferer from pseudologia phantastica, President Ronald Reagan – the man who, according to the American physician Peter E Dans, 'raised cognitive dissonance to an art form'.

Among other fantasies, Reagan claimed, and seemed to believe, that he'd been part of a photographic unit accompanying troops that liberated German concentration camps near the close of World War Two. Yet he remained quite unfazed when army records showed he had never left the United States during the war.

This indissoluble link between chronic dissembling and self-deception was described in 1727 by Jonathan Swift in his *Tale of a Tub*. 'When man's fancy gets astride of his reason; when imagination is at cuffs with the senses; and common understanding, as well as common sense, is kicked out of doors; the first proselyte he makes is himself.'

In Britain, pseudologia phantastica is more recognisable as pseudologia toxophilus – the Archer syndrome – named after the noble lord whose penchant for fabricating his biography ensured that his life story was his most imaginative work of fiction and led eventually to his imprisonment for perjury. Those who need to 'medicalise' the Archer syndrome could define it as a compulsive disorder that drives people to rewrite their personal history in a way that stretches the credulity of everyone except themselves.

The strangest case of this condition was reported in 1988 by Dr Graham Reed, chairman of the department of psychology at York University in Toronto. In his book *The Psychology of Anomalous Experience,* Reed describes how a young woman arrived late for her appointment looking distraught and giving the impression of bravely fighting back tears. She asked for time to compose herself, saying, 'I feel a bit shaken. You see, I'm afraid something just happened that rather upset me.' Then after a show of reluctance, she explained she had caught her bus in good time and was late only because, as she was about to get off the bus, the conductor raped her. Reed acted with sympathy, but remarked that it was an unusual occurrence in mid-afternoon on a main road in the city centre, not to mention on a crowded bus. When he asked if she had reported it to the police, she replied with wide-eyed sincerity that she hadn't because, 'That would have made me late for my appointment here.'

After the session, Reed took her back to the waiting room

where her mother was waiting. The mother was dismayed by the story her daughter had told – they had travelled together to the clinic and she had seen 'nothing untoward'. Yet the young woman was not at all put out by her mother's denial of her version. The rape, she explained, had taken place as she was about to follow her mother down the stairs. And she hadn't mentioned it during the walk from the bus stop because the conductor had also tried to strangle her with his ticket-punch strap and she was temporarily unable to speak.

DEAR SIR OR MADAM

ALBORG, DENMARK, 1987; LONDON, 1999

Doctors, as individuals, are capable of impressive acts of understanding and compassion. Yet, when they get together in a group, they are capable of public acts of extraordinary insensitivity. In October 1987, thirteen international experts met in Alborg in Denmark for a 'consensus meeting' on the prevention and treatment of osteoporosis – a thinning and fragility of bone that can afflict women after the hormonal changes that occur during the menopause.

The idea of consensus meetings is commendable. In Alborg, the experts listened to presentations of the published scientific data about osteoporosis before going into a huddle and emerging with a 'consensus statement' which defined the forms of treatment they believed had been established by reputable research as opposed to treatments that might be advocated by enthusiastic hobby-horse jockeys.

Their statement included a recommendation that post-menopausal women should take regular doses of hormones, even though this might increase their risk of getting cancer. When the experts presented their conclusions at a press conference, a journalist – male – pointed out that this recommendation came from a panel of which every member was a man.

The chairman agreed that this was 'unfortunate' but explained that the panel needed experienced experts, 'and, when research started in this field, only men were involved'.

'But all your patients are women,' said the journalist. 'Why not invite a couple of patients to join the group?' The reaction of the 'experts' suggested that the journalist had lost his mind.

Insensitivity to the implications of gender has a long and dishonourable history in medicine. Yet attempts in the 1990s to eliminate discrimination created a strange new problem. NHS bureaucrats discovered that in addition to facing their traditional enemies – grammar and syntax – they now had to grapple with the notion of 'correctness' without quite understanding what it was.

In February 1999, Dr Dick Ford, a GP in Bideford, wrote to the then secretary of state for health, Frank Dobson.

I was amazed to read your missive (Statutory Instruments 1999 No 326) which refers to all doctors as he, and all nurses as she. When I was a child, I wallowed in the misbelief that all dogs were male and all cats were female. It didn't take me long to discover otherwise. I can assure you that not all doctors are male and not all nurses are female. Perhaps in this era of political correctness, regulations ought to be couched in these terms.

Dr Ford got a reply not from Frank Dobson but from M A Garley (sex and administrative position undisclosed) at the NHS Executive.

I should explain that Section 6 of the Interpretation Act 1978 provides that any reference in legislation to the masculine includes the feminine, and similarly any reference to the feminine includes the masculine. Consequently all references in the Statutory Instrument to male or female include the other sex, and the regulations, of course, apply equally to all doctors and nurses. In this particular case, the regulations were drafted to refer to male doctors and female nurses solely to avoid any possible confusion and to make it absolutely clear when the reference was to the nurse and when to the doctor.

Dr Ford, a charitable man, wondered if he might have stumbled upon a bureaucrat (a word which may or, on the other hand, may not include the feminine) with a sense of humour.

I fear not.

WHAT NATIONALITY IS YOUR ILLNESS?

BRITAIN, FRANCE, GERMANY, UNITED STATES, 1989

One of the strangest areas of medicine, particularly to those who regard it as a science, is the way that national cultural traits can affect the nature of an illness and its treatment. At their lowest level, these cultural traits determine each nation's label for those vague aches and pains that are less an illness than an inconvenience. The British will attribute them to constipation or a 'chill', the French to a *'crise defoie'*, Germans to *'Herzinsuffizienz'*, and Americans to an allergy.

But national differences go deeper than saloon-bar tales of British people visiting France and swallowing the suppositories, or rumours of what French visitors do with our antibiotic capsules. Heart disease, for instance, is no more common in Germany than it is in Britain, yet Germans consume six times as many heart drugs as the British and their doctors diagnose *Herzinsuffizienz* – poorly functioning heart – on grounds that would not lead to a diagnosis of heart disease in other European countries. A German businessman will take his heart medicine publicly and with pride because it enhances his status; the British tend to swallow their tablets in secret because the knowledge that they were 'flawed' might inhibit their advancement.

The French seem equally obsessed with their livers. An American researcher comparing national survival rates was

275

alarmed by the high death rate attributed to liver disease in France. What he was measuring, of course, was not the disease rate but the attribution rate.

The Americans themselves have more macho obsessions. Their surgeons operate on twice as many of their patients as do British surgeons – one survey found that women going to US east coast centres with breast cancer were three times more likely to have their breasts removed than women treated in England or Sweden. Yet the rate of breast cancer in all three countries is the same. European doctors criticise American doctors for 'over-doctoring'; American doctors criticise their European colleagues for 'backwardness'.

Medical information sometimes has trouble crossing national boundaries. Chilblains have been described in British textbooks for over a century yet, when they occurred in Virginia in 1980 in women who exercised horses in cold weather, they were reported as a new disease: 'equestrian cold panniculitis'.

Other national barriers are aesthetic. In France the ideal bust measurement is 33 inches, in America, 39 inches. Breasts reduced by cosmetic surgeons in France would be treasured in America. As a result, US surgeons perform breast augmentation twice as often as breast reduction. In France, reduction is nearly four times more common than augmentation. Cosmetic surgery is a useful mirror of cultural attitudes. Face lifts are less common in France than in the United States because, as a Parisian surgeon explained, 'In France, to age is to enter into a social category that has its place.'

In 1989, Lynn Payer, an American journalist of French, German and English ancestry, investigated the medical differences between the four nations that endowed her with her genes and suggested some reasons for the disparities. French attitudes, she said, were heavily influenced by the Cartesian love of reasoning and disdain for practical data. As a result, French research was often more concerned with the process than with the outcome. This explained the French habit of taking the temperature with a thermometer in the rectum rather than the mouth. Rectal temperatures are indeed more accurate than oral temperatures, but British doctors claim such a degree of accuracy is unnecessary; French doctors revere the intellectual quality of accuracy and attribute their critics' attitude to British prudishness.

Medicine in Germany, Payer concluded, was characterised not just by patients' eagerness to obey their doctors' orders but by a rich Wagnerian romanticism. For Germans, the heart was not just a pump but the seat of the emotions. Hence the high consumption of heart drugs and the pride with which they were taken. Germans could enjoy bad health because the acceptable national mood was pessimism. The German language, which has more composite nouns than most, has no word for 'happy ending' but uses the English phrase 'das Happy End'.

American medicine, said Payer, prided itself on its aggression, a frontiersman approach that encouraged 'heroic' treatment. (Oddly, when doctors talk of heroic treatment they believe that it is they rather than their patients who are showing the heroism.) Some British doctors who, as students, were taught the art of 'masterly inactivity', refer to their hyperactive American colleagues as Godsakers: 'For God's sake, let's do something.' And Godsaking lays its mark on American surgery. In 1989, an American woman was two or three times more likely to have had a hysterectomy than a European woman. And an analysis of surgical mistakes in Boston revealed that two thirds were errors of commission rather than omission, arising from misplaced optimism, unwarranted urgency or the desire to use fashionable new procedures.

Americans, unlike Germans, still assume that their natural state is to be healthy. If they are not, there has to be a cause and it has to be removable. This applies not just to physical illness. Their Saniflush concept of psychotherapy derives from the belief that all Americans have it within them to achieve greatness if only some therapist can flush out those inhibitions that hold them back.

In 1989, Payer thought British medicine was characterised by a kindly but sternly protective paternalism. (With the increasing number of women now becoming doctors, we ought to call it parentalism.) British doctors, she said, were trained to think empirically and accept that knowledge came from experience rather than from theory. Or, as the French put it, 'English doctors are the accountants of the medical world.'

British kindliness was seen at its best in the development of the hospice movement. American doctors see death as the ultimate failure; British doctors accept that their job has as much to do with caring as with curing. But kindliness grows less attractive when it is corrupted by parentalism. British doctors, like British civil servants, have a tradition of keeping information to themselves. If you ask British doctors for information, they will assume that what you're really after is reassurance.

British patients conspire with their doctors to preserve the parentalism. One survey showed that a third of patients didn't question their doctors because they feared the doctor would think less of them and one in five was scared of provoking a hostile reaction. In 1989, a Briton's first line of defence against disease or discomfort was still the stiff upper lip. Payer saw an English woman explain on television how, when she'd given birth to twins on an Italian train, her main concern was that she might wake up the other passengers.

Most of the national differences are hangovers from the days before medicine began its move towards scientifically evaluated treatment. And they persist because, even today, only about 15 per cent of treatment is backed by scientific evidence that it does any good. Successful doctors treat their patients not just with science but by exposing them to that complex interplay of personality and sensitivity that makes people good healers. And, just as cultural tradition determines which treatment is acceptable – a French suppository, a British purgative, an American allergy detoxification, a German heart stimulant – so it defines which qualities make the healer impressive: the French are impressed by the qualities of a philosopher, Germans by those of a senior officer, Americans by those of a Godsaker, and the British by those of a parent.

DUBIOUS ENTITLEMENT

LIMEHOUSE, LONDON, 1989

NHS management demands particular skills, most of them to do with running an under-funded service while upholding the party line that it doesn't need more funds. This paradox has ensured that, since its inception, the NHS has been subjected to regular and increasingly desperate managerial 'reorganisations', each heralded as the final radical solution.

One of the more memorable NHS reorganisations took place on 31 January 1989, though it is remembered not because of what it achieved but because of the extravagance of its introduction. Department of Health officials claimed proudly at the time that it was the most lavish launch accorded to a government initiative. Over a million pounds was spent on a telecast from a Limehouse studio to other studios and hotel ballrooms in six British cities in which sat an audience of 2,500 Health Authority chairmen, NHS managers and carefully selected doctors and nurses.

The star of the show, Kenneth Clarke, the secretary of state for health, was ferried in ceremonial style by river boat from the House of Commons to the Limehouse studio, where he proclaimed yet another dawn of yet another new era – a sure sign to reorganisation aficionados that they were about to endure a spell of intensified administrative muddle that would eventually produce deterioration rather than enhancement.

Yet every NHS reorganisation includes details remembered by those subjected to them long after the original grand design has been consigned to oblivion. And, when the 1989 reor-ganisation eventually went the way of all the others that included no extra funds, one quirky relic of the night that Mr Clarke failed to set the Thames on fire was the passion it aroused in NHS managers for the creation of strange occu-pations, a passion so great that, for a time, pretentious job titles conferred the status that some seek to achieve with personalised number plates.

In 1994, Fritz Spiegel, musician, writer, and indefatigable pursuer of oddities, listed the NHS posts he'd found advertised in just one newspaper. They included a primary care strategy development officer, a joint planning and development worker substance misuse, a reprovision consultant, a mentoring project co-ordinator, a human resources health management advisor, a motion analysis scientist, numerous clinical studies co-ordina-tors, audit facilitators, operations directors (for administrative, not surgical operations) . . . and counsellors by the score.

In an unusual, maybe unique, episode in NHS history, this one element of the 1989 Thatcherite reorganisation, the passion for high-sounding job titles, re-emerged ten years later in the Blairite reorganisation, though naturally in a different guise. The Blairite technique was to create not a multitude of decorative titles but a handful of truly impressive ones, the health tsars: a cardiology tsar, mental health tsar, children's health tsar and so on.

It seemed odd that such a gender-sensitive administration didn't appoint even a token Tsarina; odder still that it went foreign to find an unsuitable title. The tsars, after all, were absolutist Russian rulers whose behaviour, on occasion, was not quite what people would expect in their caring health service. A nation so rich in ridiculous titles could surely have devised something more appropriate and British, such as paediatrician-in-waiting to the minister's bedchamber. And, if the new men in charge were determined to add a touch of Eastern exotica to NHS governance, they could have turned to their childhood story books and given us a grand vizier or two.

Though, once you start delving into story books, you realise the most appropriate title might be grand panjandrum.

The NHS tsars are still in power, but security of tenure is not assured. The serfs are growing restless and already there is talk of yet another reorganisation, guaranteed, like all the others, to end the need for further reorganisation.

WHAT'S MY LINE?

LIVERPOOL, 1990

During a great chunk of the twentieth century, a nasty gap existed between what students learned at medical school and what they needed to know when they went into general practice. One symptom of that gap was the panic that could afflict fledgling GPs when they tried to deal with something their patients thought was perfectly straightforward – a request for a doctor's note, a certificate or, in some parts of the country, 'a doctor's line'. The panic was engendered by the need to find the appropriate form and, more dauntingly, the appropriate words for a note for 'the insurance', 'the sick', 'the housing', 'the benefit', 'the school', 'the welfare', 'the council', 'the coal', 'the milk', 'the labour' and, in parts of the country that retained the vernacular of the old panel system, for a 'Lloyd George'.

The power of a doctor's note in the post-war years was confirmed in a letter that the Rev. Donald Soper wrote to the *Hampstead and Highgate Express:* 'I remember one Sunday afternoon at Speakers' Corner in Hyde Park being challenged by a heckler to prove that I was not mad. I found the situation somewhat tricky so, hoping to play for time, I challenged the heckler to prove that *he* was not mad which, to my discomfiture, he did by producing his discharge certificate from a mental institution.'

In the closing decades of the twentieth century, the demand for medical certificates revealed the pivotal role that GPs played in modern Britain. When, for instance, heavy rain struck Kirbyin-Cleveland in North Yorkshire and softened the fairways on the local golf course, players were forbidden to use trolleys unless a GP had certified that they were unfit to carry their bags.

Sometimes, requests for certificates reflected the social problems of the day. When a patient of Dr Linda MacConnell, a GP in Portsmouth, was found with two pounds of cannabis in her possession, she asked for a certificate explaining that she needed it to treat her ten-year-old daughter's asthma. And, in Chesterfield, a man who'd been charged with driving while over the limit asked Dr Frances Fermer to certify that his condition was provoked by the stress he had suffered ten days before when he was admitted to an intensive care unit after overdosing on methadone supplied by a friend and Prozac stolen from his mother.

Some requests are difficult for a sympathetic doctor to resist. As when a woman desperate to get her son out of the French Foreign Legion asked Dr John Davies, who practises in Great Ayton in North Yorkshire, for a note explaining the effect that her son's continuing service was having on her nerves. And a Luton GP, Dr Paddy O'Donnell, was able to render valuable service to a stranger who turned up at his surgery. The visitor, a policeman, had been accused of sexual harassment by a woman PC who claimed he'd boasted noisily in her presence about his sexual attributes, including his decorated penis. He wanted a certificate stating that his penis was unpierced. The good doctor examined him and certified with due solemnity that the vital organ was unadorned.

Even late in the century, a doctor's note was still regarded as the ultimate verification. In 1995, Dr J M Griffin, a GP in Northampton, received a letter from the solicitors of a patient who had recently died.

We have been instructed to act in the administration of the estate of the above named deceased. Following Mr X's death, the Executors now wish to cancel a holiday booking which Mr and Mrs X had made in September of this year and which was to be taken during the Christmas holiday. We completed the insurance claim form and had forwarded this to the insurance company together with the original Death Certificate. The insurance company have, however, advised that the Death Certificate is insufficient for their purposes and have requested that the Medical Certificate on the reverse side of the insurance claim form be completed by Mr X's usual doctor.

Yet any award for the strangest doctor's note would surely go to that issued in 1993 by a member of Dr John Winter's practice in Liverpool. A family in Grassendale Park had made a claim for disability living allowance on behalf of a nine-month-old baby on the grounds of 'inability to walk'. Dr Winter's colleague earned the practice £16.40 from the Department of Social Security by certifying that, in the practice's professional opinion, the child's disability was likely to improve with the passage of time.

AGREEABLE INFECTIONS

BRITAIN, 1990–2000

In the last decade of the twentieth century, the streamlined world of electronic communication was invaded by computer viruses. As panic over these viruses waxed and waned, I began to collect cases of infection with organisms that appeared to target computers and word processors left unprotected in medical surroundings. I received enthusiastic assistance from the readers of the journal *Medical Monitor* and we decided that, to avoid over-reporting, a true virus infection should be diagnosed only if the change it produced actually enhanced the original message.

The viruses we found fell into three categories:

1. **Type O** viruses penetrate the DNA of a single word and enhance its meaning by altering its spelling:

> Thank you for sending this woman along. I have started the ball rolling by requesting a semen analysis.
> *Letter from Hertfordshire infertility clinic, May 1995*

> We had an expensive discussion of his symptoms.
> *Letter from consultant to Dr Anthony Abrahams of Oxford,*
> *January 1995*

> They should also consider using lubricants to re-juice the resistance when Mr X penetrates his wife.
> *Letter from consultant to Dr Margaret Thomson of Luton,*
> *April 1996*

Dr X felt that the distended colon was related to his chronic consternation.

> *Report sent to Michael O'Ryan, a GP in Prescot,*
> *August 1997*

This lady finds herself pregnant for the third time having had a termination in 1978 and a normal delivery under Jim's car in 1991.

> *Letter to Paul Sackin of Alconbury, December 1997*

2. **Syntactical viruses** penetrate the DNA of whole sentences and determine the order of the words. As with **Type O** viruses, the diagnostic feature is enhancement of the original message.

The bulletin published by the Novartis Foundation announced it had convened 'a distinguished panel of genetically modified food experts'. The group photograph published alongside proves conclusively that a modified expert is indistinguishable from the standard suit-wearing variety.

> *Medical Monitor,* 13 January 1999

An obstetrician wrote to Kevin McBride, a GP in Warminster, telling him his patient was 'off to Cornwall to live in the near future'.

Dr McBride, who prefers to live in the distant past, accepts that Cornwall attracts folk who like to dabble in the paranormal but hadn't heard they were experimenting with limited time travel.

> *Medical Monitor,* 12 November 1997

Diet of premature babies affects IQ.

> *Guardian* headline, 27 November 1998

Barium enema symposium fills auditorium.

> Newsletter, *British Society of Gastroenterology,*
> Winter 1993

3. Homophone insinuating virus is a retrovirus that integrates with a word's chromosomal DNA to produce a homophone or near homophone that enhances the original message.

Contraceptive pills are not suiting her and other methods make her soar.

Letter found in patient's notes by Dr Kiaran O 'Sullivan of Northwich, December 1994

A letter to a Sheffield GP told him that one of his patients had 'suffered this bazaar attack while at the *Antiques Roadshow'*.

Medical Monitor, May 1999

Ian Lacy, a GP in Lincoln, thought he'd happened upon remarkable new technology when a note from a consultant explained he was considering treating a patient with a 'tumour defying device'. Only when Dr Lacy read on did he discover it was a mere humidifying device.

Medical Monitor, 14 December 2000

Amanda Corlett, a clinical medical officer at Trafford NHS Trust, was invited to a meeting to be held 'in the lecher centre in the education centre'. (It can't have been a misprint because the phrase appears twice.) Sadly the notice arrived late so she missed an 'educational opportunity' of special interest to her department dealing as it does with sexual health.

Medical Monitor, 8 August 1999

Dr Clare Wilkie, a GP who practises in Brixton, rounded off our collection with a rare example of a virus shamelessly declaring its identity. She received a notice from Lambeth police announcing that they had established a gay liaison line for 'the reporting of cases of homophonic abuse'.

DEAD BEYOND REASONABLE DOUBT

CAMBRIDGE, MASSACHUSETTS, USA, 1993

When transplant surgeons showed it was technically possible to remove organs from the recently dead and use them to renew the lives of others who were seriously ill, they provoked much debate about the moment at which death occurred. The surgeons wanted to remove the organs as soon as possible after death, yet they needed to be sure that the organ donors, as they came to be called, really were dead.

One of the problems was that the moment of death was more difficult to diagnose than it used to be. People could be kept 'alive' by mechanical devices that artificially ventilated their lungs and kept their blood circulating long after their brains had ceased to function. After much debate, medical institutions evolved the concept of 'brain death', a condition that exists when the brain has not just stopped working but reached the point when it will never work again. They also defined the tests that had to be done to confirm that brain death had occurred.

In 1993, two American doctors decided to measure how these tests matched up to a widely accepted definition of death. In a magnificently irreverent experiment, Doctors Mike Dubik and Brian Wood were able to verify that the criteria laid down by America's leading medical institutions for diagnosing brain death were valid when tested against a universally accepted standard.

In the summer of 1993, they kept a large seven-year-old

doornail under close observation for 24 hours and reported that, during that time, the nail:

- showed no signs of vocalisation or volitional activity
- exhibited no respiratory movements or spontaneous eye movements
- offered no evidence of postural activity (decerebrate or decorticate)
- made no spontaneous or induced movements

The doornail therefore met the established 'physical examination' criteria for the diagnosis of death.

They then moved on to the designated neurological investigations. They wired up the doornail to a standard machine designed to measure electrical activity in the brain and were able to record thirty minutes of electro-cerebral silence. They also found that when they subjected the nail to 'rousing stimuli' they evoked no electrical or any other form of response.

At the end of this exhaustive study, Drs Dubik and Wood concluded that 'the criteria for death as described in modern medical literature are valid and may be used with confidence by clinicians'.

Two years later, they published their results in the *Annals of Improbable Research,* a journal dedicated not just to making scientists smile but to encourage them, while smiling, to rethink some of the routine assumptions they make about their work.

THE SMOKE CONSUMERS
OF THE FENS

CAMBRIDGE, 1993

In the 1990s, a strange new language invaded two national institutions – the NHS and the BBC. In some hospitals, consultants of a certain age who'd grown bored with the unending routine of outpatients, operating theatre or laboratory embarked on passionate affairs with the new language and, like many who embark on passionate affairs in middle life, quickly lost all sense of reason and discretion.

The decorated platitudinous gothic style in which the language was cast had been evolved by management consultants, public relations gurus, spin doctors and folk of similar ilk who needed impressive phrases to hide the threadbare nature of the thought, if any, that lay behind their words.

Some medical institutions were so concerned by the corruptive force of this language that they employed Tim Albert, one of those rare journalists who is also a good teacher, to bring meaning to their utterance. The sort of NHS 'communication' Albert had to tackle is exemplified by this admonitory note:

The whole purpose of reaching agreement in respect of maintaining disagreements that occur within an internal framework have been known for many years. We would therefore ask you on this occasion as we have done in the past to continue to use the further stages in the internal procedure if you so desire in order that no accusations can be levelled at either side for failing to abide by agreements.

Albert reduced it to, 'Please follow the internal grievance procedure.'

The first reported corruption of doctors, rather than managers, by the new language was a memorandum sent to consultants who worked for the Addenbrooke's NHS Trust in Cambridge and signed not just by the chief executive but by the medical director, who in all other matters was a bright, intelligent, and erudite man.

You need to be aware that effective 9.00 a.m. on 13th December, the Executive Board has agreed that a ring-fence shall apply to the bed envelope of each general management grouping across the hospital. Thus the intention is that the Medical grouping, the Surgical grouping and Specialist service grouping for example will consume their own smoke in meeting bed requirements.

The memorandum achieved notoriety when one of the consultants who'd received it sent it to a medical journal with a request for advice. 'Through which orifice,' he asked, 'am I expected to consume my own smoke?'

THE NORDEN SYNDROME

BRITAIN, 1993

One of the strangest medical conditions reported in the last quarter of the twentieth century was defined not by a doctor, nor a medical scientist, but by one of Britain's most accomplished comedy writers, Denis Norden. The condition is a compulsive interpretative disorder, possibly congenital, that makes people accept only the literal meaning of words. Norden called it literalism and, because he himself was a literalist, gave an occasional airing to his symptoms on the BBC Radio Four series *My Word*.

In one programme, he offered what has since been recognised as the definitive account of the disease. 'On being confronted with the headline "Public borrowing down", my instinctive response was "What a strange thing for members of the public to be borrowing. Just shows how many people must be stuffing their own duvets."

'And when I turned to the arts page and found a story headed "Hockney draws large crowds", the immediate thought was, "Well, I suppose it must make a change from drawing swimming pools."

'But by far the greatest source of misinterpretation for those condemned to take words and phrases at their face value is the public notice. These can range from the increasingly common stickers saying "Neighbourhood Watch" – for which the cinema inside my head never fails to screen a picture of local people popping round to see what time it is – to a little placard they used to have on certain Northern Line trains that read "Passengers Alight Both Ends".'

Norden's literalism often complicated his dealings with doctors. When one of them advised him to drink more fluid, his immediate reaction was, 'What else is there that I can drink more of?' And in 1993, when a medical journal publicised his condition, cases were reported from all over the country. Many of the reports came from doctors who had diagnosed the condition in themselves.

Before he realised he was a literalist, Dr Peter Kersey, a dermatologist in Plymouth, couldn't understand why there were so many signs in his hospital pointing the way to a 'disabled toilet' when people, some of them in urgent need, were looking for working ones. Another doctor who developed insight was Dr A P Harrison, a GP in Keighley. Before he diagnosed his own condition, he used to suffer feelings of deprivation every time he visited a department store in Cardiff where a notice in the cafe read: 'All our tea is served in China'. Not much use, said Dr Harrison, to a person dying of thirst in South Wales.

A relieved Peter Moody, clinical director of the pharmacy and therapeutics directorate at Furness General Hospital, discovered there was at least one other literalist in his hospital. When a corridor was being washed and was protected by the notice 'Wet floor', a graffitist had added the line, 'This is not an instruction'.

Many doctors wrote approvingly of the sensible advice that pharmacists print on the labels of drugs they dispense for elderly people, 'Keep away from small children', but Dr Ramindra Seth, a GP in Nottingham, posed a question which no others could answer. Why, he asked, did farmers talk about cows being 'in calf' when, to his literal eye, it was clearly the calf that was in the cow?

Thanks to the response from its readers, the journal was able to publicise aspects of our environment that the rest of us take for granted but could be hazardous for literalists. The public car park at Wareham in Dorset, for instance, was identified as dangerous territory for female literalists. Above a doorway in the wall that borders it is the traditional sign 'Ladies'. But alongside is another: 'Have you paid and displayed?'

The journal also published evidence that literalism is not an exclusively British disease. One case report, tinged with something close to poignancy, came from Dr Julian Churcher, a GP in south-west London. He had treated a visitor from France and given her an NHS temporary resident form to sign. When she returned it, it included the entry: 'Name of doctor at home: *Docteur.*'

NEANDERTHAL MEDICINE MEN

BIRMINGHAM, 1995

An enduring feature of medical schools is the adulation that medical students have accorded down the ages to the school's 'characters' – often their most bigoted, reactionary and chauvinistic teachers who win the 'character' accolade by being outrageous or outspoken, usually both. Egged on by students the characters soon become caricatures, a potentially dangerous process if impressionable students start to model themselves on the characters they feel they should admire.

As those students grow older, they come to regard themselves as the embodiment of those they once admired, and this natural progress from admiration to imitation has helped perpetuate some of the most dangerous stereotypes in medicine: the decisive surgeon who is sometimes mistaken but never in doubt; the reactionary grouch who prides himself on being 'one of the old school' which, as Dickens points out in *Bleak House,* is any school that seems never to have been young; and the medical chauvinists whose exploits are noted by colleagues like Dr Luisa Dillner. 'When considering the attitude of male obstetricians and gynaecologists,' she wrote in her column in the *Guardian,* 'you have to remember they are predominantly surgeons. This makes them automatically autocratic. Many genuinely have difficulty with the concept that what's yours isn't necessarily theirs to remove.'

The most grotesque case of caricature in recent times was reported by Dr Phil Hammond in his book *Trust Me I'm a*

Doctor. When he was lecturing in Birmingham in 1995, he heard a student describe what happened when she assisted a surgeon:

> First he asked me if I was from the home counties. When I said yes, he started calling me Tinkerbell and said I looked the sort of girl who'd had a horse between my legs. Then he asked me if I'd lost my virginity up against the wall of a horse-box while my mother was outside watching a gymkhana. The registrar and the other theatre staff started laughing too. It was like being in a monkey house. At the end, he asked me if I minded him being sexist in theatre? 'Women like to know what men want.' Then he made a hole in the gall bladder and said, 'Look what you've made me do.'

This incident happened at a time when half the doctors qualifying each year in Britain were women.

MR BRITON CHANGES TRAINS

BRITAIN, 1995

So many conversations in GPs' surgeries are riddled with euphemism that, in the early 1970s, the Department of Health issued a glossary designed to help overseas graduates interpret the vernacular in which British patients talked to their doctors. The booklet included over twenty euphemisms for being pregnant, ranging from the familiar – 'in the club' and 'up the spout' – via the nostalgic – 'in an interesting condition' – to some so obscure that they could only have been tracked down by civil servants with time on their hands. One quite new to most doctors was 'being overdrawn at the bank', which seemed guaranteed to provoke interesting consequences if the doctor was a dedicated reader of the glossary and the patient was trying to explain why she needed a certificate for social security benefit.

Despite the fact that people now talk more freely about sex than they did even in the 1970s, discussion of intimate matters in a GP's surgery can still be strangulated by euphemisms – not all of them uttered by the patient.

High on the list of strangest euphemisms are those that men employ to describe that most unreliable of contraceptive practices in which a man tries to withdraw his penis before he ejaculates – still described by the diminishing number of doctors who learned Latin at school as *coitus interruptus*.

In 1995, the medical journalist Dr David Delvin, who also worked in family planning clinics, set about collecting the

297

phrases that men use. The list he produced is remarkable for its consistency of image, its rich regional variation, and its confirmation of the British male's abiding love of trains. Here is a selection:

Cheshire and Merseyside:	I get off the train at Edge Hill, doctor.
Cambridgeshire:	I get out at Saffron Waldon.
Hampshire:	I stop at Fratton.
Rural Sussex:	I disembark at Haywards Heath.
London:	I always change at Clapham Junction.

An Edinburgh GP, Dr Patricia Santer, told Delvin that Lothian men talk of 'Getting out at Haymarket', the last station before Edinburgh. She also added a Freudian frisson to her observation by pointing out that those who stay on the train will pass though a long dark tunnel before emerging, indeed bursting, into the delightful gardens of Princes Street. Quite so.

A SWEET MEASURE

BATH AND CARDIFF, 1996

In 1996, two British hospital doctors, one a consultant, the other a junior, devised an odd but ingenious way of assessing how much time a hospital doctor spends on the wards. Fiona Cooke, a senior house officer at the Royal Brompton Hospital in London, and Rhian Morse, a consultant physician at the University Hospital of Wales, made use of one of the commonest gifts that grateful patients give to the nurses and doctors who have looked after them, a box of chocolates.

The boxes are traditionally kept on the wards where those who work there can help themselves. It's a useful tradition. The caffeine in chocolate has a stimulant effect that can help the weary – a state that often afflicts staff on hospital wards, particularly the most junior doctors. As a result, say Drs Cooke and Morse, newly qualified housemen and women 'have a massive exposure to a wide range and quantity of chocolates – one of the many early and challenging experiences for the new doctor'.

They decided to test the ability of doctors and nurses to recognise popular chocolates and to see if chocolate recognition was in any way related to the number of years a doctor had been qualified. A random selection of 76 nurses and doctors, senior and junior, at the Royal United Hospital, Bath, and the University Hospital of Wales, Cardiff, agreed to take part in the trial. Each volunteer was shown a grid containing twelve popular chocolates and asked to identify the flavour and make of each. Prodding, smelling and tasting were not allowed.

299

The research, published in the *British Medical Journal*, produced some clear-cut results. All the volunteers, except the consultants, turned out to be better at recognising the make of chocolates than the flavour. Consultants were equally bad at recognising both. Among junior doctors, the chocolate-recognition scores of those who had been qualified for more than a year were significantly higher than those of senior doctors and of fellow juniors in their first year after qualification. The nurses performed as well as the best of the junior doctors. The results also showed that the longer a doctor had been qualified, the lower the chocolate-recognition score. There was one exception to this general rule. Most nurses and doctors, regardless of how long they had been qualified, could recognise the coffee crème.

After analysing the statistical data, the researchers concluded that a doctor faced 'a steep learning curve for chocolate recognition' in the first year after she or he qualified, though they admitted that this is true of other medical skills. They found it difficult to determine whether the learning process with chocolate was an active or a passive one. Their results suggest it is a deeply personal accomplishment. Chocolate recognition is unlikely to be taught by senior colleagues, or even acquired from them, because the skill appears to deteriorate with increasing seniority.

Despite the poor recognition skills of senior staff, they certainly knew which chocolates they liked and which they did not, even if they couldn't recognise them. Senior registrars and consultants commonly used phrases such as 'the yucky one' or 'the yummy one' to indicate their preference. Drs Cooke and Morse suggest that this behaviour is in line with the more instinctive approach that doctors take to medical problems as they become more senior. Many consultants, they point out, have been heard to say, 'I don't know what's wrong with this patient, but he's definitely sick.'

The most significant finding of the research was the near universal recognition – and dislike – of the coffee crème. The researchers' comment on this finding was the traditional, 'The reason for this is unclear.'

The bad news for consultants was that, even before the results were published, NHS managers had expressed interest in the chocolate-recognition score as a surrogate measure of time spent on the wards.

LEGAL NICETIES

NORFOLK, VIRGINIA, USA, 1996

A senior barrister who, before he became a judge, acted as an adviser to the General Medical Council, once said how much he enjoyed the 'professional niceties' that went with the job. He defined these as 'the civilised exchanges that occur when members of the learned professions engage in discourse'. Those words, spoken in 1987, already seem dated thanks to the eagerness with which Britain has imported aggressive elements of USA legal culture, like the 'ambulance chasers' who advertise for clients with a promise of 'no win, no fee'.

In the United States, where lawyers have become national hate figures – one huge internet site is devoted simply to recording jokes in which lawyers are portrayed as greedy, ruthless and amoral – the professional niceties have lost much of their niceness, particularly in cases where doctors who consider themselves blameless find themselves embroiled in protracted litigation over alleged malpractice.

The doctors are beginning to bite back, and when the learned professions meet in US courtrooms, the exchanges could often be described more accurately as 'professional acerbities' – as in these excerpts from court transcripts published in the *Massachusetts Bar Association Journal*.

Lawyer: Do you recall the time that you examined the body?
Doctor: The autopsy started around 8.30 p.m.

Lawyer: And Mr Dennington was dead at the time?
Doctor: No, he was sitting on the table wondering why I was doing an autopsy.

Lawyer: Before you began your autopsy, did you check if the victim was breathing?
Doctor: No.

Lawyer: Did you check if he had a pulse?
Doctor: No.

Lawyer: Did you check if he had brain activity?
Doctor: No.

Lawyer: But why not?
Doctor: Because his brain was sitting in a laboratory dish on top of my desk.

(Pause)

Lawyer: But is it still not possible he could still have been alive, nonetheless?
Doctor: Well, yes, it is possible he was alive. But he would only have been fit to study law.

After that, it will come as no surprise that the oddest medico-legal case of recent times was reported from the United States. There, in 1996, in circumstances that were already pretty strange, a group of lawyers managed to make them even stranger by trying to get doctors to pay for an alleged error that, if it had been a mistake, had been made by a lawyer.

The case arose after Thomas Passmore, a citizen of Norfolk, Virginia, discovered that his right hand was possessed by the devil and cut it off with a circular saw. He had seen the malignant number 666 appear across his palm, so had followed the biblical injunction, 'If thine right hand offend thee, cut it off.'

When the ambulance took him, and his hand, to a local

hospital, he refused permission for the surgeons to intervene because the bible offered no authority for the surgical reattachment of offending body parts. The hospital, thinking it was acting in his best interests, sought a court injunction to override his instructions on the grounds that he was grossly deluded and incapable of making a rational decision.

The law, in the person of a judge, refused to grant an injunction. Mr Passmore's lawyers then sued the hospital for $3.4 million for obeying the judge's instruction.

Time was when the British would say, 'It couldn't happen here.' Now we can't be quite so sure.

ANALYSING AN ALIEN IMPLANT

BRISTOL, 1997

In March 1997, James Basil came to interview Dr Susan Blackmore for a student media project. Dr Blackmore, who is a parapsychologist at the University of the West of England, grew interested when Basil told her how, five years before, when he was thirteen, he had reached out a hand from his bed and found he was touching another hand that was smooth, lizard-like and had curled fingers. That experience triggered memories of lying in bed with two aliens standing at his bedside and of floating into a UFO outside his bathroom window. Eventually, he told Dr Blackmore, he was able to recall memories of many abductions by aliens and could prove his experiences were real because they had implanted a small object in his mouth. He had later removed it and wondered if Dr Blackmore would be interested in analysing it.

She found it hard to resist this unique opportunity to investigate purportedly alien material. Many abductees claimed that aliens had implanted small tracking devices into their bodies. Some said the aliens did not want the implants removed or subjected to X-rays or scanning; implants alleged to have been removed had usually disappeared in mysterious ways.

The implant measured about two by three millimetres and its surface appeared to be made of dullish grey metal. To determine whether it contained miniaturised alien technology, Dr Blackmore solicited the help of a colleague, Dr David T Patton, who had access to more high-powered equipment than exists in a university psychology department.

On 9 April 1997, Drs Blackmore and Patton and the abductee James Basil got together to conduct an investigation. First, they examined the implant through a stereo light microscope, which revealed it had irregular edges and that part of the surface was covered with yellow-brown material, which they assumed was dried organic matter from Basil's mouth.

Next, for about an hour, they used a scanning electron microscope to examine the surface of the implant at different magnifications. James Basil was keen that they should seek out fibres because these were said to have been found on previous implants. They found several and also some small rounded surface features similar to ones that Basil had heard had been found on other alien implants. Nothing they saw looked like miniature technology or mechanical components but, as Blackmore and Patton pointed out, alien technology may be unrecognisable to human eyes.

For their final investigation they used energy dispersive X-ray microanalysis, an investigation which, by determining the implant's composition, would reveal any combination of elements unlikely to be found on Earth. And it did, indeed, come up with the answer. The implant contained mercury, silver and tin in the proportions usually found in dental amalgum.

As a result of their high-powered investigation, Drs Blackmore and Patton concluded that the implant was a displaced dental filling and the fibres and small rounded objects were dried organic material which, because the object had been in James Basil's mouth for about two weeks, most likely came from him.

Reporting their results in the *Skeptic*, Susan Blackmore and Dave Patton speculate on how far scientists should go in using time and expensive equipment to test extraordinary claims. They conclude that, in this case, the effort was worthwhile. If they had refused to help, believers in UFOs and conspiracy theorists would have used their refusal as evidence that the 'scientific community' was biased against them. And, of course, their university could have been the first place on Earth to find a piece of alien technology.

TREASURE HUNT IN
SOUTH LONDON

WANDSWORTH, LONDON, 1997

In April 1997, the Merton, Sutton and Wandsworth Health Authority circulated a letter to local doctors and police:

> This Authority has received information from the Church Lane Practice at 2 Church Lane, Merton Park, SW19 that the following patient may attempt to obtain drugs irregularly.
>
> Name(s):   John Silver
> Date of birth: Not Given
> Home Address: Not Given
> Drug(s):   Rum; Opiates
> Description: Above average height, grey hair, faded
>   blue greatcoat with bird droppings on
>   left shoulder. Above-knee amputation
>   on right but very mobile with one
>   crutch

This patient visited the above mentioned practice claiming to have been discharged from the Navy where he had been serving as a cook. He had a pleasant and convincing manner, but became threatening and abusive when his requests for rum and opium were declined. Before leaving the surgery, he insisted on handing the receptionist a small piece of paper blackened with what appeared to be charcoal on one side. It is believed he may return.

If approached by this patient requesting medication, please bear the contents of this letter in mind and, if necessary, contact your local police station.

The letter also included the date on which the information was sent from the Church Lane practice – 1 April.

Andrew Mills, the GP who sent it, later claimed he did so to lighten the morning of the 'oppressed workers' and expressed no regret over the greater exposure it was given by what he called the Health Authority's illiteracy. 'Clearly,' he said, 'the most recognisable character created by Robert Louis Stevenson could today pass unnoticed through the Health Authority's portals along with the rest of Flint's crew.'

Merton, Sutton and Wandsworth Health Authority defended itself by saying that descriptions of addicts were often this colourful. Dr Mills riposted that that, of course, was his inspiration.

This strange case is proof, if proof were needed, that an essential attribute of a successful bureaucrat is a congenital deficiency in the humour department. When this is combined with a lack of knowledge of our literary heritage, the result can be engaging.

BRITAIN'S SERIAL KILLERS

BRITAIN, 1997

The most dangerous job in Britain was defined in 1997 by a rigorous epidemiological study conducted by three researchers from the department of public health and epidemiology at King's College Hospital, London. The job, more likely to be predicted now than it was then, was being a character in a soap opera. Characters in *EastEnders* were way ahead of Formula One racing drivers on the danger list; life as a character in *Coronation Street* was far more risky than life as a bomb-disposal expert or as a steeplejack.

After a 'cohort analysis' of deaths in *EastEnders* and *Coronation Street,* supplemented by an analysis of deaths in *Brookside* and *Emmerdale,* the investigators discovered that the death rates for soap opera characters were higher than in any of the other dangerous occupations they investigated. Not only that, but deaths in soap operas were almost three times more likely to be from violent causes than would be predicted by the character's age and sex. Some soap operas were more dangerous than others. A character in *EastEnders* was about two times more likely to die during an episode than a similar character in *Coronation Street.*

After what they described as their 'hard-hitting analysis', the investigators explained – with an ill-disguised air of satisfaction – that the results confirmed what they had long suspected: that Brookside Close, Coronation Street, Albert Square and Emmerdale were extremely dangerous places. Characters who lived there tended to die young and from a variety of obscure and often violent causes, ranging from the mystery virus in *Brookside,* which killed three, to a plane crash in *Emmerdale,* which killed four. Other violent causes of death included car accidents, murders, drug overdoses and suicides.

Five-year survival rates for characters aged under 29 were the same in all the soap operas. But when it came to characters between the ages of 30 and 44, 'people moving to Coronation Street went on to lead charmed lives, while their peers living in Albert Square dropped like flies'. Staying alive in a television soap opera was not easy: 'Standardised mortality ratios for characters were among the highest for any occupation yet described.'

Conscious of the truth of the cliché that prevention is better than cure, the good doctors of King's College Hospital, Tim Crayford, Richard Hooper and Sarah Evans, suggested that characters in these serials would be well advised to wear good protective clothing (designed to withstand sharp implements, sudden impacts and fire) and to receive regular counselling to help them cope with the psychological impact of living in an environment in which the risks were akin to those in a war zone.

They presented their research as 'the first quantitative estimate of the size of the pinch of salt which should be taken when watching soap operas'.

A SOUND DIAGNOSIS

CALIFORNIA, 1999

One evening in northern California, a distinguished American physician, Faith Fitzgerald, sat in a hospital ward, writing up a patient's notes. Nearby, at the ward telephones, the duty nurses were growing increasingly distraught as they tried to get hold of the intern on call. Eventually admitting defeat, they asked Dr Fitzgerald if she would see the patient they were worried about – a 75-year-old woman who had had a surgical operation and had been sent back, still groggy, to the ward from the anaesthesia recovery room.

Within hours, according to her nurse, she started to babble incoherently when alone, though she appeared to be fully oriented when the nurse spoke to her directly. The nurse feared that she was 'sundowning' – doctorspeak for the confusion and agitation that sometimes afflicts elderly patients in the early evening – and wanted to give her a tranquilliser.

Dr Fitzgerald agreed to see her and, as they approached the patient's room, could hear 'rhythmic speech, unintelligible but punctuated by modulations of intensity ranging from prayerful quietude to vigorous exhortations'.

'There,' said the nurse. 'See what I mean?'

Through the door they saw the woman lying on the bed and declaiming at the ceiling. Then, as they watched, Dr Fitzgerald began to recognise words: Hrothgar, Herot, Beo, Grendel.

She walked into the room.

'Hello,' said the patient brightly.

'Hello back,' said Dr Fitzgerald. 'You're doing *Beowulf?*'
The patient smiled. 'Yes,' she said.

She'd been an English professor at a small university, where she had specialised in Old English literature. As a result, she was on familiar terms with the epic tale of Beowulf and his companions in their battle with the monstrous Grendel and Grendel's Dam.

Before her operation, she had decided to recite the poem in Old English when she recovered. As she explained, 'I thought it would be a way I would know whether or not I had all my brain left after anaesthesia.'

That evening, a sensible patient had met a literate doctor: a happy conjunction that should occur more often.

SELECTED BIBLIOGRAPHY

Asher, Richard, *Richard Asher Talking Sense,* London, Pitman Medical, 1972.

Blackmore, Susan, and Patton, David T, *The Skeptic,* 11:3, 1997.

Bondi, Hermann, 'Risk in Perspective', *Risk: Man-made Hazards to Man,* Oxford, Clarendon Press, 1985.

Clark, R W, *The Life of Ernst Chain,* London, Weidenfeld and Nicholson, 1985.

Cockayne, Edward, 'Talking Shop', *World Medicine,* 18 October, 1980.

Cronin, A J, *Adventures in Two Worlds,* London, Gollancz, 1952.

Dean, Geoffrey, 'The Curse of the Pharaohs', *World Medicine,* 18 June, 1975.

Dubik, M and Wood, B, 'How dead is a doornail?' *Annals of Improbable Research,* November/December, 1995.

Fitzgerald, Faith T, 'Helen Glaser – The Lighthouse Keeper', *The Pharos,* Fall, 1999.

Gordon, Richard, *The Alarming History of Medicine,* London, Sinclair-Stevenson, 1993.

Gould, Donald, *The Black and White Medicine Show,* London, Hamish Hamilton, 1985.

Grant, Roger, *Scottish Medical Journal,* 32: 57–59, 1987.

Hammond, P, Mosley, M, *Trust me I'm a Doctor,* London, Metro, 1999.

Hare, Ronald, *The Birth of Penicillin and the Disarming of Microbes,* London, George Allen and Unwin, 1970.

Hirst, Stephen, 'Talking Shop', *World Medicine,* 20 September, 1980.

Hofmann, Albert, *LSD: My Problem Child*, New York, McGraw-Hill, 1980.

Jolly, G M, 'Talking Shop', *World Medicine*, June, 1977.

Kenin, Richard and Wintle, Justin, *Dictionary of Biographical Quotation of British and American Subjects*, New York, Knopf, 1978.

Macfarlane, R G, *Florey, Brief Lives, Selections from the Dictionary of National Biography*, Oxford, Oxford University Press, 1997.

Medawar, P B, *Advice to a Young Scientist*, New York, Harper & Row, 1979.

Munk, William, *Munk's Roll*, Royal College of Physicians, 1861.

Norden, Denis, *The Utterly Ultimate 'My Word' Collection*, London, Mandarin, 1991.

Owen, David, *Time to Declare*, London, Penguin, 1991.

Payer, Lynn, *Medicine & Culture*, London, Gollancz, 1989.

Pigache, Philippa, 'Blinded by Psychology', *World Medicine*, 6 November 1974.

Porter, Roy, *The Greatest Benefit to Mankind*, London, HarperCollins, 1997.

Reed, Graham, *The Psychology of Anomalous Experience*, New York, Prometheus Books, 1988.

Rosin, R D, *The Broadway Clinical Supplement*, 6 September, 1966.

St Clair Symmers, William, *Exotica*, Oxford, Oxford University Press, 1984.

Silverman, William A, *Retrolental Fibroplasia: A Modern Parable*, New York: Grune and Stratton, 1980.

Thornton, J L, *John Abernethy*, London, Marshall, 1953.

Timmins, Nicholas, *The Five Giants*, London, HarperCollins, 1995.

Wasserug, Joseph D, *Modern Medicine*, November, 1985.